THE QUEER CINEMA
OF DEREK JARMAN

INTERNATIONAL LIBRARY OF CULTURAL STUDIES

THE QUEER CINEMA
OF DEREK JARMAN

Critical and Cultural Readings

NIALL RICHARDSON

I.B. TAURIS

LONDON · NEW YORK

Published in 2009 by I.B. Tauris & Co Ltd
6 Salem Road, London W2 4BU
175 Fifth Avenue, New York NY 10010
www.ibtauris.com

In the United States of America and Canada distributed by Palgrave Macmillan,
a division of St. Martin's Press, 175 Fifth Avenue, New York NY 10010

The International Library of Cultural Studies: 1
ISBN 978 1 84511 536 4 (hb)
      978 1 84511 537 1 (pb)

A full CIP record for this book is available from the British Library
A full CIP record for this book is available from the Library of Congress

Library of Congress Catalog Card Number: available

Printed and bound in Great Britain by CPI Antony Rowe, Chippenham
from camera-ready copy edited and supplied by the author

Dedicated to my beloved Natalie – one of the 'queerest' women I've ever known.

CONTENTS

ACKNOWLEDGEMENTS

I should like to thank my PhD supervisors – Professor John Hill and John Deeney for all their help, support and guidance over the years it took to finish the project. I should also thank Professor Paul Willemen for acting as a temporary supervisor and also Professor Martin McLoone whose kind words of encouragement helped me more than he realised. Dr Angela Smith proof-read drafts of the manuscripts and was vigilant in hunting out all my mechanical errors. Finally I should like to give a big word of thanks to Sarah Shrive-Morrison for her hard work in preparing the manuscript for publication.

INTRODUCTION

I was 18 when I saw *Edward II* – my first Derek Jarman film. I chanced upon it, quite by accident, on a dreary Sunday night while flicking through the channels. *Edward II* sticks in my memory as one of those remarkable viewing experiences where I became spellbound by a film that I hadn't intended to watch in the first place and didn't really know anything about. I suspected that the film was based upon the Marlowe play of the same name which depicted the problems which King Edward experienced in maintaining a 'relationship' with Piers Gaveston of France but I was not prepared for Jarman's interpretation of this play. After the film I was fired up with excitement. Who was Derek Jarman? Why had I never seen any of his films before? And, most importantly, where can I get video copies of his other work?

Edward II had a huge effect upon me at a time when my life was at one of its lowest points ever. Like other 18 year-olds I was slogging through soul-destroying A-Level revision. Yet unlike other 18 year-olds (or so it seemed to me) I was also wrestling with issues of my own sexuality. Growing up in a tough, provincial town in Northern Ireland (a place famous for its intolerance of religious difference let alone sexual difference) I was wracked with what I now realize was a stereotypical sense of isolation and self-loathing. In a time preceding the media deluge of *Will and Grace*-type saccharine images, I had only a televisual diet of camp queens trilling across the sitcom stages or else the sanitised soap-opera/TV movie gays who consummate their frigid relationship through the act of holding hands. Before seeing *Edward II* the soap-opera/TV movie narratives had convinced me that all gays were suburban married men who suddenly decide that they're gay and then leave their wives only to settle into pseudo domesticity with another man. Eventually all the other characters accept these 'homosexuals' – but only if they're quietly closeted about it. In the world of soap operas and TV movies (at least in the late 1980s and early 1990s) a gay man always loses a wife simply to become some other man's wife (see Watney, 1982: 116).

Edward II represented the very opposite. Here was 'same-sex passion' which refused to be quiet and domesticated. Here were characters who demonstrated that leading an alternative lifestyle was a constant struggle. As a result these queers were furious about their oppression and vented violent rage against the church and the state. Most importantly, *Edward II* also made same-sex passion explicit (or at least for the early 1990s, *relatively* explicit). My only knowledge of Marlowe's original play was through my A-level English Literature syllabus where a fossilized teacher (who given her time and location was probably trying her very best) had insisted that there was no same-sex passion suggested in the text. The play was an examination of friendship – or something like that. In Jarman's interpretation I suddenly found many of the themes that I had wanted to read in the original text made explicit on the screen. I experienced a great sense of excitement, like an archaeologist unearthing a lost treasure, and the thrill of feeling part of something – an insider group who knew how to read Marlowe 'properly'.

Most importantly – and hardly surprising given that I was a sexually frustrated 18 year-old – I was in awe of the abundance of nude male bodies represented in *Edward II*. Homoeroticism glistened across the screen: nude rugby scrums, gorgeous gym queens crunching their abs in the gym and sailors in Gaveston's bed engaged in some sort of threesome or fourgie. I also developed a massive crush on King Edward. His sandy hair, alabaster skin, downy freckles glittering across his shoulders and his gym-toned physique represented a physical type which – more than ten years later – I still consider my ideal.

That was my first reading of *Edward II*: a sense of excitement at the explicit 'same-sex passion'; an erotic pleasure from seeing so much male flesh and a feeling of triumph at the film's representation of queer militancy. I was both inspired and also slightly overwhelmed by the overt sexual politics represented in the narrative. However, a second viewing (I had slammed a video-tape into the machine after the first few minutes) yielded some different responses. On watching the film again, my revulsion for Gaveston increased. Not only did I find him physically unattractive – skinny, rough and ginger – but he was also a particularly nasty character. Similarly, I started to question the efficacy of Gaveston and Edward's 'queer' politics. Was all this anger actually 'getting' the characters anywhere? This confrontational approach – a 'them' versus 'us' mentality – only seemed to further marginalize the queer characters and render them an easily excisable tumour in the side of the heteronormative dominant. Likewise, I started to become more intrigued by the secondary aspects of the film. Who was that androgynous woman playing the campy, deliciously glamorous Queen Isabella? Why was I becoming more and more intrigued by and attracted to Isabella? Why was her representation so exciting and so different from any other representation of femininity that I'd seen before? Why was there so much violence represented in the narrative with sexuality often configured within paradigms of sadism or self-tortured masochism? Also, I started to take more notice of little Prince Edward (Isabella and Edward's only son) who punctuated the narrative like a Sophoclean Chorus, his gaze of surprise at the queer goings-on often echoing my own reaction. The film's 'happy-ending' was Prince Edward, dressed in almost full drag, dancing on a cage containing the dusty Isabella and Mortimer. What was Jarman trying to say in such a 'queer' image?

This book is, in many ways, the continuing musings of that frustrated 18 year-old who chanced upon *Edward II* one dreary Sunday night. It is an attempt to analyse the two different responses inspired by my first and second viewing of the film. While my first response marvelled at the film's uncompromising and aggressive sexual politics, my second reading found more intriguing 'queer' themes at work in the film text. Therefore, this book is intended as the first full-length study devoted to analysing Jarman's cinema through the critical lens of 'queer'. Unlike other studies, this book will not simply praise Jarman's films as political allegories (gays versus straights) but will examine *how* Jarman's images explore many of the debates in current queer theory – especially its challenge to fixed ideas of gender, sexuality and the body.

Who was Derek Jarman?

Derek Jarman has always held a rather uneasy position with both audiences and film critics. His films were never 'crowd-pleasers' placating homophobia or supporting the 'false-optimism' (Jarman, 2000: 68) of a 'gay-is-good' sensibility. Similarly, Jarman has always endured a stormy relationship with both academic and journalistic critics. For example, the film journalist Alexander Walker originally described Jarman as one of the most 'prodigiously gifted' (1985: 228) of the young British filmmakers but, by the end of Jarman's career, Walker was writing scathing – if not even downright bitchy – criticism of his films. Reviewing *Edward II*, Walker suggested that the film had 'a strong streak of wishful martyrdom' and that it was really 'getting on people's nerves to hear Jarman advertising himself – or being advertised – in every branch of the media as the most famous living HIV positive victim' (Walker, quoted in Peake, 1999: 487).

Academic criticism, although less malicious, was, until recently, hardly more favourable. Jarman was largely ignored by the new wave of academic film critics writing for the journals *Screen* and *Monogram* in the late 1970s and early 1980s. *Screen* criticism was intrigued by new analytical tools (especially psychoanalysis) in reading classic (Hollywood) film texts (especially Hitchcock and Sirk) and by the avant-gardism of Godard and Brecht. Jarman's cinema was seen not only as rough-edged and unsophisticated but even vulgar and heavy-handed.

Jarman, however, has actually referred to himself as 'cine-illiterate' (quoted in Lippard, 1996: 3) and indicated that he thought of himself primarily as a painter who also made films (Lippard, ibid.: 2). Indeed, Jarman's artistic output was extremely varied. He was not only a painter, writer, set designer and filmmaker but also a writer, queer activist and respected gardener whose Dungeness garden was featured on the BBC television show *Gardener's World* (BBC2, 23 June, 1995). It should also be noted that his academic background was English, History and Art History at Kings College London and, unlike other filmmakers who then progressed to film school, Jarman followed his undergraduate studies by enrolling as a fine art student at the Slade School of Art.

Jarman's first real involvement with film was as a set designer for Ken Russell's *The Devils* (1970). He then worked with Russell on *Savage Messiah* (1972) and also on Stravinsky's opera *The Rake's Progress*. In 1976, however, Jarman released his own first feature film – *Sebastiane* – which was made from a suitcase of money donated by an anonymous Italian businessman.

Sebastiane is noteworthy for being one the most (homo)sexually explicit feature films ever (it is still, to my knowledge, the only film which managed to show an erection on screen) and for its foregrounding of the male body and alternative paradigms of masculinity – themes which would be developed throughout Jarman's later works. *Sebastiane* tells the story of the Roman centurion who refuses to fight and, as a result, is tortured and eventually executed. The film raises interesting questions about the representation of the male body on screen and the thorny issue of male masochism.

Jarman's second feature was the punk-inspired *Jubilee* (1978). *Jubilee* presaged much of the political anger which would appear throughout Jarman's work. Tony Peake suggests that *Jubilee's* inversions 'are a metaphor for gay life' (1999: 249) while Nayland Blake even describes punk's 'poses and strategies' as 'tied to queerness' (1995: 20). *Jubilee* also introduced Jarman's interest in English heritage and the Elizabethan Renaissance as the film represents Elizabeth I being conducted on a tour of her future, nihilistic, anarchistic country by her magician John Dee.

These themes are developed in *The Tempest* (1979) which draws obvious parallels between John Dee and Prospero (played by Heathcote Williams). The film again attracted both criticism and praise for the way it revised Shakespeare's script, notably through its campy ending in which sailors dance the hornpipe while Elisabeth Welch sings *Stormy Weather* – a reference to a party where Jean Cocteau brought 21 sailor-boys as a birthday present.

In 1985 Jarman released *The Angelic Conversation* – his cinema of small gestures – which is arguably one of his most beautiful and moving films. Shot entirely on Super 8 and then transferred to 35mm, *The Angelic Conversation* represents the journey of love between two beautiful boys while Judi Dench reads from Shakespeare's Sonnets in a voice-over narration.

Caravaggio (1986) was the closest Jarman ever came to making a mainstream feature film. It tells the life story of the Renaissance artist Michelangelo de Caravaggio and the strange/queer relationship which he has with his model Ranuccio and the street urchin/prostitute Lena. Jarman himself found the collaborative process of making a feature film extremely exhausting and vowed that he would never repeat it. *Caravaggio*, however, develops many of the themes implicit in the earlier films: the relationship between sex, desire and the body and the coercion of desire through financial and physical power. The film also introduces the divine Tilda Swinton as Lena. As evidenced by her sensitive portrayal of Lena, Swinton seemed to have an almost intuitive understanding of what Jarman was trying to achieve and would continue to have an important presence within all his later works.

The Last of England (1987) is Jarman's bleakest work, containing some of his most violent and truly frightening images. Rage permeates every scene, especially Jarman's hatred of Thatcherite politics and the state of the British Nation. In this respect, *The Last of England* is often regarded as a companion piece to *Jubilee*. In 1986, while editing *The Last of England*, Jarman was diagnosed HIV+ and bravely decided to reveal his HIV status to the public. Although Jarman would not directly address the issue of AIDS until *Blue* (1993), his next films all represented the ubiquitous threat of AIDS through colour imagery and metaphor.

War Requiem (1988) is Jarman's examination of war and death. The soundtrack of the film was Benjamin Britten's *War Requiem* (1962) and also incorporated Wilfred Owen's war poetry. Undoubtedly influenced by his HIV diagnosis, *War Requiem*'s images emphasise suffering, grief and eventual death.

The Garden (1990) is arguably one of Jarman's most powerful works in that it wrestles with the problem of synthesising both his own personal artistic vision with his interest in militant queer politics. Based loosely on the Gospel stories, *The Garden* documents two male lovers (a metaphor for Christ) who are tortured by the establishments of church, military and state. The scenes of brutality in the film are even more excessive than those in *Jubilee*, yet *The Garden* also presents moments of tenderness between the two lovers and a sense of hope in the film's ending.

Edward II (1991), based loosely on the Marlowe play of the same name, is Jarman's most discussed film and probably his best known. Where Marlowe represented implicit 'same-sex passion' between King Edward and Piers Gaveston of France, Jarman rendered it explicit. In *Edward II* all the powers of the church and court conspire to prevent the relationship between Edward and Gaveston and eventually assassinate Gaveston. As can only be expected from such a narrative, separatist, if not even radical politics are implicit throughout the film. Yet *Edward II* also develops many of the interesting themes which Jarman was wrestling with in his earlier films, especially thanks to Swinton's superb portrayal of Queen Isabella – Edward's spurned wife.

Wittgenstein (1993) was commissioned by Channel 4 and was supposed to be the first in a series of films about famous philosophers, although this series was eventually cancelled. *Wittgenstein* is considerably lighter in tone than most of Jarman's other films and presents an often 'comic portrait' (Lippard, 1996: 6) of the tortured genius's life and work.

Towards the end of his life Jarman suffered extreme ill-health due to AIDS-related opportunistic infections and was nearly blind when he made *Blue* (1993). Arguably *Blue* is (still) one of the most successful films in representing an invisible virus without either dehumanising the sufferer or trivialising the condition. The continuous blue screen is accompanied by a soundtrack in which four voices describe many of the symptoms and experiences of the virus. *Blue* signifies the way in which Jarman's style has evolved full circle. From the excessive, often Baroque style of the early work which featured (in abundance) the nude male body, *Blue* is minimalist and notable for avoiding the representations of the actual body while still maintaining a sense of the physical in its voice-over narration.

Queer Readings

This book is the first study devoted to an analysis of how the political and cultural debates of 'queer' are represented throughout Jarman's cinema. Jarman himself was particularly keen to describe his work as 'queer' yet, surprisingly, there have been few studies addressing this aspect of his work. Many film and cultural critics have been interested in Jarman for issues other than his representation of sexuality and sexual politics – such as his representation of England/Englishness and how his cinema fits (or does not fit) into the tradition of British filmmaking. One of the key studies of Jarman is Michael O'Pray's book *Derek Jarman: Dreams of England* (1997) which offers a superb introduction to Jarman's films placing them in their historical and thematic context. The focus of O'Pray's book is 'authorship' and the artistic development in Jarman's oeuvre and, as such, is still one of the finest introductions to Jarman's films. If there is a criticism to be made of O'Pray's book, it is that the writing is a little light on critical analysis and avoids (largely) the question of sexuality and sexual politics in the films. More recently two new 'introductions' to Jarman's cinema have appeared. Rowland Wymer's *Derek Jarman (2005)* gives detailed critical readings of all eleven of Jarman's films and, as is hardly surprising given that the author is a respected literary scholar, the book places particular emphasis on Jarman's adaptation of Renaissance literature. Likewise, William Pencak's *The Films of Derek Jarman* (2002) is another 'introductory' guide to Jarman's cinema. Pencak is an historian rather than film critic and so his book is not concerned with critical readings but with creating 'program notes to Jarman's films from a historical perspective' (Pencak, 2002: 4).

In a very different vein, John Hill's *British Cinema in the 1980s* (1999) offers an interesting section on Jarman which analyses Jarman's cinema in terms of its position within the British film tradition. Hill asserts that Jarman's cinema 'may be seen to straddle a number of tensions' (1999: 155) as it is a part of British art cinema yet also adopts 'a more extreme approach to narrative'. It is 'indebted to modernist avant-garde' but yet is also emblematic of the personal politics 'more characteristic of 'underground' cinema' (ibid.). Similarly, writers such as Lawrence Driscoll (1996), David Hawkes (1996), Colin MacCabe (1992), Peter Wollen (1993) and, most recently, Steven Dillon (2004) have been very interested in Jarman's unique cinematic style and have foregrounded similar debates in their writing: the representation of Englishness; is Jarman's work art cinema, counter cinema, lyric cinema and how does this fit into a tradition of British filmmaking (heritage cinema versus British realism)?

However, there is not the same breadth of writing focused on sexuality, sexual politics and, most importantly, 'queer' in Jarman's films. One of the most sustained academic studies of Jarman's cinema to date has been the collection of essays edited by Chris Lippard, *By Angels Driven: The Films of Derek Jarman* (1996). This interesting collection touches upon 'queer(ish)' debates but has a tendency to collapse 'queer' (which emphasises anti-identity politics) with 'gay' (which asserts separatist identity politics) (see Chapter 1 for consideration of the difference between 'gay' and 'queer'). Gardner's chapter in Lippard's collection, 'Perverse Law: Jarman as gay criminal hero' and Quinn Meyler's 'Opposing "Heterosoc": Jarman's counter-hegemonic activism' – focus upon Jarman's political activism yet largely configure 'queer' as a more aggressive version of Gay Lib. Both authors praise Jarman's work for being oppositional to oppressive norms. Quinn-Meyler even asserts that the violent sexuality represented in Jarman's cinema is 'an act of subversion with the potential to destabilize the control of 'Heterosoc' (1996: 120). Far from being an exploration of alternative sexual dynamics, Quinn-Meyler argues that Jarman's images of sado-masochism are deliberate acts of political resistance. While Quinn-Meyler undoubtedly makes a valid point, the problem with his analysis is that it praises Jarman's work solely as an allegory of political struggle rather than focusing on the more intriguing aspects of dissonant gender and sexuality represented in the images.

However, one of the more interesting writings on Jarman (certainly from a queer cinematic perspective) is Jose Arroyo's 'Death, Desire and Identity: The Political Unconscious of "New Queer Cinema"' (1993). The chapter offers detailed textual analysis of both *Edward II* and another example of New Queer Cinema – Gus Van Sant's *My Own Private Idaho*. Yet in one of the chapter's footnotes, Arroyo suggests that Jarman's representation of 'identity' is influenced by separatist, quasi-ethnic politics of Gay Lib (1993: 95). Although this reading is certainly possible from all Jarman's films, this book will argue that issues of subjectivity are rather more complex in Jarman's cinema than the assertion of essentialist, political separatism. In this respect the book will attempt to answer Arroyo's question: 'what (aside from AIDS) makes *Edward II* […] a New Queer Film?' This book will argue that the answer lies not with reading the political allegorical content of Jarman's narrative but recognising Jarman's queering of gender, sexuality and their prescription of the body.

One of the most inspiring 'queer' critiques of Jarman's cinema is Leo Bersani and Ulysse Dutoit's short monograph on *Caravaggio* (1999). As can only be expected from two such respected scholars (Bersani continues to be one of the academy's leading queer theorists) the monograph is an insightful reading of the queer resonances in *Caravaggio* (and a number of other Jarman films as well). Indeed the monograph is probably the first piece of criticism to delve into Jarman's representation of sexuality, analysing the psycho-sexual foundations for these images, rather than merely praising Jarman's portrayal of tendentious political battles. For Bersani and Dutoit, *Caravaggio* is an examination of the power of sexual desire and how this challenges the subject's sense of identity. Reading *Caravaggio* as an examination of gender and sexual identity – especially sexuality's 'self-lacerating passage from life to death' (1996: 75) – Bersani and Dutoit argue that the film is a testament to the power of desire and culture's (failed) attempt to circumscribe sexuality with the gendered body.

This book will develop many of these themes and argue that they feature throughout Jarman's canon – despite the fact that Bersani and Dutoit are dismissive of most of Jarman's films as being mere political tracts (1999: 16). Therefore, the emphasis throughout will not simply be on how the films' images can be read as political allegories for aggressive, separatist sexual politics but on how Jarman illuminates the debates in current 'queer theory'. I want to argue that although it is very possible to read Jarman's cinema as a political tract or slogan (and indeed Jarman himself was not adverse to such interpretations), the films' 'queer' status is more indebted to the way in which the images interrogate the normative continuum of sex, gender and sexuality. Jarman's work is consistently challenging preconceived notions of gender, sex, sexuality and, most importantly, how this circumscribes the 'body'. His work is not merely a slogan for queer political activism but a subversion of normativity – both gay and straight. It is too reductive to read Jarman's work as a more aggressive version of Gay Lib – a hetero versus homo battle. Instead the films actually contradict many of the normative ideas cherished by 'gay politics' such as the quasi-ethnic style essentialist politics and the notion of a homogenous gay community.

Therefore, the main arguments raised in this book are largely the key debates found in academic queer theory. Queer theory is concerned with two main issues. Firstly, queer theory is largely underpinned by the theories of performativity (see Chapter 1: section on Butler) which views gender as a performative effect – a doing which, within a recognised cultural matrix, constitutes a being. Like feminism, it has been one of queer theory's main agendas to expose the incoherencies in the sex-gender continuum and show that masculinity and femininity are not the inherent, respective qualities of male and female. However queer theory then emphasises that the sex-gender grid largely supports the heterosexual matrix (gender is still the defining attribute in sexual object choice). It is queer theory's belief that the exposure of gender as a performative effect will destabilise the sex-gender matrix and therefore rattle the dominance of heterosexuality. Secondly, queer theory develops this argument by questioning if desire is necessarily circumscribed by the gender of the subject's sexual object choice (see Chapter 1: sections on Sedgwick and Dollimore). Surely factors other than gender, may equally determine sexuality – such as a preference for a specific activity or sensation? The goal of both debates is the destabilization of sexual identity.

Therefore, the first chapter of this book does not offer film analysis at all but is devoted to an examination of 'queer' as it appears in both theory and politics. There is, of course, an irresolvable tension between queer theory, which 'has largely been the creation of academics' (Seidman, 1996: 13), and queer politics which was a response to the everyday problems faced by 'queers'. While queer theory (in its broadest sense) focuses on mismatches or incoherencies in the assumed stable continuum of sex, gender and sexuality – exposing heterosexuality as simply one of a myriad of performative effects – queer politics (rightly or wrongly) was often seen as a 'stroppier' (Healy, 1996: 179) version of gay liberation politics. Yet much queer political work cherished the same intention as queer theory – the destabilization of the heteronormative landscape through the exposure of sexuality as an identification rather than identity and thus challenging the hetero/homo hierarchical binary. However, it achieved only moderate success in mobilising such radical aims. Theory may argue that identity is a performative effect but trying to mobilise this agenda in the mainstream is a hefty task by any standards.

To a great extent Jarman's work falls into the same trap. His narratives (especially *The Garden* and *Edward II*) continually represent failed attempts to overthrow the dominant sexual hierarchy. Instead of achieving their goal, Jarman's images often only succeed in martyring or sentimentalising queer love. The overt separationist politics, founded on 'in-you-face' aggression, only constrict the queer lovers within the crippling, yet ironically heroic, position of victimhood.

However, this book will stress that some of the 'queerest' images in Jarman's work are those not explicitly connected to allegorical political activism. Therefore, Chapter 2 explores the thematic and stylistic concerns of the movement known as 'New Queer Cinema': a cluster of queer-themed films which attempted to address the tensions between queer activism and its theoretical cousin – queer theory. There is always a difficulty in trying to analyse the salient features from such a diverse range of films, especially considering that much of queer cinema was heavily influenced by American underground filmmaking while Jarman represents his own unique brand of British 'art cinema-inclined work' (O'Pray, 196: 184). Yet the similarities throughout queer cinema are not to be found simply in issues of style but in its representation of cultural themes. The Queer New Wave is largely a cinema of anti-identity politics, postmodern and dystopic in its representations and politically incorrect. It also questions the position of the male body within cinematic traditions and normative representations of gender. Finally, the pandemic of AIDS is evident throughout queer cinema whether addressed directly or metaphorically.

The rest of the chapters are then devoted to expanding the themes raised in Chapters 1 and 2 in more direct relation to Jarman's Cinema. In contrast to other studies of Jarman, this book will not proceed chronologically (one film per chapter) but, in keeping with the agenda of analysing the 'queerness' of the films, the book will be ordered thematically. As a result some Jarman films will receive more attention than others. Chapters 3 to 6 are largely concerned with Jarman's 'queer' representation of gender. Chapters 3 and 4 look at Jarman's representation of masculinity and consider the politics of Jarman's self-tortured male masochists while also analysing how Jarman deliberately subverts many gay stereotypes or tropes in his work, such as the gay cliché of 'straight identified rough trade'. Chapters 5 and 6 offer an analysis of femininity in Jarman's cinema and, as can only be expected, Chapter 5 focuses upon Jarman's beloved icon of the screen: Tilda Swinton. Jarman has often been accused of misogyny in his representation of the female body but I challenge this criticism by arguing that Jarman continually employs Swinton's famous androgyny and her command of Brechtian acting style in order to expose gender as a performative effect. Swinton's acting style consistently evidences a distinction between Swinton the actor and her character's role, drawing attention to the performed femininity or this role or, to use Mary Ann Doane's famous term, her 'feminine masquerade' (1991). Although locating her politics firmly within feminism, Swinton's performances are undeniably some of the 'queerest' (in the sense of non-normative) images in Jarman's films. While Chapter 5 defends Jarman's representation of 'monstrous' women, Chapter 6 focuses upon occasions when Jarman's cinema notably avoids the representation of the female body altogether, such as *The Angelic Conversation*, where the Dark Lady of the Sonnets does not appear. Drawing upon psychoanlytical theories (largely Kristevan), the chapter analyses Jarman's representation of sublime femininity and his recurrent motifs of water imagery and narcissistic reflections.

Chapter 7 tries to unite all these themes within broader paradigms and draws parallels between Jean Genet and Jarman. Jarman has often been described as the successor to Jean Genet so this chapter attempts to discern the thematic and stylistic links between Jarman and the films of Genet. Genet's work has often been (mis)read as the internalization of oppression and self-loathing – a criticism which has been levelled at Jarman too. Yet drawing upon Bersani's theories, I argue that Genet and Jarman are both attempting to move beyond the confining limits of transgression itself.

All the chapters draw attention to Jarman's representation of the 'body' but this theme is further developed in Chapter 8 in the analysis of *Blue*. Jarman is, of course, (in)famous for his explicit representation of the body and *Sebastiane* became famous, predominantly, because of its male nudity. *Blue*, however, is remarkable for the way in which the physical body is absent from the imagery but, despite this, the film actually manages to inspire an awareness of the body, without representing the body itself.

In many ways this is the third key theme of the book (after the 'queering of heterosexuality' and the how 'desire is a solvent of identity'): desire *as* the body versus desire *beyond* the body. Jarman's work is not about trying to disavow the body, its desires and physical attributes, in order to impose some bogus sense of sublimity beyond the physical. Instead his work emphasises that transcendence is attained through the physical. As Andrew Moor summarizes 'the *melding* of matter and spirit forms the basis of Jarman's romantic quest' (my emphasis, 2000: 52).

It is true that Jarman was never a populist filmmaker and his films were certainly never 'crowd pleasers' at lesbian and gay film festivals. Instead his cinema was uniquely personal, emphasising his own political, philosophical and erotic vision, regardless of whether it appealed to a 'gay' audience or not. Yet Jarman's cinema offers great pleasures to the spectator. Campiness/humour feature throughout all his films so that even the bleak and profoundly disturbing *Last of England* has moments of visual irony while *Blue*, made when Jarman was suffering extreme ill-health, offers moments of wry humour in the voice-over narration.

Therefore, I hope that this queer analysis of Jarman's cinema will not commit the crime which Leo Bersani accuses Judith Butler of doing in much of her 'queer' theorising: namely making 'heavy stuff for some silly and familiar campiness' (Bersani, 1995: 48). I hope this book, in all its chapters, conveys the sense of pleasure which the films offer and doesn't reduce the films to comic-book illuminations of queer theory. Finally, although this book is an academic study, I hope the writing still suggests a sense of the 18 year-old who was not only inspired by *Edward II*'s dynamic images of queer sexuality but who also fell in love with King Edward's glistening shoulders.

1

WHAT'S QUEER? QUEER THEORY VERSUS QUEER POLITICS

Are Derek Jarman's films simply political slogans? Leo Bersani and Ulysse Dutoit argue that *Edward II* 'is a gay and lesbian rally' (1999: 18) while José Arroyo (1993: 85) points out that Jarman's work was substantially influenced by the politics of second wave gay liberation which emphasized a separatist, minority style, identity politics. Therefore, it could be argued that many of Jarman's films, especially works such as *Edward II* and *The Garden* merely represent tendentious battles between 'good' queers and 'evil' straights or (to use Jarman's word) 'heterosoc'.

It is very possible to read Jarman's cinema as a political tract and Jarman himself was very happy to have his work interpreted as such – for example, the accompanying script to *Edward II* subordinates the Marlowe text to a huge queer slogan on every page. However, this book will argue that although it is feasible to read Jarman's work as a political slogan, the films' 'queer' status owe more to their representation of 'queer' in its theoretical sense rather than through the portrayal of vanguard political activism.

Therefore, this chapter seeks to explore the tension between 'queer' as an academic theory and 'queer' as it is mobilized politically. Although Teresa de Lauretis argued that queer theory had little to do with queer politics of the early nineties (1991: xvii) this was a slightly narrow view. The 'zaps' of Queer Nation, and its British counterpart OutRage, never intended to be jazzed up second wave Gay Lib. Queer zaps were not attempting to proclaim the presence of a quantifiable minority and carve a niche for it in the heterocentrist landscape. Instead, queer zaps sought to destabilize that very landscape itself. Queer was not opposed to the dominant but attempted to rupture it from within. Hence queer politics' emphasis on the subversion of heteronormative spaces (public places such as shopping centres), breaking down normal/queer boundaries and turning dichotomies inside out. Queer was never about offering an assimilationist agenda – representing a quantifiable minority which pleaded for acceptance – but instead attempted to expose the cultural contingency of the normal/queer dichotomy itself. In short, queer politics, like queer theory, attempted the deconstruction of the limiting labels of sexual and gender identities.

However, there is a tension between politics and theory. Although 'queer' may offer tantalising theoretical possibilities, these often encounter barricades when activists attempt to mobilize them in the political arena. This chapter will review the debates central to queer theory and then explore the attempts which have been made politically to mobilize these theories.

A Queer Background

Early lesbian and gay studies often employed a methodology similar to early women's studies in that it strained to unearth all the 'queer'-identified characters in the historical and cultural landscape. The belief was that by claiming the leading literary and artistic figures of the past, the status of 'queer' would be elevated. We may be 'queer' but we're in good company. We have Shakespeare, Marlowe, Wilde, Michelangelo, Leonardo da Vinci and so the list can continue. Jackie Stacey (1991: 293-6) aptly terms this the 'Oscar Wilde approach'.

This approach is not as empowering as it initially appears. Firstly, it is difficult to label a figure such as Shakespeare as 'gay' or 'queer' when such terms did not exist in Renaissance England. The Elizabethans did not possess appropriate vocabulary for condemning a man on the grounds of sexual dissidence. He could either be a cuckold – a doddery, old codger who allowed his wife to be seduced right under his nose – or he could be slighted on grounds of gender transitivity (effeminacy).

Secondly, the Oscar Wilde approach only locates famous 'queer' figures within the historical landscape but does little to change that landscape itself. What is the benefit, either politically or academically, of arguing that a leading figure is 'queer'? Does it actually do anything to change the heterosexist bias of the landscape in which those figures are located?

Thirdly, the Oscar Wilde approach assumes that history is an immutable canvas whose events are indelibly inked upon its surface. History, however, is a changing picture whose documents are always subject to new interpretations. For example, scholars do not read Shakespeare in the same fashion now as they did in the Victorian era or even in the 1970s.

Queer theory, therefore, instead of simply trying to locate 'queer' characters within the landscape, attempts to overthrow the heterosexist landscape itself. Rather than locating 'queerness' as a quantifiable entity, queer theory questions the very idea of a sexual identity and, in doing so, challenges the regimentation of sexuality into a clean-cut homo/hetero binary.

In this respect queer theory is a postmodern practice based upon issues of social constructionism, the decentring of the subject and the dissolution of identity. As Stuart Hall summarizes, the postmodern subject is:

conceptualized has having no fixed, essential or permanent identity. Identity becomes a 'moveable feast': formed and transformed continuously in relation to the ways we are represented or addressed in the cultural systems which surround us.

(1992: 277)

Therefore identity is 'an effect of identification with and against others: being ongoing and always incomplete, it is a process rather than a property' (Jagose, 1996: 79). The writer who developed these theories in relation to sexual identifications was Michel Foucault whose extensive body of writing set the precedence for queer studies and queer theory. Arguably, Foucault's most important contribution to these debates is his theory about the socially constructed nature of sexuality.

This socially constructed nature of sexuality, or 'Foucaultian constructionism' has, however, often been misinterpreted as arguing that sexual object choice is a cultural construct. Misreadings of Foucault have argued that human subjects are sexually attracted to someone of the same/opposite sex because of cultural interpellation. In what is termed a 'sloppy folk constructionism', people 'learn' to be attracted to the same/opposite sex because of peer pressure. Yet this was not Foucault's thesis. Instead Foucaultian constructionist theory tried to explain how sexual identities are the result of culture labelling and classifying various sexual acts. Before the modern stigma of 'the homosexual' was invented, many people may have engaged in 'same-sex acts' but simply did not claim an identity from those acts. Foucault cites Ancient Greece as an example of a culture which did not categorize someone in the same fashion as modern Western culture does (1975: 97). In Ancient Mediterranean cultures an adult Greek male could have sexual relations with anyone he wanted, provided he remained the active or penetrative partner during intercourse. The objects of the adult Greek's attentions could be women, slaves or boys – anyone who did not enjoy the same social position as he did. The point is that in Ancient Mediterranean culture, the sexual act did not signify the same sexual identification as it does in contemporary Western culture. The concept of the homosexual/heterosexual identification system, predicated upon *whom* someone had sex with, held no validity in Ancient Greek culture.

Similarly, in contemporary times there are cultures which do not delineate sexual identity in the same way as Western culture. In Latin American culture, for example, 'there is no cultural equivalent to the modern "gay" man in the Mexican/Latin American sexual system' (Almaguer 1993: 255). In Latin culture it is only the passive, penetrable man who is labelled as 'gay'. The active, penetrative man is straight identified. In this culture, sexuality is not delineated in terms of *whom* someone has sex with, but in terms of *how* someone has sex.

Constructionists therefore view the concept of a 'gay' identity as dependant upon the culture in which the sexual subject is located. Many people may be subject to some form of homoerotic desires but it is only modern, Western culture which classifies those desires into a distinct homo/hetero binary.

Foucault posits 1879 as the inception of the homosexual subject (although historians such as Alan Bray contest this date and argue that the taxonomy 'the homosexual' was first used towards the end of the seventeenth century in the subculture of 'molly houses' (Bray, 1988: 16-17)). No longer someone who simply indulged in a range of sexual acts, the 'homosexual' was now constituted by those very activities. To have sex with another man bestowed a homosexual identity upon the subject. Most importantly, this identity was deemed to be 'visible' in the body of the homosexual and the main signifier was what Foucault termed an 'interior androgyny, a hermaphroditism of the soul' (1978: 43) or what we now term 'gender transitivity' or 'effeminacy'. Homosexuality was identified and stigmatized by a crude yet rigid conflation with gender. This 'hermaphroditism of the soul' lingered well into the twentieth century as the supreme signifier of homosexuality and was perpetuated in Western culture by figures such as Quinten Crisp who defined the predicament of homosexuals by writing that 'they set out to win the love of a "real" man. If they succeed, they fail. A man who "goes with" other men is not what they would call a real man' (1968: 62).

This leads to Foucault's other main development for queer studies in which he argued that sexuality was the insidious effect of networks of power. Foucault argued that, contrary to popular belief, there was not a social repression of sexuality in the Victorian era but a huge incitement to speak about it because this helped to regulate, classify and control sexual subjects. Sexuality is not a 'stubborn drive' (1978: 103) but a 'dense transfer point for the relations of power' (ibid.). According to Foucault, power is not something which certain groups of people 'have' but instead is a network of forces. These forces are not simply random but occur in specific historical contexts in which certain groups or factions *do* have control or dominance. Foucault argued that modern power does not function through repressing sexual desires but instead by classifying, marginalising and therefore morally ranking these various sexualities. Yet, where there is power there is always resistance and the formation of the homosexual subject facilitated the development of a unified group who could, through what Foucault termed 'reverse discourse', claim the label as a useful identity:

> Homosexuality began to speak on its own behalf, to demand that its legitimacy or 'naturality' be acknowledged, often in the same vocabulary, using the same categories by which it was medically qualified.
>
> (1978: 101)

The queer theorist who developed these ideas – the conflation of gender with sexuality; the constructionism versus essentialism debates and how sexuality is endemic to networks of power – is Eve Kosofsky Sedgwick.

Eve Kosofsky Sedgwick

Labelled the 'queen of queer studies' whose work 'can be seen as initiating the field of queer theory' (Campbell, 2000: 159), the importance of Eve Sedgwick in queer studies cannot be overemphasized. Although often criticized for her indulgent queer readings of classic texts (see Siegel, 1998: 36), in which she claims to 'find' fist-fucking in Henry James (or rather 'fisting-as-*écriture*') and masturbation in Jane Austen, Sedgwick has certainly offered many valuable developments in debates on sexuality.

The thesis which first made Sedgwick's name was *Between Men: English Literature and Male Homosocial Desire* (1985) – an exploration of 'homosociality' (a phenomenon which can *roughly* be termed 'male bonding') and its fraught relationship with homosexuality. Sedgwick explains that although there was no tension between Ancient Greek homosociality – men identifying with and promoting the interests of other men – and homosexuality – men having sex with men (see Dover, 1980) – modern culture is structured by an exaltation of the one and subordination or abjection of the other (1985: 5). Developing Irigaray's formulation of 'hom(m)o-sexuality' (1985: 170-1), Sedgwick argues that homosociality or male bonding is dependant on two factors: homophobia and the objectification of women. The homoeroticism which develops between close friends is displaced onto the abject other of the stigmatized homosexual and also sublimated into desire for the woman. It has been Sedgwick's project to illuminate how this operates not only within classic literary texts but contemporary Western society.

Sedgwick's approach, therefore, is deconstructionist. She makes this clear (or as clear as her swirly prose can ever be) within the first few pages of *Epistemology of the Closet*:

one main strand of argument in this book is deconstructive, in a fairly specific sense. The analytic move it makes it to demonstrate that categories presented in a culture as symmetrical binary oppositions – heterosexual/homosexual, in this case – actually subsist in a more unsettled and dynamic tacit relation according to which, first, term B is not symmetrical with but subordinated to term A; but, second, the ontologically valorized term A actually depends for its meaning on the simultaneous subsumption and exclusion of term B.

(1990: 9-10)

In her numerous writings, Sedgwick has explored the relationship between homo- and heterosexuality, showing that homosexuality – far from being the bogeyman of modern, bourgeois culture – is actually heterosexuality's defining other. Sedgwick's project has been the destabilization of normative heterosexuality and of the homo/hetero binary which she has attempted to achieve through two main agendas.

Firstly, Sedgwick reworks Foucault's 'constructionist' versus 'essentialist' argument into the paradigms 'universalising' versus 'minoritising'. The minoritising approach sees homosexuality as something relevant to only a specific or distinct minority. On the other hand, the universalising approach reads homosexuality as something which pervades, in one way or another, the entire spectrum of sexualities in modern culture (Sedgwick, 1990: 1-2). 'Universalising' and 'minoritising' are therefore not synonyms for 'constructionist' and 'essentialist' but offer a more malleable theory. The minoritising view offers an identity politics founded on the sense of immutable sexual identity but the universalising view, rather than focusing on the idea of identification as an effect produced by culture, suggests that sexual desire moves in excess of the limiting labels of *any* sexual identification. Arguably, it is impossible to regiment sexual desire. As Sedgwick writes, 'sexual desire is an unpredictable powerful solvent of stable identities' so that 'apparently heterosexual persons and object choices are strongly marked by same-sex influences and desires' (1990: 85).

Sedgwick also reworks Foucault's argument that sexuality is the effect of networks of power into the symbol of 'the closet' which she sees as 'the defining structure for gay oppression in this century' (1990: 71). Sexuality and, more importantly, knowledge of sexuality are intrinsically linked to the web-like structures of power pervading modern culture. Homosexuality holds an important relation to the 'wider mappings of secrecy and disclosure' (1990: 71) and to issues of public and private that maintain a sexual hierarchy throughout the Western world. 'Queers' are deemed 'tolerable' provided they remain conveniently closeted. It's not the homosexuality as such which is closeted but the knowledge of the knowledge: the idea of the open secret.

Secondly, Sedgwick, drawing upon the innovative writing of Gayle Rubin (1975 and 1993), emphasizes that sexuality is fluid and cannot be accommodated by the rubric established to describe gender (1990: 29). In her analysis of gay male sexuality, Sedgwick questions the historical paradigms which have been used to describe sexuality through a conflation of sexuality with gender. Foucault's 'hermaphroditism of the soul', which sees homosexuality as characterized by the homosexual's liminal positions between genders, is still read as an axiom in contemporary culture. Sedgwick asks why it is assumed that 'anyone, male or female, who desires a man must by definition be feminine' (1993: 157).

In a similar vein, Sedgwick questions why the sole defining feature of sexual identity has historically been the gender of the subject's sexual object choice? Sedgwick stresses the dizzying eclecticism of sexuality in order to emphasize that many other features *may* be the defining agency instead of gender (1990: 31). Some people, such as those who engage in SadoMasochsim (S&M), may eroticize a specific act or sensation rather than the sex or gender of their partner. Indeed some S&Mers may be equally happy to engage in a sexual 'fix' with a partner of the same sex as with a partner of the opposite sex. Some people may enjoy only group sex and engage in threesomes. Others may eroticize age difference and be 'cradle-snatchers' or 'daddy-seekers' while others may eroticize body-types and be muscle-worshippers or chubby-chasers. All these features may be equally important (if not even more important) for the subject than the sex or gender of his/her sexual partner.

In light of this argument, Sedgwick's most (in)famous contribution to queer theory has been her revival of a category from archaic sexology: the onanist or chronic masturbator. Sedgwick (when not moaning about how fat she is (1998: 629)) has announced in her critical writing that she herself does not identify as homo- or heterosexual because for her, sexuality *is not* predicated upon sexual object choice but is masturbation (1998: 626). Indeed, for Sedgwick the gender or sexual object choice is irrelevant as she does not even like sex with anyone else but instead only enjoys sex on her own and therefore identifies as an onanist – neither heterosexual nor homosexual but 'queer'. Therefore, in light of Sedgwick's argument, are we often not too reductionist in the way we label sexual identity? For example, if a straight identified female straps on a dildo and fucks her male partner can this 'queer' activity be labelled 'heterosexual'? Although the activity is between a male/female couple the sexual act itself violates the traditional performance of heterosexuality. Similarly, if a straight identified women gains considerable erotic pleasure from watching hardcore gay porn is it not more than a little reductionist to label her desire as 'heterosexual'?

The effect of both these Sedgwickian approaches – universalising versus minoritising and the calibration of sexuality outside the axis of gender – is to fracture the hetero/homo binary and challenge the importance of sexual identity politics. The goal of Sedgwick's project is to destabilize heteronormativity and to shift the emphasis from traditional identity politics to a broader examination of how sexual taxonomies are labelled and regimented by the cultural landscape.

Judith Butler

If Sedgwick has been called the Queen of Queer Studies then Judith Butler is undeniably the herald of queer theory. Although Butler wrote *Gender Trouble* (1990) as a feminist project, the book's exposition of gender instability and how heterosexuality is universally privileged, held great importance for queer studies. In her influential thesis Butler argued that gender – the matrix on which traditional heterosexuality is predicated – is a self reflexive, performative effect. In an often quoted passage, Butler asserts that 'there is no gender identity behind the expressions of gender; that identity is performatively constituted by the very "expressions" that are said to be its results (1999: 33).'

Performativity was a term first developed by the philosopher John Austin who argued that language could be divided into two broad categories: the constative and the performative (1966). The constative is descriptive language – a saying which describes what is already there. (An example of a constative utterance might be: 'It's a sunny day.)' The performative, on the other hand, is a 'saying' or 'doing' which constitutes a 'being' when interpellated within an accepted matrix of conventions and witnesses. The most often cited example of a 'performative' is the marriage ceremony where the priest or vicar *pronounces* the man and woman to be husband and wife. This utterance or gesture has altered the ontological status of the male and female subjects standing in the church before the vicar. No longer simply a man and woman now the vicar has *pronounced* them to be husband and wife. However, performativity cannot exist in a vacuum. It can only make sense within an established and accepted social matrix. If the proverbial 'man off the street' pronounced the male and female to be husband and wife then the utterance would mean nothing. Similarly the performative always requires witnesses who validate its legitimacy within this accepted culture.

Therefore, it is important not to confuse performativity with performance – as some early critics of Butler's work did. Performance is voluntary and applied (the actor is on the stage 'performing' King Lear) while performativity has an anti-voluntarist aesthetic which cannot be separated from the concepts of iterability and ritualization. Butler, in her sequel, *Bodies that Matter*, stresses that 'performativity must not be understood as a singular or deliberate "act", but rather as the reiterative and citational practice by which discourse produces the effects that it names' (1993: 2). If this were not the case, Butler speculates, the subject could simply go to the wardrobe, put on a 'gender of the day' and then take it off at night (1993: x).

In order to illustrate how all gender is not only performative but imitative, Butler cites the entertainment spectacle of drag which she argues exposes the apish nature of gender as 'in imitating gender, drag implicitly reveals the imitative structure of gender itself – as well as its contingency' (1999: 175). Where previous feminist critics read drag as a mockery of the idea of essentialized femininity, Butler argued that drag demonstrated that there was no original or inherent femininity to be caricatured or mocked. Drag exposed that *all* gender is a performative effect.

The problem, however, with Butler's argument is that it cites only a drag act of supreme quality. Butler's theory is certainly appropriate to a drag act where the gender parody is seamless and imperceptible. The frisson or thrill of such an act is how it exposes gender as imitative and not related to chromosomal sex. Unfortunately other drag acts (such as the classic British end-of-the-pier type drag show) where the artist is perceptibly a man in woman's clothes actually have the opposite effect and support an essentialist view in which gender can be argued to be inextricably linked to chromosomal sex.

Again many critics misinterpreted Butler's theories and often conflated day-to day gender performativity with theatrical drag which Butler offered simply as *an example* of performativity. Sheila Jeffreys, for example, asks:

> When a woman is being beaten by the brutal man she lives with is this because she adopted the feminine gender in her appearance? Would it be a solution for her to adopt a masculine gender for the day and strut about in a work shirt or leather chaps?
>
> (1993: 81)

Jeffreys certainly asks a remarkable question. Not only does she believe that dressing as a stereotypical gay leatherman is going to defeat the problem of domestic violence but she also thinks that gender can be 'adopted'. This is diametrically opposed to Butler's anti-voluntarist argument. These mis-readings of Butler, though, may well have more to do with Butler's excruciating writing style (Medhurst calls it 'barbed-wire prose' (1997: xxiv)) than the academic ability of her readers.

However, although Butler was writing from a feminist agenda, her work not only revised feminist politics but had a tremendous influence on emerging queer studies. Although Sedgwick has pointed out that gender may not be the defining characteristic of sexual object choice, gender performativity has traditionally been thought to underpin heterosexuality. Hetero-sexuality literally translates into the sexuality of difference (hetero = difference) and it is the gender difference (masculine/feminine) which is thought to be the scaffold of hetero-erotics. Masculinity is attracted to its binary opposite – femininity. Butler terms this the 'heterosexual matrix' and points out that 'the institution of a compulsory and naturalized heterosexuality *requires* and regulates gender as a binary relation in which the masculine term is differentiated from a feminine term, and this differentiation is accomplished through the practices of heterosexual desire' (1999: 30). Put simply, Butler is arguing that for heterosexuality to appear as 'natural' it requires the gender binary to also seem essential or natural. However, if gender is destabilized, by exposing it as a performative effect through performances such as drag or camp, then the scaffold for heterosexual desire is challenged. Much 'queer' art therefore has tried to represent gender as a 'regulatory fiction' (Butler, 1999: 180) and force the spectator to realize that gender may actually be a flimsy scaffold for eroticism. If a heterosexual man is watching a 'quality' drag act and finds the drag-artist 'sexually attractive' then this will challenge his sense of sexual identification and ask him to reconsider how something as 'fictional' as gender can actually be a scaffold for eroticism. Queer representations therefore ask if desire is *necessarily* circumscribed by the gender of the sexual object choice. And, if desire is predicated upon gender, how can desire be viewed as stable if gender is such a flexible fiction?

Jonathan Dollimore

While Butler argued that gender is a performative effect and Sedgwick attempted to separate sexuality from the constrictions of gender, Jonathan Dollimore has examined the potential of this 'queerness' to disrupt normativity. It has been Dollimore's project to analyse how queerness subverts the dominant from within. Dollimore asserts that the power of queerness/perversity/sexual dissidence is not (despite what people like to think) that it threatens from without. Instead the power of queerness is that it fissures from within.

Dollimore's *Sexual Dissidence* argues that what is culturally classed as perversion is often 'a displacement of disorder from within the dominant onto the subordinate, achieved via a mapping of the natural/unnatural binary onto the dominant/subordinate hierarchy' (1991: 111). Dollimore asserts that 'the proximate is often constructed as the other' (ibid.: 33). There is a continuous displacement from the dominant, onto the subordinate, which Dollimore terms 'transgressive reinscription' (ibid.: 103).

Yet Dollimore argues that sexual dissidence has the power to turn these binaries inside/out and reveal that perversity *really* stems from the inside but is only culturally constructed as being outside the normal. The power of perversity to disrupt and dishevel lies in the fact that it is intrinsically linked to the inside – the so-called natural or normal. Dollimore calls this the 'paradoxical perverse'. The power of perversity is that it 'is very often perceived as at once utterly alien to what it threatens, and yet, mysteriously [is] inherent within it' (ibid.: 121). The outsider may be outside the normal but it is only by being in opposition to the centre or 'normal' that the outsider is considered deviant or strange in the first place. In this respect, while the outsider may be outside heteronormativity (s)he is simultaneously inside it. The power of the 'paradoxical perverse', to dishevel and even destabilize heteronormative binaries, Dollimore terms 'the perverse dynamic' (ibid.: 121). In an analysis of texts ranging from Shakespeare's *The Tempest* to Milton's *Paradise Lost*, Dollimore shows how 'transgressive reinscription' is employed time and again in cultural representations but that the 'perverse dynamic' can dishevel and upset this hegemony.

Dollimore, however, is certainly one of the first queer theorists to put theory into practice and has mobilized his own version of the 'perverse dynamic' in his everyday life. Queer's emphasis on anti-identity – sexuality moving beyond the confines of gender and fissuring from within – not only inspires Dollimore's writing but fuels his personal life as well. Indeed Dollimore's much publicized sex life (of which, it must be noted, he has recently been the main publicist (2001: 23)) has attracted as much interest as his academic theories. Although Dollimore claims (or should that be 'brags'?) that throughout his academic career he has been 'fucked from pillow to bedpost by other guys' (2001: 23), he recently found himself 'in a relationship with a woman' (ibid.: 22). Apparently this propelled various academic colleagues into apoplexy. Some snarled that Dollimore was a 'traitor' who had become a 'breeder' (ibid.: 23) while others sneered that Dollimore had only ever been pretending to be gay to further his career (ibid.: 23) because, as we all know, being gay identified is such a jolly career booster.

However, Dollimore's radical shifts in sexual identifications certainly place a queer slant upon the theory of 'sexual dissidence' fissuring from within. Dollimore has not only challenged heteronormativity but the oppressive limitations of hegemonic gay identifications. Understandably therefore, Dollimore's other research strand has always been similar to Sedgwick's: the calibration of sexuality outside the matrix of gender. Yet while Sedgwick formulates 'universalising' sexual theory, Dollimore (as could only be expected) focuses on the issue of bisexuality (1996; 1997; 2001) and even asserts that, in the future 'the norm will surely be bisexuality' (2001: 17). For Dollimore, bisexuality does not signal the weakening of identity politics but is, in fact, the fruition of a queer agenda, offering 'a liberating, dynamic state of unfixity' (1996: 526). Bisexuality not only signifies instability in the subject's sexual identification but also questions the sexual subjectivity of others.

Dollimore therefore suggests that gay identity politics are not simply Foucault's 'reverse discourse' but may, in fact, be a way to salve the difficulties of regulating desire itself (2001: 32). Gay identity politics may actually be a 'protection' (ibid.: 26) against the frightening complexity of sexual desire and, as such, may be stiflingly 'normative' (ibid.: 34). Identity politics may suffocate people by making them anxious about conforming to established straight/gay sexual scripts. Dollimore therefore argues (in words echoing Sedgwick) 'that desire always retains the potential to disturbingly unfix...identity' (2001: 35). Yet for Dollimore, this is not something which the subject should strain, at all costs, to reject but instead is something which should be embraced as a powerful 'perverse dynamic'.

Alan Sinfield

One of the most prolific queer theorists in the British Academy and (arguably) the *first* chair of Lesbian and Gay Studies, Sinfield has produced an extensive body of writing on theatre, literature and queer culture and politics. Sinfield's project has been the examination of an English queer identity/identification. Yet, unlike Sedgwick, Butler or Dollimore his work is less abstract and favours a cultural materialist approach rather than psychoanalysis or deconstruction.

Cultural materialism (indebted to the theories of Marx and Althusser) regards any cultural/social formation as an ongoing process of self-reproduction. Any social formation has to prevent its own extinction and it does this through the Ideological State Apparatuses such as church, education and the law. People are interpellated or hailed up by these dominant ideologies which socialize them into acceptable subjectivity. The social formation will then repeat this socialization for the next generation.

Therefore, the dominant ideology always appears to be normal or natural or (if we credit Christianity) God-given. Most importantly, for Queer Theory, all the ideological state apparatuses cherish normative ideas of gender and sexuality. The idea of the nuclear family, for example, is inscribed in and reinforced by the dominant ideologies of the Western world. Yet these dominant ideologies are in a constant state of flux and readjustment. Continuous pressure from sub-cultural formations and other disturbances force dominant ideologies to adapt. Rather than employ the psychoanalytic vocabulary of Dollimore or the deconstructive literary gymnastics of Sedgwick, Sinfield posits dissidence in cultural/historical terms. Perversity is created by a struggle between dominant ideologies. It is these fractures in ideologies or 'faultlines' (Sinfield 1992) which are labelled as dissidence.

One of Sinfield's most influential theses is his example of the history of effeminacy and its relation to British homosexuality. Using Oscar Wilde as a key example, Sinfield asserted that the conflation of homosexuality with effeminacy is a relatively recent occurrence in British culture. In Wilde's time, male effeminacy may not have been anything to be proud of, but it certainly didn't stigmatize the subject as homosexual. Wilde was exonerated from such accusations by his social class. Effeminacy was read as representative of upper (or upper middle) class laxity and effeteness but it was not indicative of same-sex passion (1994: 71).

However, since the public disgrace of Oscar Wilde the dominant ideology has conflated effeminacy with homosexuality. Effeminacy is now commonly perceived as the signifier of same-sex passion so that a film or television spectator now knows to interpret an effeminate man as homosexual (see Russo 1981; Dyer, 1984). Arguably, homophobia is not the reason why many gay men are harassed. Sometimes the harassment should be more correctly termed 'effeminophobia'. Many schoolboys suffer playground bullying and hear that bitter taunt 'queer' not because their sexual behaviour is non-normative but because they are gender transitive/effeminate and therefore transgressive the sex/gender 'framework' (Sinfield 1994: 126) which supports the normal/queer binary.

Sinfield points out that the Oscar Wilde trial had a tidal-wave effect (indeed, preceding the mass media, Wilde was arguably one of Britain's first 'celebrities') and effeminacy came to be perceived as the signifier of homosexuality. This is one example of the dominant ideology reacting to a fissure within its ranks and policing the sex-gender grid upon which the heterosexual matrix teeters.

Sinfield's exploration of homosexuality and its conflation with gender returns us to the debates raised by Sedgwick, Dollimore and Butler. How do we challenge the hierarchical hetero/homo binary and how do we calibrate sexuality without collapsing it into the heterosexist rubric used to define gender? Although it has been queer theory's agenda to deconstruct heteronormativity within the pages of academia, queer activism attempted the difficult task of mobilising these theories in everyday life.

Queer Politics

Queer politics, then, absorbed some of the theoretical moves made in queer theory, which also emerged at this time – a post-structuralist, postmodern, constructionist view of sexual identity, which the very term 'queer' tried to capture, in an attempt to erase the boundaries that had previously riven sexual communities.

(Bell and Binnie, 2000: 37)

Queer politics attempted to mobilize the same agenda as appeared on the pages of academic texts. Queer was not simply a feistier version of Gay Lib or a 'stroppier' identity politics (Healy, 1996: 179). It was not attempting to carve out a niche in the heteronormative landscape for a quantifiable minority but instead sought to destabilize the very concept of heteronormativity itself and minority identity politics.

However, it is particularly difficult to mobilize these theories. Writing about a 1991 Lesbian and Gay Studies conference, Angelia Wilson lamented that Judith Butler had stunned her audience with 'streams of impenetrable prose' (1997: 99) and, understandably, asked 'where is all this getting us?' (ibid.: 100). For a political scientist like Wilson, Butler's abstract theories of gender performativity, how drag exposes the cultural contingency of gender and how this can have a radically subversive effect upon sexual identifications, lack relevance for the realities of everyday existence. Understandably, Wilson argues that our main concern should be with 'the gap between queer theory and the practicalities of political activism' (ibid.: 100).

Yet how can theories which insist upon the deconstruction of identity be mobilized effectively? In order to answer this question I want to review the history of organized lesbian/gay/queer politics as it progressed through First and Second Wave Gay Liberation into Queer.

First Wave Gay Liberation

Apart from early homophile movements in major cities, the first organized gay political activism was Gay Liberation which can be divided into two eras. The first era offered a utopian liberation politics which 'aimed at freeing individuals from the constraints of a sex/gender system that locked them into mutually exclusive homo/hetero and feminine/masculine roles' (Seidman, 1997: 110). Although this agenda, with its emphasis on deconstructing exclusive identity categories and binaries, may seem similar to 1990s Queer Politics, there were some key differences.

Firstly, Gay Lib maintained that sexism was the backbone of gay oppression (Jay and Young, 1992: 7). Curiously this agenda was not intended solely for the liberation of lesbians. Gay men also claimed that they were oppressed by sexism. Employing the post-Foucaultian trope of reading gender and sexuality as collapsible categories, gay men really did argue that they were equally oppressed on the grounds of sexism. The argument runs that if homosexuality is considered emblematic of gender transitivity, gay men are therefore like women who, within a sexist society, are deemed inferior.

On the other hand masculinity and heterosexuality were thought to be virtually coterminous. This lead to 'semiotic guerrilla warfare' (Weeks, 1985: 198) in which gay men strained to appropriate the 'accepted' signifiers of masculinity, for example, muscularity and hairiness.

Secondly, First Wave Gay Lib was insistent upon liberating sexuality. The Gay Lib belief, however, was very different from Queer's flaunting of disreputable sex. Indeed Gay Lib emphasized the importance of tender sensuality as opposed to carnal sexuality. As Alan Young summarizes:

> This sexual freedom is not some kind of groovy life style with lots
> of sex, doing what feels good irrespective of others. It is sexual
> freedom premised upon the notions of pleasure through equality, no
> pleasure where there is inequality.
>
> (Jay and Young, 1992: 28)

However, the emphasis upon sexual pleasure through equality is a fragile
idea. There is always an imbalance of power in sexual activity although
this, within consensual sexual activity, is always a negotiated imbalance.
Therefore writers who were influenced by the idealism of early Gay Lib
politics often wrote the most fantastic accounts of sexuality. Brian
Pronger, in his interesting yet wild and wayward book, *The Arena of
Masculinity*, asserted that:

> Heterosexuality [...] is the eroticization of the power men have over
> women, the eroticization of the basically subordinate position of
> women in patriarchal culture; it is the eroticization of power
> difference.
>
> (1990: 61)

By contrast, Pronger reads homosexuality as 'the eroticization of basic
gender equality' (ibid.: 70). This leads him to make the ludicrously
sweeping statement that 'the equality of homoeroticism is demonstrated
by the relative absence of intimidation and violence in the openly sexual
environments of parks, bathhouses and backrooms. Men forcing
themselves on each other in these settings is very rare, almost unheard of'
(ibid.: 134). Just because Pronger hasn't heard of it doesn't mean it hasn't
happened. Only someone with no empirical knowledge of gay life
whatsoever could even consider making such a statement.

Thirdly, First Wave Gay Lib is further distinguished from Queer Politics
in the emphasis that it placed upon 'choice'. As Gary Lehring points out
'the liberationists did indeed argue that gays and straights alike needed only
to choose to be gay to make it so' (1997: 176-77). This was not Foucaultian
constructionism which argued that it was culture which labelled specific
sexualities in an attempt to regiment them. Instead this politics was what
we now term 'folk constructionism' which read sexuality as something

which may voluntarily be imposed or, on the other hand, disposed of.

However, if sexuality is supposedly voluntary then gay politics is weakened as bigots can ask why gays don't simply choose to be straight identified. Therefore First Wave Gay Lib 'gave way in the 1970s to an ethnic/minority socio-political agenda' (Seidman, 1997: 110), more commonly referred to as 'Second Wave Gay Lib'.

Second Wave Gay Liberation: the ethnic/minority agenda

Most commentators would argue that it is inaccurate to classify gays and lesbians as an ethnicity. However, Steven Epstein, in his stirring essay 'Gay Politics, Ethnic Identity: The Limits of Social Constructionism' offers a postmodern reading of 'ethnicity' which he sees as 'something that is neither an absolutely inescapable ascription nor something chosen and discarded at will' (1987: 43) and, in this respect, suggests that ethnicity is a suitable designation for gays and lesbians:

> It would seem to be precisely the fact that ethnic culture has been evacuated of content that has permitted the transposition of the category 'ethnicity' onto a group that, in the traditional sense of the term, clearly would not qualify for the designation. Thus it is true that lesbians and gay men don't really fit the original definition of what an ethnic group is: but then, neither really, do contemporary Jews, or Italian-Americans, or anyone else. In this way, the decline of the old ethnicity permits and encourages new groups to adopt the mantle and revive the phenomenon.
>
> (1997: 39)

From this politics of 'gay' ethnicity sprang the sweetly reassuring fantasy of the homogenous gay community 'wherein all were united by the commonality of homophobic oppression' (Healy, 1996: 176). The mythic, homogenous 'gay community' is a very comforting fantasy and gays and lesbians constantly 'dream up communities as utopias of belonging' (Taylor, 1997: 10). There will, of course, always be a superficial sense of community established in the face of oppression. Indeed, if there is one thing which distinguishes 'gay', in the sense of Second Wave Gay Lib, from 'homosexual' it is the emphasis placed on oppression. As Simon Watney argues:

> Gay Liberation insisted […] that what lesbians and gay men share is not some identical, personal essence of homosexual desire, but the social experience of discrimination and prejudice, which are mobilized by the workings or power – the law, the press, education, the church, social science, and so on – upon the terrain of sexuality as a whole.
>
> (1994: 17)

Being united against the monster of oppression is a poetic image but the problem with this politics is its reductive nature. There are (and will continue to be) many gay men who do not encounter oppression on a daily basis. Indeed some gay men (and if I'm being honest I should include myself) manage to earn a living from being gay identified and making a song and dance about it. This, of course, exposes the main problem with the mythic homogeneity of the gay community in that it will always be fractured by differences of race, class, age, sex and gender. Added to this we can offer a Sedgwickian point and fragment those who are even white, middle-class, male and gay identified along the intricate matrix of sexuality and corporeal sensuality in which the emphasis can be changed from the sexual object choice to the preference for an activity. Do white, same-sex practitioners of S&M identify more by the gender of their sexual partners than by the activity in which they engage?

Similarly, a great deal of nonsense has been written about the 'gay ghetto' – a misnomer inherited from Second Wave Gay Lib which, despite its inaccuracy, has entered common currency. There never has been and never will be a gay ghetto. Historically ghettos have been places where a minority has been *forced* to live – the prime examples have always been Jewish ghettos – or they have been areas where people have been confined due to crippling poverty and New York's 'Bronx' has almost entered into popular mythology as the prime example. However, an area created in terms of entertainment and freely entered by middle-class people can only be termed a ghetto by those who have absolutely no cultural knowledge whatsoever.

Second Wave Gay Lib, therefore, offers a paradoxical politics. On the one hand it emphasizes oppression. Gays are united under the crushing boot of 'hetero scum' (Warner, 1992: 19). On the other hand it represents a reverse discourse in which gay – which usually means white, middle-class, educated, gay man – is conveniently assimilated back into the mainstream. Being gay in a major city is predicated upon sex and consumerism. Metropolitan cities are crammed with professional, well-to-do gay men who, like 'Stepford Boyz' (Burston, 1995: 99) happily support the Pink Pound with their shopping, clubbing and gym membership.

With tensions rising between the internal factions of the supposedly homogenous gay and lesbian community, there was a need to readdress the umbrella term of 'lesbian and gay'. Dissent along the lines of socio-economic class, race, gender, ethnicity and, most importantly, sexual practices started to be vocalized. The idea of the community began to fracture and, by the early nineties, the marriage of lesbian and gay politics had given birth. But 'the child is queer, and a problem child it surely is' (Hayes, 1994: 14).

A Queer Agenda

It has now become popular to dismiss the minority/ethnic style politics of Second Wave Gay Lib yet it should be remembered that it is only possible to dismiss the politics of Second Wave Gay Lib because they have actually happened. Like early Feminism and the Black Rights Movement, a moment of unity (at least superficial unity) was necessary in order to make a protest. How can a minority contest the arbitrary oppression of a minority without congregating around and mobilising that characteristic minority status? In every political movement, a cursory moment of unity has always been important.

However, as the two waves of Gay Lib evidenced, both the essentialist minority politics and its corollary of an homogenous ethnic community as dictated by Second Wave Gay Lib, or the emphasis upon 'folk constructionism' and sexual choice as dictated by First Wave Gay Lib, offer limits and shortcomings in terms of political activism. While the First Wave's emphasis on sexuality as a 'choice' facilitates arguments that gays should therefore 'chose' to be straight, the Second Wave's insistence on essentialist politics can inspire eugenicist arguments or the belief that medical science should hunt for a 'cure'.

The key point is that the essentialist/constructionist debate is only raging, and we only hunt for different theories to explain how we turned out this way (not heterosexual), because it is implied that we turned out the wrong way. Until Queer Theory nobody questioned heterosexuality as it simply stands as an exalted monolith: the aspirant template of contemporary culture. Indeed as Calvin Thomas points out, 'straights have had the political luxury of not having to think about their sexuality, in much the same way as men have not had to think of themselves as gendered and whites have not had to think of themselves as raced' (2000: 17).

Queer Politics, therefore, tried to change the emphasis. Instead of asking why there is homosexuality, it inverted the question and demanded to know why there is homophobia? Most importantly 'queer' did not set itself in opposition with heterosexuality but against the idea of 'normal' (Warner, 1997: xxvi). Normal is, after all, a problematic word which holds a ridiculously lofty status. When examined in a cultural context it doesn't even make sense. How did society ever come to term something which should more accurately be labelled 'common' as 'normal'? To use a silly, yet comparable example, a great many people in the world are overweight or fat. That is something which is average or 'normal' yet certainly not exalted. Few people, on the other hand, look like supermodels. Supermodels are not 'normal' yet many people aspire to their extreme proportions. How therefore did we come to exalt a sexuality (heterosexuality) which is merely common or average?

Queer Theory, therefore, draws a distinction between the 'normal' and the 'normative'. 'Normal' refers to necessary biological or medical conditions – for example, human hearts should beat in a certain way or else people will drop down dead. It is therefore *necessary* that someone has a 'normal' heartbeat. The 'normative' by contrast is something which is a cultural construct but yet is deemed to be natural or necessary. There is, of course, a power in normalcy as when something is taken to granted, viewed as normal, then it is accepted as axiomatic. As Richard Dyer points out, it is heterosexuality's claim to 'naturalness and rightness' which 'oppresses us' (1997: 261).

Therefore Queer Politics sought to destabilize this hegemony. Not pleading for tolerance of homosexuality and a niche in a major city, queer tried to overthrow the workings of power. It is irrelevant why there is homosexuality and why queers turned out this way. Why the hell is there homophobia?

Queer Nation

American Queer Politics drew strongly upon the counter-politics deployed by ACTUP (AIDS Coalition To Unleash Power). Queer Nation was actually formed at an ACTUP meeting in New York, April 1990. The devastation which AIDS wrought in New York was comparable only with that in San Francisco. In Britain, however, even when the epidemic was at its highest, it never matched the decimation of AIDS-ridden New York and so, as can only be expected, Queer Nation was more influenced by AIDS politics than its British counterpart was.

From the start, Queer Nation's agenda, like ACTUP, was the fight to attain visibility. Queer Nation tried to break down the boundaries which delineated queer and straight or queer space and straight space. Queer disrupted the homophobic safety fence which kept queer/straight as mutually defining others. As symbolized by Queer Nation's lavender flag (the colour achieved by blurring the 'red, white and blue') the colours of straight and queer are not clearly delineated but do blur. No longer did queers want to be bounded in a subculture and entertained in gay villages. Instead queer concentrated on exposing the shifting dynamism of sexuality and the internal tensions and contradictions within identity categories.

Challenging homophobia, however, is a difficult task. Homophobia differs from, say, racism in that it 'is entirely a response to an *internal* possibility' (Bersani, 1995: 27). A racist may well believe ridiculous notions such as 'blacks are evil' but not even the most extreme racist would fear that blacks will persuade him to 'turn' black. Homophobia is the very opposite and, literally translated, means 'fear of same' (homo = same). It is the fear that someone might be labelled as homosexual or, even more threatening, that homosexuality may be all too enticing and incite unwanted desires, that causes acts of homophobia. Homophobic actions are therefore intended to distance or even abject the 'dangerous' homosexual body as 'to let gays be open about their gayness [...] is to risk being recruited' (Bersani, 1995: 27).

It was for this reason that Queer Nation emphasized the importance of 'actions' or 'zaps'. Very often these took the form of 'kiss-ins' in hyper-spaces – spaces which shouldn't 'belong' to anyone – such as shopping malls. The emphasis was often upon physical displays of affection which heterosexual couples take for granted (holding hands, kissing) but which are denied to same-sex couples unless they are confined to gay quarters. By claiming the shopping mall – a hyper-space usually claimed by the family – Queer Nation tried to show that all spaces could be queer. Queerness was everywhere – hence the ironic use of 'nation' in the group's title.

It is, however, important to differentiate 'actions' or 'zaps' from the pickets or protests initiated by previous Gay Lib organizations. Henry Abelove suggests that:

> Unlike a demonstration or a protest or a picket [...] an action expresses a felt need to create a wholly non-domestic site of excitement, outrage and interest. An action is, structurally speaking, a response to an experience or expectation or ennui, an ennui that is culturally produced by the absence in queer life or aspiration of those family excitements and interests to which we are all, queer or not, required to be habituated.
>
> (1992: 25)

As Abelove suggests, the sense of edginess and speed which an action entails is all important to queer politics. If queer is about destabilizing fixed identities and exposing categories as contingent, then it is important to maintain a sense of dynamics and edginess. As soon as queer becomes classifiable then it can be conveniently located back into the pigeonhole of the gay village. It can once again become the defining other to the normal heterosexual family and can be assimilated, provided it is confined to its safely locked-up box.

OutRage

Queer Nation's British cousin was OutRage. Unlike Queer Nation, OutRage was more indebted to the politics of the Gay Liberation Front (GLF) – which had become famous for employing the aggressive tactics of Second Wave Gay Lib – than it was to the politics of AIDS awareness. Although a British chapter of ACTUP was formed in January 1989, its tactics were never as extreme as its American counterpart because London had not been massacred by AIDS in the way New York had suffered. Therefore, OutRage was formed as a response to homophobic queer bashings and Thatcherite politics, especially the infamous Section 28 which prohibited the 'promotion' of homosexuality in educational institutions.

OutRage was unrelenting in its attempt to challenge legal and political problems. Unlike Queer Nation, the emphasis was not upon gaining visibility in the mainstream but instead aimed to challenge homophobia and political discrimination in a retaliatory fashion. One of the first, and most successful OutRage 'zaps' was the 'kiss-in' organized around the Eros statue in Piccadilly Circus because OutRage had learned that the police had the 'right' to arrest gay men for kissing in public. Under Clause 25 of the Criminal Justice Bill, police had the right to arrest gay men for solicitation, procuration of homosexual acts and indecency between men. 'Solicitation' could range from winking to exchanging telephone numbers; 'procuration' could be anything which helped two gay men to have sex such as introducing two gay men at a party, while 'indecency' could simply be kissing or even holding hands. These offences could be punishable by up to five years' imprisonment.

The other target of OutRage's wrath was the now infamous Section 28 which, more than any other policy, has distinguished the homophobia of Thatcherite politics. As a conference in October 1987, Mrs. Thatcher lamented that 'children who need to be taught to respect traditional moral values are being taught that they have the inalienable right to be gay' (quoted in Marie Smith, 1997: 116). Section 28 is emblematic of the pseudo moderate approach offered by Thatcherite politics. More than any other political party of the time, the New Right sought to construct the mythic figure of the assimilable, good homosexual who could fit – subtly closeted – into the mainstream. This was juxtaposed with the evil, promiscuous 'queer' who was, of course, typed as predatory and a threat to vulnerable children. Politicians have always used children as political bait and they have only to claim to do something for the benefit of 'our wives and children' to secure respect. By conjuring the evil queer as the children's bogeyman, Thatcherite politics could occupy some mythic, pseudo-tolerant middle-ground.

Section 28, established on 24 May 1988, is particularly representative of Thatcherite politics and, as can only be expected, is problematic in its choice of words. Prohibiting 'the promotion of homosexuality' offers a stifling ambiguity. According to Section 28:

1. A Local Authority shall not:
• intentionally promote homosexuality or publish material with the intent of promoting homosexuality
• promote the teaching in any maintained school of the acceptability of homosexuality as a pretended family relationship

2. Nothing in subsection 1 above shall be taken to
• prohibit the doing of anything for the purpose of treating or preventing the spread of disease.

(quoted in Watney, 1991: 388)

Such linguistic gymnastics emphasize the pseudo-tolerant, contradictory approach of Thatcherite politics as the clause should not prevent 'the spread of disease' but, at the same time, homosexuality is not allowed to exist as the very mention of it could be construed as 'promotion'. Therefore any form of safe-sex education becomes problematic. Section 28 is also emblematic of the contradictory nature of New Right politics. Where, on the one hand, Thatcherism saw homosexuality is an essentialist light, it also trembled with a fear that 'promotion' of homosexuality in schools could somehow have a proselytising effect. There is a corrupt equation between the 'queer' as a cultural and historically intransigent monster and vulnerable children who can, ironically, be turned into such a monster.

Therefore OutRage, unlike Queer Nation, had to respond to such direct political action. Although both OutRage and Queer Nation were animated by a need to attack homophobia and destabilize heteronormativity, OutRage had more specific targets upon which to focus its energy. As a result OutRage was seen as more reactionary – something which attacked specific institutions rather than trying to challenge the heterosexist landscape itself.

However, the key problem for both Queer Nation and OutRage was that both attempted to destabilize the hetero/homo binary by continuous appropriation and reshuffling of the dominant terms. Both tried – through camp or postmodern or queer spectacles – to evoke a revision of normative identifications and a subversive breakdown in sexual and gender taxonomies. Yet, as I want to consider now, neither faction of queer politics was totally successful in its approach.

How Queer Can We Be?

While queer theory tried to expose the incoherencies in the assumed stable continuum of sex/gender/sexuality and unmask identifications as being performative effects, queer activism tried to mobilize it politically. Both theory and politics tried to destabilize and therefore dethrone heterosexuality. However, while this may be a valid theory within the pages of an academic textbook, how successful can these ideas be on the street? How can a politics, which takes as its very basis the deconstruction of identity, be mobilized effectively? How can queers contest oppression and heteronormativity without first congregating around an identity category?

Judith Butler has argued though that 'the deconstruction of identity is not the deconstruction of politics; rather, it establishes as political the very terms through which identity is articulated' (1999: 189). Butler calls for a 'disruption' of identity concepts or a parodying or 'camping up' of the very limits and confinements of identity. Butler suggests that political emphasis should shift from regarding queer as something which supposes sexual deviancy as a foundation into something which attacks the very fibre of sexual taxonomy (see also Gamson, 1993: 412).

This, however, is dense Butlerian theory which, as Anamarie Jagose (1996: 103) points out, may work well on the page but becomes a little limp when transferred to the street. Therefore, while queer politics attempted to fissure the matrix of heterosexuality and expose identity as contingent and constructed, it was not entirely successful. There may have been some who were 'postmodern' enough or 'intelligent' enough, or 'queer' enough to read queer 'zaps' and 'actions' correctly but, for many others, queer zaps simply looked like a bunch of gays and lesbians flaunting their sexuality in a public place. It is difficult to eradicate sexual taxonomies when a specific action will always lead to someone being labelled by someone else. As Elizabeth Wilson famously asked, 'how transgressive is transgression' (1993: 107)? In order to prevent queerness being assimilated back into the mainstream, to maintain it as something which fissures the idea of the 'normal', queerness has to keep moving. Queer politics needs to maintain a sense of edginess, to shuffle continuously the boundaries of queer/straight and prevent assimilation. Yet how long can queer politics do this? Can queer ever move quickly enough? As Wilson points out, all transgression defines itself against the dominant:

> Yet just as the only true blasphemer is the individual who really believes in God, so transgression depends on, and may even reinforce, conventional understandings of what it is that is to be transgressed.
>
> (Wilson, 1993: 109)

The crossing of one boundary only produces another boundary which must also be transgressed. To continue shuffling the boundaries in order to expose the contingency of identifications and, in doing so, challenge assimilation is a very difficult task. If queer doesn't maintain a sense of dynamism and flux it risks becoming atrophic and being incorporated back into the mainstream. The Pink Pound (exemplified by Manchester's gay village – now one of the city's leading tourist attractions) is a key example of how this may happen. Something once considered radical has now been assimilated and is marketed as a tourist sight. Alan Sinfield therefore suggests that 'queer' must 'keep devising strategies to outmanoeuvre hostile appropriations: to keep moving' (1992b: 25). The task is never to solidify but to keep progressing; to keep shifting the boundaries of identification and to keep baffling the dominant culture.

Yet, even more worrying is the fact that exposing heteronormativity as constructed may not necessarily disempower it. As Leo Bersani points out, the dominant factions do not need to be 'natural' in order to rule and 'to demystify them doesn't render them inoperative' (1995: 4). It has been one of queer theory's main projects to expose 'heterosexuality as the epitome of a wretchedly destabilized sexual identity' (Dollimore, 2001: 39). Yet, as Dollimore asks, is this happening in reality? Although dominant ideologies such as the nuclear family and legally/church-sanctioned marriage may be under pressure, 'heterosexuality *per se* is proving adaptable to say the least' (Dollimore, 41). Even if queer activism succeeds in exposing heterosexuality as simply another gymnastics in the array of sexualities, this is not necessarily going to destabilize its dominant position.

On the other hand, queer's deconstructive tactics also raises another dilemma; if queer insists upon destabilizing identity categories, then it eventually dissolves itself and this begs the question of what actually is 'queer'? If 'queer' is a movement founded on anti-identity politics, the goal of which is to expose sexual and gender identifications as performative, surely anything can consider itself queer? David Halperin humorously suggests that, in the future, queer could even stretch to 'include some married couples without children, for example, or even (who knows?) some married couples with children – with, perhaps, very naughty children' (1995: 62).

However, the backbone of queer – something which maintains its political unity despite internal contradictions – is the politics of shame. Queer will never be something which is trendy or fashionable when the subject must *earn* the right to the painful dignity of the appellation 'queer'.

Shame On You!

Many people still cannot bear the sound of the word 'queer' as its core bristles with shame. As both Sedgwick (1993b: 4) and Butler have stressed, 'queer' can never be extricated from all those years of abuse as

'"Queer"derives its force precisely through the repeated invocation by which it has become linked to accusation, pathologisation, insult' (Butler, 1993: 226). The word 'queer' still conjures the horror of childhood (and sometimes lifelong) abuse which ranges from name-calling to physical violence. It is only by fighting through all the years of shame that the subject can earn a right to, and a pride in, the title 'queer'. As Butler emphasizes, no amount of reclamation can ever remove 'queer' from its signified of shame. 'In this sense, it is always an imaginary chorus that taunts "queer"!' (Butler, ibid.).

Russell Davis's television drama series *Queer As Folk* was criticized for its breezy deployment of the term queer (see Mason, 1999: 4). Arguably there was nothing queer about the series. The gay men simply wanted to spend Pink Pounds and have sex all the time while the lesbians wanted to have babies. Indeed the lead character – Stuart Jones – seemed to conform to the worst stereotype of 'gay' as synonymous with white, middle-class, urban and interested only in fashion and sex. Also, Stuart's promiscuity was not really transgressive because it was absorbed and maintained by Manchester's gay village.

Sally Munt, however, cited the shame/pride dichotomy in the series as something which validated the 'queer' in the title. In the first episode Stuart's car is defaced by graffiti which reads 'queer' in bright spray paint. Yet Stuart almost seems to revel in the shock value which the graffiti facilitates. Likewise he enjoys silencing the homophobic school boy by telling him that he will give him a 'good fuck'. Although Stuart's actions certainly have immediate effect, there is an immaturity to this approach. Shame cannot simply be turned into pride like the spin of a dial. Stuart's flaunting of his sexuality which he continues to do throughout the series (unsettling straight clients and police) is reminiscent of the childish petulance which revels in its own naughtiness; the vicarious and transitory empowerment of shocking others into momentary submission. It is not a development of pride but simply a redistribution of shame.

By contrast, the only character in *Queer as Folk* who genuinely earns a right to the appellation 'queer' is the schoolboy Nathan who, by the final series, is able to pronounce himself 'queer' in front of his homophobic teacher and classmates by answering 'queer' instead of 'here' during class registration. Far from being something which is flaunted for its momentary stun value, Nathan's proclamation claims an actual pride in his queer status. It is not simply a deflection of shame through social embarrassment but an open embrace of queer, with all its sexual indignities, and a kindling of pride for the status it bestows.

It is important to remember that shame is a performative effect (Sedgwick, 1993b: 5). If someone, in the sight of witnesses, makes the performative (rather than constative) utterance, 'Shame on you!', then this performative declaration bestows upon the shamed one an identity effect. There may be others listening who do not wish to condemn the shamed one or there may be others who want to pistol-whip the shamed one, but the point is that shame has interpellated the shamed one into a performative, identity effect. Therefore shame offers a paradoxical constituency. While simultaneously abjecting the body of the shamed one it also imposes upon it an identity. Shame and pride, therefore, exist in a tacit dynamism. Reinscribing or flaunting one does not lead to a triumph of the other.

The problem, however, lies with mobilising this politically. How do we find 'a queer ethic of dignity in shame' (Warner, 1999: 37)? It is for this reason that I have always believed that 'queer' – both politics and theory – was unfortunate to happen *too early*. Most academic critics were introduced to queer theory in the early nineties and this fostered some delicious and still on-going debate. Yet politically, I feel we have not been able to mobilize queer effectively. Queer politics ignored the fact that, for many people, coming to terms with the minority identity of 'gay' was, in itself, a struggle. For many gays and lesbians, trying desperately to maintain some standard of dignity and self-respect in a remote area where homophobia hangs in the air like a stench, being gay is difficult enough. The very last thing these people need is 'queer' questioning the very idea of identity itself. In times of crisis people need stability not mobility. Therefore, I should argue that queer attempted too much too soon. Many people are only just coming to terms with gay identity now and queer's attempt to dissolve the very concept of identity was too ambitious by anyone's standards.

What we find throughout Jarman's cinema is a similar wrestling match between queer theory and politics. On a superficial viewing, the films' images can be read as representing a separatist, gay identity politics: the films contain gay rallies, brutal acts of homophobia and an exaltation of gay love. The narratives, arguably, establish a separatist agenda between gays and straights which, although attempting to overthrow the regimes of power, are shown to be very unsuccessful.

Yet, on the other hand, Jarman's films also often question the idea of a sexual identity itself with many of the images offering a Sedgwickian deconstruction of sexual identity, showing that desire is a solvent of identifications. Likewise, Jarman's cinema is continually intrigued by the politics of shame, the performativity of gender and the separation of sexuality from the gendered body.

While the tension between queer theory and queer politics is not likely to be resolved in the near future, it is perhaps this very tension which gives 'queer' its important sense of edginess. Perhaps, as can be seen in Jarman's cinema, it is the very problem with actually trying to mobilize queer which maintains its dynamic status and will continue to baffle and challenge both assimilationist and segregationist agendas. If 'queer' ever does become something which can be readily summarized by academic formulae then its very status of 'queer' would disappear.

2

QUEER CINEMA

Arguably, 'Queer Cinema' 'has been in existence for decades' but merely 'lacked a label' (Hayward, 2000: 307). The films of Jean Genet, Jack Smith, Kenneth Anger and Andy Warhol (to name only a few 'queer' identified filmmakers) are arguably just as 'queer' as anything labelled 'Queer Cinema' and indeed various film scholars have recently argued that the title 'Queer Cinema' should be used to describe *any* films which contain representations of 'queers' (see Griffiths, 2006).

However, critics usually apply the term 'Queer Cinema' to a brief cinematic moment in the late 80s and early 90s when a collection of queer-themed films attempted to revise issues of queer representation and queer subjectivity (see Aaron, 2004). The term 'Queer Cinema' itself was coined by the film journalist Ruby Rich at the Toronto Festival of Festivals:

> There, suddenly, was a flock of films that were doing something new, renegotiating subjectivities, annexing whole genres, revising histories in their image [...] They're here, they're queer, get hip to them.
>
> (Rich, 1992: 31)

And what were these new queer films? *Poison* (Todd Haynes, 1991), *My Own Private Idaho* (Gus Van Sant, 1991), *Young Soul Rebels* (Isaac Julien, 1991), *Edward II* (Derek Jarman, 1991), *Tongues Untied* (Marlon Riggs, 1991), *Paris is Burning* (Jennie Livingston, 1991), *The Hours and the Times* (Christopher Munch, 1992), *The Living End* (Gregg Araki, 1992) and *Swoon* (Tom Kalin, 1992) to name some of the most renowned, although by no means all, of the films showcasing under the banner of 'queer'.

The subject matter of all these films seemed very different. Jarman's *Edward II* was based on the Christopher Marlowe play; *Poison* was loosely indebted to the writings of Jean Genet, the conventions of 1950s horror films and television documentary while Araki's *The Living End* was an homage to both the road movie tradition, inspired by *Bonnie and Clyde* (1967, dir: Penn), the political counter-cinema of Jean Luc Godard and the iconography of gay pornography. *My Own Private Idaho* (the film to achieve the greatest commercial success) was, in many ways, the heir to Fassbinder's cinema – especially in its self-conscious reworking of American popular culture – while *Swoon* represented the Leopold and Loeb story in an eclectic style which was as much indebted to the opulence of the heritage film as the art house cinema. In this respect, classing the films together in terms of cinematic style or subject matter is problematic.

Yet, the films are all united by their attempt to represent 'queer' in their images. Queer Cinema captured the zeitgeist of a cultural moment when queers rejected a 'tolerated', minority position, refused to allow the pandemic of AIDS to be conveniently ignored and challenged heterocentrist squeamishness about queer visibility. In this sense, Queer Cinema was not only political but, very often, didactic.

This reactionary quality, however, is represented differently throughout the films. Araki's *The Living End* is traditional narrative cinema, indebted to both Hollywood's road movie and 'buddy movie' tradition, in which its romanticized outlaws are driven as much but their hatred of homophobic society and their resentment of 'picking up the tab' for earlier generations' sexual liberation, as they are united by their passion for each other. On the other hand, Kalin's representation of the psychotic, swooning flappers – Leopold and Loeb – is a striking attempt to emphasize the queerness in an event which previous representations, such as *Rope* (1948, dir: Hitchcock) and *Compulsion* (1959, dir: Fleischer) had masked. *Swoon* 'puts the homo back in homicidal' despite the fact that such a representation may fuel homophobic paranoia. In one striking scene, *Swoon* represents Leopold and Loeb in bed together in the courtroom thus emphasising that their homosexual activities were always at the forefront of the jury's mind. The film therefore explodes the open secret of Leopold's and Loeb's sexuality which other representations had tastefully erased but which was burning in the mind of the public and jury at the time.

In this chapter I want to analyse the salient themes of Queer Cinema. It is, however, difficult to critique such a diverse collection of films, which were not only influenced by different cinematic traditions but were created in different cultures throughout the western world. Although Queer Cinema is predominantly an American cinematic moment, whose inventors are schooled in cinematic history and film aesthetics (especially Haynes, Araki and Van Sant), Jarman, on the other hand, is not only British but also 'not a film-maker immersed in film history at all' (O'Pray, 1996: 9). Yet Queer Cinema shares many cultural themes and ideas in common. The films are not only united by chronological proximity but by an attempt to mobilize many of the political and theoretical aims of queer and AIDS activism. This chapter will attempt to outline some of the main debates surrounding Queer Cinema: debates which later chapters will develop in relation to Jarman.

Firstly, all the queer films can be described 'loosely' as postmodern cinema or, as Rich describes it, 'homo pomo' (1992: 32). Secondly, Queer Cinema was unconcerned with notions of political correctness and the gaze of the film at the spectator is undoubtedly a queer one. Thirdly, constructionist ideology (in some cases anti-identity politics) is evident throughout all the films. Fourthly, the films challenge preconceived notions of gender, especially in relation to the male body and the way masculinity is traditionally represented. Fifthly, although Queer Cinema is often accused of misogyny, this chapter will argue that its representations should be read as attempting to subvert traditional notions of gender rather than outright misogyny. Finally, Queer Cinema is a response to AIDS and represents the pandemic in both direct and metaphoric fashions.

Homo Pomo

As a political cinema, the Queer New Wave has its roots in avant-garde film-making practice, especially the Counter Cinema of the 1970s (exemplified by Jean-Luc Godard) and the American Underground Cinema (especially the work of Warhol, Smith and Anger). Even Jarman has remarked that the films of Warhol and Anger had an influence on his work (O'Pray, 1996: 9).

Queer Cinema is not merely trying to break with dominant ideologies but is often attempting to subvert the traditional cinematic codes and conventions which support those ideologies. Like Underground Cinema, the queer filmmakers are also united in an attempt to challenge censorship and reinstate the 'queerness' which previous cinematic representations had often elided. Similarly, Queer Cinema can also be described as 'avant-garde' cinema because of the way it interrogated or questioned the established cinematic practice and attempted to challenge dominant themes and ideologies. ('Avant-garde' was originally a military term describing the 'advance party who *interrogate* the terrain ahead of the main army' (Smith, 1998: 39; see also Hayward, 2000: 27).

Avant-garde is a problematic term, though, if only because there is so much disagreement in how 'avant-garde' is to be distinguished from 'modernism'. Modernism was a reaction against realism and, more importantly, the rise of photographic realism. In contrast to realism, modernism is characterized by a self-reflexive concern with its own formal qualities, a foregrounding of the artistic medium and less emphasis on verisimilitude. Modernism, in this sense, was exemplified by Clement Greenberg's critical writings which insisted that:

> The purely plastic or abstract qualities of the work of art are the only ones that count. Emphasize the medium and its difficulties, and at once the purely plastic, the proper values of visual art come to the fore.
>
> (reprinted 1990: 71)

Therefore, it could be argued that because all modern art challenges traditional regimes of representation it is, by its very nature, avant-garde (Sitney, 1978). For this reason, the art critic Hal Foster (and indeed most of the other critics associated with the journal *October*) championed the idea of the avant-garde as different from modernism. For Foster (1996) and Krauss (1985, 1993) modernism is characterized by its formal innovation, its foregrounding of the art object itself as a vehicle for the artist's expression rather than what it claims to represent. (Cubism, for example, can be read as supremely modernist.) The avant-garde, by contrast, attempts to shock and subvert. It is not simply formal experimentation for its own sake but offers a disruptive critique. So, for example, Dada and Surrealism can be seen as key examples of avant-garde art because both movements attempted to subvert the dominant orders. (The infamous eye-slicing scene in the surrealist film *Un Chien Andalou* (dirs: Bunuel and Dali, 1928), which forces every spectator to squirm in horror, is a rather apt emblem of the film's shock tactics.) Therefore, it is fair to say that not all modernism is avant-garde but all avant-garde work is modernist.

As can only be expected, avant-garde film-making practice has always offered an opportunity for the expression of minority groups such as blacks, women and queers. Understandably, therefore, Queer Cinema, drew upon the legacies of avant-garde film-making and was not merely attempting to subvert traditional ideologies and destabilize homo/hetero binaries but was also attempting to question traditional cinematic practice and its implicit heterocentrist bias. For example, all the films not only subvert the intra-diegetic gazes of the film (men gaze at men in Queer Cinema) but question the male, heterosexual bias of the pro-filmic gaze itself.

Preceding the Queer New Wave, the most (in)famous exponents of queer desire in avant-garde cinema (excluding Genet's *Un Chant D'Amour*) have been Kenneth Anger, Jack Smith and Andy Warhol. While their work is often termed 'Underground Cinema' – an organized movement which actually signed a manifesto accusing dominant cinema of moral corruption – the work of Anger, Smith and Warhol could arguably be termed 'proto-queer'. Firstly, these filmmakers' work was characterized by a rejection of traditional film-making conventions. Anger employed collage techniques and montage-editing or else, as in *Scorpio Rising*, returned to a more tableaux appearance foregrounding the characters' costume and movement in a style which is more presentational than re-presentational (Suárez, 1996: 148). Warhol, by contrast, often employed the use of a single long take eschewing traditional editing and cinematographic conventions. Yet both Anger and Warhol's films were united in their explicit representation of queer sexuality and, most importantly, by a foregrounding of contemporary gay iconography.

From the 1950s onwards, gay art was starting to openly articulate is homoeroticism without cowering behind a veil of neo-classicism. Bob Mizer's *male*-order magazine, *Physique Pictorial*, represented young toughs (often urchins straight out of prison) who were depicted in everyday environments. Although *Physique Pictorial* hid behind the mask of being a fitness/bodybuilding magazine, it represented a more contemporary gay iconography as opposed to the work of, say, Whilhelm Von Gloeden or Wilhem Von Pluschow whose homoerotic images used Classical Greek motifs and sweetly androgynous youths. Similarly, the sketch artist Tom of Finland was starting to represent commonplace gay accessories (motorbikes, uniforms, check shirts and jeans) (see Snaith, 2003) while the translated writings of Jean Genet, which revelled in the same subversion of stereotypical masculinity, were growing in circulation in the 1960s. In a similar vein, both Anger and Warhol, despite employing avant-gardist film-making techniques, represented commonplace macho culture which, by the 1950s, had been appropriated by gay subculture (see *Scorpio Rising* (Anger) or *My Hustler* (Warhol)). In so doing, both Warhol and Anger elided the division between high and low culture: the films rejected the tenets of traditional film-making yet represented 'earthy' subject matter. Indeed the work of Anger and especially Warhol helped set a precedent for much of what is now termed postmodern art.

Postmodernism is, of course, a notoriously difficult area to summarize, not least because each strand of scholarship perceives the debates differently. For philosophers, postmodernism signalled the death of 'les grands récits' or meta-narratives which characterized 'modern' thought of Enlightenment philosophy (Lyotard, 1984). Lytoard famously described postmodernism as 'a crisis of narratives' (1984: xxiii); a world fragmented by the catastrophes of the twentieth century – world wars, atomic bombs, viral warfare, mass genocide, global warming and AIDS – thus negating the Enlightenment philosophy of intellectual and social progress. This distrust of universalising theories (such as religious or secular philosophies), which sought to unmask the so-called 'truths' of human existence, signified the postmodern death of the essential subject.

However, for sociologists and cultural materialist critics, postmodernism is more generally referred to as 'postmodernity' and is seen as signifying the break from the modernist tradition of industrialization to alternative means of capitalist production. Postmodernity is read as synonymous with post-industrialization: the decline in industrial services, the growth in alternative means of production and the rise in other industries such as tourism and, most importantly, the media. More than anything else, the growth in media communication has ushered in the rise of postmodernity as it signifies the transition from physical industrialization (the production of actual goods) to an industry premised only on the production of signs and images (the media and, to a lesser extent, tourism). Jean Baudrillard therefore suggests that the postmodern world is not simply dominated by signs but that these very signifiers actually *form* the postmodern world itself. We now exist in a world of 'hyper-reality' which has no reality beyond itself (Baudrillard, 1983).

Art critics, on the other hand, read postmodernism as a break with modernism which had emphasized 'pure' art at the expense of figurative imagery. Not only did the modernist approach to art disregard the historical determinacy of the art object but it had started to forget art's 'transformative' potential. Modern art – including avant-gardist work – had become institutionalized as 'high art'. Picasso and Braque were housed in museums and 'appreciated' by only an elite group of people while even subversive movements such as Dadaism were being studied on university art history courses. Modern art was therefore criticized for failing to 'speak' to more than a minority of educated art critics and, arguably, had lost its power to move the spectator. Even avant-garde art, in the jaded, fragmented, postmodern world, seemed to have lost the power to shock and Greenberg asked in 1967, 'Where is the avant-garde?'.

Reacting vehemently to this (or as vehemently as anyone claiming to be devoid of emotions and wanting to be a 'machine' could react) was the artist usually credited as the forefather of artistic postmodernism: Andy Warhol. Warhol is most famous for his repetitive silk-screens (such as *Campbell's Soup Cans*) which figured every day items in boring succession – the only addition being a synthetic, lurid colour. Perhaps the most disturbing aspect of Warhol's work is that, despite being figurative representations, Warhol is unable to make use of an actual, worldly image. In order to appeal to Warhol's sensibilities the image must firstly have been processed and reproduced in some way. Warhol then adds yet another level of re-presentation to the image – often a highly inappropriate, garish colour wash. A Warhol canvas, therefore, consists of layers of blank re-presentation built up like a teetering tower of children's building blocks.

Warhol is often compared with Duchamp, whose 'ready-mades' (every day objects which Duchamp 'named' art, such as *Fountain* (a urinal) or

L.H.O.Q.Q. (a defaced copy of the *Mona Lisa*)) scandalized the art world of the 1920s. Yet Warhol is subtly different. While Duchamp was challenging the art world, exposing the idea of fine art as simply being a language game and stressing the conceptual quality of art, Warhol was moving one stage further. Warhol's work insists upon an equation between art and commodity culture. Warhol's art drained the object of its original semiotic meaning and added a second level of 'financial' signifiers. In so doing, Warhol mimed the system of capital which attributes 'price' as 'meaning' to goods in the marketplace. This industrialization of art was emphasized by Warhol's often quoted quip that he 'wanted to be a machine' and the title which he gave to his studio: 'The Factory'.

Not surprisingly, Warhol's work is often deemed the perfect illumination of the philosophical and sociological debates about postmodernism. Firstly, he offers the apocalyptic vision of post-industrialization in which the actual products have simply become simulations or representations – the tension between a soup can (cheap and nasty food source) and its million dollar advertised representation. Warhol therefore effects the separation of signifier from signified; the Baudrillardean sense of hyper-reality. In Warhol's art there is only the regurgitation of artistic signs and a frightening sense of aesthetic and emotional vacuity throughout all his work.

Secondly, if the avant-garde had supposedly lost the power to shock, Warhol attempted the very opposite and created images which are excruciatingly boring. In stark reaction to the glistening sensuality of an Abstract Expressionist canvas, which foregrounds the 'pure' quality of the art and ignites aesthetic shivers, Warhol seeks only an *an*-aesthetic response. More than any other artist, Warhol aims to dull the spectator's senses. Indeed, one of Warhol's most ingenious silk-screens was the repetition of the electric chair, colour washed in a pretty pink pastel. The electric chair – one of the most horrific inventions of the twentieth century which kills by literally frying the internal organs – simply becomes another image reproduced ad infinitum across a Warhol canvas. Drained of its emotional resonances, the electric chair simply becomes another sign in the postmodern world of simulation and hyper-reality. When the electric chair is re-presented as a pretty motif, the hybridity of utopia/dystopia is grotesquely emphasized. The electric chair – a monster of modern invention, shattering any faith in humanity (Enlightenment, humanist, Christian) – becomes a lurid, hyper-real image drained of its signified. This becomes even more obvious in Warhol's films such as *Sleep* (1964) which represents a man sleeping for six hours (essentially a parody of the trance or dream film) or *Blue Movie (aka Fuck)* which, despite representing two nude characters lounging around the house together and having lots of sex, is one of the most un-erotic films ever made. The film only inspires an an-aesthetic response and the characters even nod or wink at the camera thus emphasising the constructed nature of the film, the commoditization of imagery and the acknowledgement that this blue movie is yet another boring, generic porn flick.

However, the impact of postmodernism on mainstream film-making was intense. Although the Hollywood film industry can be seen to embody the post-industrial, post-Fordist sense of postmodern economy (Storper and Christopherson, 1987), debates on filmic postmodernism have tended to be in the area of artistic criticism. Firstly, critics have noted the representation of postmodern themes and philosophies in recent films. Much of New Hollywood is coloured by postmodern cynicism (a lack of faith in human and intellectual progress) and a sense of dystopia pervading futuristic images (see especially sci-fi films such as *Aliens, The Terminator, Blade Runner* and *The Matrix*). Hollywood is constantly imaging worlds of technological sophistication, where images don't merely dominate but actually *are* the world itself (*The Matrix*).

Yet it has been New Hollywood's tendency to consistently quote from not only other films, past and contemporary, but from other art forms – and also its increasing self-consciousness and self-referentiality – which film critics have read as emblematic of film postmodernism. Like the Warhol silk-screens, New Hollywood cinema has been read as espousing a deliberate lack of depth in which the original is negated in favour of a hyper-real, repetitive image, a pastiche of another form of re-presentation.

Film criticism, however, has been divided in its opinion about the significance of these film pastiches (see Jameson, 1984). Although Hollywood often employs parody (an appropriation of an image in order to ridicule a specific text and its ideology) much postmodern cinema is characterized by the use of pastiche or blank parodies. As John Hill summarizes:

Thus, while a New Hollywood film such as Robert Altman's *The Long Goodbye* (1973) quotes from film history and reworks genre conventions with obvious parodic intent – to debunk the myth of the private eye and the values he represents – the use of film quotations and references to a 1980s 'event' film such as *The Untouchables* (Brian de Palma, 1987) is largely characterized by the use of pastiche (as in the clever, but politically and emotionally 'blank' reconstruction of the Odessa Steps sequence from the revolutionary Russian film *Battleship Potemkin* (1925). As such, the film's use of pastiche offers less a critique of the male hero (as *The Long Goodbye* does) than an 'alibi' for the film's ideological conservatism by inoculating the film against being read too straight.

(1998: 101)

Like New Hollywood, much of Queer Cinema is characterized by parody and pastiche. Yet unlike New Hollywood these are not simply 'blank parodies' but interrogations and/or reclamations of past history. The queer filmmaker reclaims previous re-presentations/art/historical events and explodes the queer subtext which previous representations have elided. Far from eschewing depth and meaning, and rendering everything a question of style and aesthetics, Queer Cinema is concerned with the reclamation of past events/representations for a queer perspective. Kalin's *Swoon*, for example, is largely devoted to reinstating the issue of Leopold and Loeb's sexuality which other representations had elided. The film constantly evidences how the public was obsessed with the men's sexuality but yet this sexuality was an 'open secret' – something everyone was tacitly aware of but could not openly acknowledge. Likewise Van Sant's *My Own Private Idaho* is not only loosely founded on Shakespeare's *King Henry IV – Part One* (Scott (Keanu Reeves) is based on Prince Hal and he sometimes quotes Hal's speeches, such as Hal's soliloquy at the end of Act IV, Sc. II) but it is also a reconsideration of the Hollywood oedipal drama. In *My Own Private Idaho*, Mike (River Phoenix) is searching for his home and family, counterbalancing Scott's open rejection of his father and traditional, nuclear home-life. Mike's recurring fantasy is of being cradled on his mother's lap while she reassures him that everything will be all right. Yet this image initially occurs at the start of the film when Mike is receiving fellatio from one of his clients. The film's theme – the tension between the search for love as opposed to the exchange of sex for money – is made explicit in its opening sequence. Mike's orgasm is signified by a picket fence farmhouse crashing to the ground and exploding into splinters. This is not merely an inversion of the orgasm motif (usually fireworks soaring into the sky rather than something crashing to the ground) but is a direct pastiche of the most famous flying farmhouse in the history of cinema and a film which, like *Idaho*, is a quest for Oedipal resolution. The farmhouse resembles Dorothy Gale's farmhouse – a key motif in one of the most popular road movies ever: *The Wizard of Oz*. Yet unlike the *Wizard of Oz*, Mike's house does not land in Munchkin-land but instead *Idaho* subverts the *Wizard of Oz* narrative so that while Dorothy resolves her Oedipal drama, finds her family and attains traditional subjectivity, Mike's quest is destined to failure. *Wizard*'s ideology dictates the importance of the nuclear family. Dorothy yearns for Auntie Em and her secure home life and, arguably, the film's camp popularity exists because gay men, like Dorothy, feel marginalized from mainstream domesticity and therefore enjoy the fantasy of returning to, and gaining acceptance within, traditional culture. *Idaho*, on the other hand, inverts *Wizard*'s narrative and represents a bleak, dystopian image of marginality: a body on the road but never actually going anywhere.

There's neither the Emerald City nor the cradling lap of Aunty Em at the end of the road. Far from offering a traditional happy ending – the queer subject nestling back with his mother – *Idaho* ends 'openly' without traditional narrative closure as the queer subject learns sadly that he does not fit into conventional society.

In a similar vein to Van Sant, the queer filmmaker who most obviously (and sometimes rather heavy-handedly) exemplifies postmodern debates is Gregg Araki whose films, (nearly) always set in the quintessentially postmodern city of L.A., revolve on innumerable levels of parody and pastiche. *The Living End* is a queer parody of Hollywood's road movie and its lead characters are queer reclamations of gay stereotypes employed by mainstream films – 'macho type' and 'the sad young man' (see Dyer, 1993a). *The Living End* also references Art Cinema and Counter Cinema and is as much a pastiche of Godard's *À Bout de Souffle* (1960) as it is of his political work such as *Pierrot Le Jeu* (1965) and *Le Weekend* (1967). Araki has even been called the 'guerrilla Godard' and the names of his *Living End* heroes – Jon and Luke – are an obvious homage to Jean-Luc Godard.

Yet Araki's films constantly debunk this artistic heritage. In one scene Jon is slumped in front of a Godard poster, in another scene a copy of Bazin's *Theories of Cinema* ends up in the bin and Jon himself is attempting to write an article on 'The death of cinema'. What is so striking about Araki's work is that this heavy-handed referencing of high art conventions is then fused with the iconography of gay porn and *The Living End* references gay porn conventions in nearly every one of its 'oh-yeah-fuck-me-senseless' scenes.

However, Araki is not attempting some 'cynical bricolage' (Mills, 1997: 312) but offering jubilant quotations from film history. Obviously these quotations give pleasure to the spectator but the inclusion of gay porn iconography is not simply to add spice to the narrative but rather to elide the boundary between high and low art. Araki is not simply flaunting his knowledge of film history/aesthetics but attempting to fuse high and low conventions (gay porn with art cinema) and reclaim cinematic history for a queer perspective.

This postmodern collapse of high/low boundaries (as exemplified by Araki) and deliberate quotation from history/other art forms (Van Sant) is especially evident throughout Jarman's cinema. As O'Pray suggests, Jarman's films elide the boundaries of high and low art and there is an acknowledgement of modernist sensibilities yet without the *detachment* of modernism. Instead Jarman offers a directness (sometimes this can even be called 'crudeness') in the way his films address the spectator. In many ways, Jarman is 'reminiscent of Brecht sieved through the *Carry On* series and music hall' (O'Pray, 1996: 9). His cinema often has a brashness and irreverence emblematic of bawdy music hall and popular entertainment, yet the work is also poetic and capable of many sensitive images. Jarman's final film *Blue*, for example, could be considered a modernist work in its foregrounding of the medium and distinct reference to Abstract Expressionism. Yet the soundtrack is decidedly postmodern in its description of everyday activities, deliberate fragmentation of identity ('I am a cock sucking/Straight acting/Lesbian man') and wry use of humour.

In a similar fashion to other Queer Cinema, Jarman's films often employ quotations and pastiche. Yet unlike Araki, Haynes or Van Sant – filmmakers immersed in cinematic genres and traditions – Jarman usually quotes from art and other historical texts and includes anachronistic detail. The effect of this jarring anachronism is to collapse the intervening years and emphasize the relevance of his images throughout history. As Arroyo argues, 'films like *Edward II* try to place gays in history because imagining gays in history is to a certain extent a way of legitimising present existence and more importantly, a way of imagining a future' (Arroyo, 1997: 79). Queer Cinema, through its use of quotation and pastiche, attempts to revise history, open a space in traditional representation and locate queer subjectivity within that historical nexus. This is not simply intellectual gymnastics but an attempt to revise modernist sensibilities and inject a directness of approach into the detachment of modern art which many critics believed was failing to make an impact. Most importantly, this facilitated an interrogation of queer subjectivity itself. Above all Queer Cinema emphasized the struggle which the queer subject faces in a postmodern world, founded on swirling media representations, transitory identifications, mitigated human reaction and the pandemic of AIDS.

Queer – Politically Incorrect?

Although film journalists such as Ruby Rich were effusive in their praise, the Queer New Wave was not without its critics. Cherry Smyth argued that this so-called Queer Cinema was essentially repackaged gay and lesbian films (Smyth, 1992b, 1992c) as the films' images did not seriously challenge preconceptions of gender and/or sexuality held by both heterosexual and queer identified viewers.

Although Smyth makes a valid argument, it is too reductive to say that Queer Cinema is merely spiced up gay and lesbian work. The earlier gay and lesbian films of the 80s and early 90s were characterized by a struggle to represent 'positive' images of gays and lesbians. Critics such as Vito Russo (1981), Jack Babuscio (1984), Andy Medhurst (1984) and Richard Dyer (1984; 1993; 1993b) have, in great detail, analysed the 'negative', stereotypical representation of gays and lesbians in mainstream films. The lesbian was usually the butch dyke while the gay man was effeminate, if not usually a 'queen', who was often lecherous and promiscuous. These stereotypes were created through a conflation of gender codes and sexuality in which the actual sexual orientation (irrespective of sexual activity) was downplayed and replaced by codes of exaggerated femininity or butch aggression. Needless to say these stereotypes could exacerbate public disgust of homosexuality and encourage self-loathing within the gay spectator. Dyer called these stereotypes 'the in-betweens' (1993) as they were represented as sad, pitiful creatures who were failing to be either one gender or the other.

Gay and lesbian films responded vehemently to this. In what came to be known as the 'identity politics films', gay stereotypes were deliberately, and often clumsily, revoked. Films often cited as characterising this genre of cinema are: *Making Love* (1982), *Longtime Companion* (1990) and *Our Sons* (1991). In the lesbian category there were: *Claire of the Moon* (1992), *Bar Girls* (1994) and *The Incredibly True Adventures of Two Girls in Love* (1995). *Longtime Companion*, for example, in its very title alone, struggles to overthrow a negative gay stereotype and show that gay men are not all promiscuous succubi who move from one random fuck to another; they can be long-time companions. Indeed, the end of *Longtime Companion* represents the monogamous couple as the only characters who are happy and healthy while the other more promiscuous gay men have all succumbed to HIV related infections or are dead.

Ellis Hanson, however, writes dismissively of these films:

> one can hear the ideological machinery grinding as the wooden dialogue strains to undo every 'stereotype' that comes to mind. Instead of psychological complexity, we find predictable types and cardboard role-models. Instead of intellectual depth, we find a political slogan disguised as a narrative. Instead of aesthetic ingenuity, we find a stilted form of social realism. Instead of 'accurate' or 'positive' images of the gay community, we find an anodyne fantasy of the gay community.
>
> (1999: 9)

Arguably, Hanson's description is a little too dismissive. Films such as *Longtime Companion* have distinct political and artistic merits, if only in trying to achieve something new. It should not be forgotten that films such as *Longtime Companion* and *Making Love* were the first gay-themed films to attract mainstream audiences and were certainly some of the first to be shown outside the security of art house cinemas. They were also the first traditional narrative films to represent gay lifestyle and gay characters rather than an occasional stereotype dropped into the narrative to provide comic relief or a flicker of horror. Nevertheless, it was evident that these identity politics films were not made for a gay audience but instead were targeting homophobic middle-America in an attempt to contradict all the stereotypes which had accumulated over the years of watching negative representations of gay and lesbians.

Queer Cinema reacted against this in two ways. Firstly, the Queer New Wave was unconcerned with images of political correctness. *Swoon* irreverently flaunted a stereotype in which the homosexual's sexual perversity crossed over into psycho-pathology. *My Own Private Idaho* and *The Living End* explored the seamy, seedy underside of life in which the boys were certainly not being middle-class, assimilable, 'longtime companions', while *Edward II* represented an immature, spoiled King Edward who was easily manipulated by his spiteful boyfriend.

Todd Haynes, director of *Poison*, is even prepared to make a joke out of the question of positive stereotypes and, with suitable irony, states:

> I think that I should be creating positive images of homosexuality to spread around the world, on television, through the mass media to show people that gays are positive, they're just like them. That's my role. That's my job (laughs). I am being sincere.
>
> (in Wyatt, 1993: 8)

With the use of obvious irony, Haynes points out how futile it is to attempt to create positive images. Rather than being a filmmaker driven by an artistic vision, the director who is obsessed with representing positive images is reduced to a slogan maker or political tract writer. More importantly, the idea of reducing all queers to a jolly uniformity in which everyone is monogamous, straight acting, attractive, educated and middle-class is a fantasy. As Richard Dyer points out, 'it might be inaccurate of straight movies and television to make out that all gay men are screaming queens and that that is something frightful to be, but plenty of gay men *do* enjoy a good scream' (Dyer, 1991: 199). Simply replacing negative stereotypes with (so-called) affirmative ones is just as artistically vacuous and, more importantly, is no more accurate a representation of queer diversity than the early stereotypes of Hollywood cinema.

Secondly, the New Queer films, 'directly addressed a non-straight audience' (Doty, 1998). There was less emphasis in the New Queer Wave, on attempting to sway public perception of gays, lesbians or queers. In fact, if the ill-educated, homophobe of middle-America were to see these films he might be forgiven for thinking that he was correct in all his assumptions. But, as Grundman points out, 'there are differences between negative stereotypes from Hollywood and those coming from our own ranks' (1993: 25). If queers choose to represent themselves in un-positive ways then that is different from the representation forced upon them by the heterocentrist monopoly of Hollywood. Therefore Queer Cinema did not try to establish a lame dichotomy in which queers are angelic while homophobes are monstrous. Instead, its representations of queers are complex and intriguing – sometimes attractive, sometimes detestable. Queerness was not simply 'good' or 'bad' in Queer Cinema but a given fact of life.

Therefore, when Doty argues that Queer Cinema directly addressed a non-straight audience, he is essentially describing what Paul Willemen termed the 'fourth look' of cinema: 'the look *at* the viewer' (1994: 107) from the film text itself. Much has been written about the male gaze in traditional Hollywood cinema (Mulvey, 1975; Kaplan, 193; Kuhn, 1985), citing it as a technological commoditization of women. Yet this 'male gaze' should not be confused with the general gaze – the Sartrean gaze (Satre, 1966) – to which all human beings are subject and which allows us to develop a sense of self through objectification in the eyes of others. Lacan termed this 'general gaze' the Other. The Lacanian Other does not simply describe a specific group of persons (the others) but refers to cultural systems of meaning in which a subject must be interpellated in order to attain valid subjectivity. The subject requires it to be validated by the gaze of the Other in order for traditional relations to make sense.

Lacan uses an anecdote to illuminate this theory (1986). This Lacanian anecdote has a certain campiness about it – a sense of ironic Hegelian grandeur – as the whole event takes place in a 'small boat', in a 'small town' and even features a fisherman called Petit Jean. The story revolves around the momentous event of Lacan fishing with Petit Jean and noticing a sardine can floating by. Petit Jean points out that although Lacan – the world-renowned psychoanalyst – may have seen the sardine can, the sardine can certainly didn't see Lacan. Lacan adds that Petit Jean 'found the incident highly amusing – I less so' (1986: 96). The reason the sardine can (a metaphor of the Other) didn't recognise Lacan was because Lacan – the academic psychoanalyst – had no right to be in the fishing boat attempting to fish. His subjectivity was not validated by the cultural Other. The sardine can did not recognise Lacan's subjectivity. He was not interpellated by the cultural system of meaning in which he found himself situated.

In 'The Fourth Look', Willemen explained that film can also have this 'sardine can' effect. 'In the filmic process, this look can be represented as the look which *constitutes the viewer* as visible subject' (Willemen, 1994: 107). This 'fourth look' is the gaze of the film itself at the spectator and this gaze validates the spectator's subjectivity. For example, a Spike Lee film may question a white spectator's 'right' to watch the film text. This should not be confused with a question of empathy in which a black spectator could arguably empathize with the narrative where a white spectator cannot. Instead the 'fourth look' questions the white spectator's subjectivity in the light of the filmic event. The film itself may not recognise a white perspective and, like the sardine can, may not 'see' the white spectator.

This theory is important in the analysis of Queer Cinema which, unlike other gay identity work, addressed the queer spectator. By contrast, a gay identity politics film such as *Longtime Companion* recognises and acknowledges a heterosexual (and also white, middle-class, North American) perspective. *Longtime Companion* evokes the Other of traditional Western ideology as the film's very mantra is the importance of nuclear monogamy and so validates gay existence in the light of traditional heterosexuality.

Queer Cinema, by contrast, did not attempt to pander to either heterosexual anxiety or gay assimilationist politics. It did not offer anodyne, fantasy images of the mythic gay community in which gay liberation is premised on the belief in conformity and assimilation. Most importantly, Queer Cinema did not validate the heterosexually-identified spectator's subjectivity and did not recognise a conservative perspective. The spectator of Queer Cinema is assailed with the most queerphobic images imaginable. Suddenly we have images of Leopold and Loeb shagging in bed together in the courtroom and shamelessly gratuitous, debauched and violent sex throughout Araki's *Living End.*

The result of the films caricaturing such clichéd prejudices is to force the spectator to re-evaluate his/her own subjectivity in the light of the film/Other. Most spectators should feel a certain amount of discomfort in seeing such negative images exploding across the screen. The film does not recognise or validate gay assimilationist or conservative perspectives. The 'fourth look' of queer cinema only acknowledges queer subjectivity and the representation of negative images should only be intelligible and pleasurable to the polymorphously perverse dykes and fags who make up a queer cinema audience.

Cinema of Anti-Identity:
Gay Identity versus Queer Identifications

Smyth's questioning of the 'queerness' of these films deserves further consideration. It would be possible to argue that, far from representing 'queerness' with its emphasis on anti-identification and rejection of sexual labels, Queer Cinema simply offers eroticized images of beautiful gay men – a 'fantasmatic recreation of gay/queer as other – gay/queer as handsome, aesthetic and criminal' (Nash, 1994: 100; see also Bruzzi, 2000: 133).

However, this reading is highly debatable. Firstly, it is important to remember that most of the films do not have a contemporary setting. *Edward II*'s Edward and Gaveston exist in Renaissance England when the term 'gay' did not exist and same sex desire was not classified by modern, bourgeois sexual taxonomies. Likewise Tom Kalin points out that his swooning flappers – Leopold and Loeb – could not be labelled 'gay' in accordance with how we perceive the term today. 'In fact, they weren't gay as we understand it. Homosexual identity in 20s Chicago was different from what we think of now' (Okewole, 1992: 5). In a similar vein, Van Sant's *My Own Private Idaho* 'bypasses 1970s Gay Lib identity politics' (Arroyo, 1993: 77) and negates the concept of a gay identity. The film represents mutable sexual identifications, especially the character of Scott who is the son of the Mayor and a hustler by choice. Scott's sexual orientation is never clearly delineated but remains ambiguous. Indeed, Scott is first represented in the film *as* a representation on the cover of a gay porn magazine, suggesting that his sexual identification should not be determined by first impressions and 'read' as fixed.

The question raised throughout the film is whether Scott is hustling simply to hurt and insult his father or is he struggling to express unsanctioned desires. As Arroyo argues, 'the film represents homosexuality as a fluid spectrum with a concomitant variety of possible identities' (1993: 76).

Likewise, Todd Haynes's *Poison* develops the Genetesque, proto-queer motif of sexual fluidity. The protagonist of the 'Homo' sections of the film is John Broom (literal translation of Jean Genet) and is homosexually identified. The taxonomy even goes on his prison registration. Yet Broom's imprisonment reworks Genet's theme that, ironically, the homosexual is only free to love when his is supposedly denied freedom. It is only in the confinement of prison that expressions of homoerotic passion are allowed to blossom. Although Broom claims the identity 'homosexual', the prison sequence testifies to the fluidity of sexual desire and even questions the relevance of Broom's homosexual identification.

However, Araki's *The Living End* is often cited as a key example of Queer Cinema (Taubin, 1993; Rich, 1992) but, more than any of the other films, *The Living End* seems to represent contemporary, gay identified, sexy 'boyz' who simply want to fuck each other senseless. Yet *The Living End* is remarkable for the way it becomes more surreal as the narrative progresses, eventually becoming the queer cinematic equivalent of a Delvaux painting. At the start of the film Jon is represented as a middle-class, well-educated film journalist who possesses all the achievements of gay middle-class success: West Hollywood apartment, good job, expensive car, luxurious lifestyle – in short, he is a proper WeHo (West Hollywood) Boy. Then, as the film progresses, Jon gradually abandons middle-class success and becomes a queer outlaw with his lover Luke.

One of the factors which distinguished gay from earlier homosexual identifications was the concept of an established social identity rather than mere orientation. As Mary McIntosh famously summarized, 'a lesbian or gay is someone for whom important aspects of their social life and identity are organized around their sexuality' (1997: 208). The problem with gay identity, though, is that it requires socio-economic privilege. In order to identify according to one's sexual orientation, and, most importantly, organize one's social life around this identity, the gay subject requires a certain economic standing not least of which is being resident in a metropolitan city. A film like *Longtime Companion* tacitly emphasizes this by featuring only well-to-do, middle-class, Manhattan resident, gay men. And, of course, the very concept of gays aping heterosexual monogamy and marriage is a class-oriented concern. Marriage is a middle-class privilege as 'poor white trash don't get married: they just 'shack up' together' (Brownworth, 1996: 82). Queer, therefore, did not simply challenge homophobia but targeted the socio-economic privilege and complacency of middle-class gays and lesbians who had carved out comfortable niches in the metropolitan landscape. For those who can afford it, it is very possible to be 'gay' within the sanctuary of LA's West Hollywood or New York's Chelsea and *The Living End*'s Jon represents just such a middle-class gay man.

Yet *The Living End* throws Jon's lifestyle into disarray. The diagnosis of his HIV status and the arrival of Luke forces an exodus from West Hollywood as Jon and Luke become road criminals. America's vast, sprawling highways have always provided the arterial lifeblood of America's landscape and, as such, have fuelled the intriguing images of the American 'road movie' tradition (see Cohan and Hark, 2000). Jon and Luke, however, literally infect the arteries of America and proclaim the queer presence everywhere. Rather than be confined to a localized minority, Araki's queer road heroes symbolize the ubiquity of queerness throughout the American landscape.

The Living End, of course, revolves on various levels of pastiche and parody, most notably Godard's *À Bout de Souffle* but also his *Le Weekend* and *Pierrot Le Fou*. As in Godard's cinema, *The Living End* forces a re-examination of the visual image, questioning how it should be read. As the film descends further into fantasy, Jon's beloved middle-class West Hollywood lifestyle slides away so that his only link with his gay heritage is through the telephone calls with his female friend Daisy who, ironically, is straight identified. The film's telephone motif – which symbolizes (in a heavy handed way) the diluted nature of human interaction in postmodern LA – is emphasized from the early scenes of *The Living End* in which a persistent caller attempts to coerce Jon into 'fone-sex'. Gay West Hollywood sexual identity is shown to be synthetic – no more concrete than a telephone call. Indeed, in the same way that *The Birds* (dir: Hitchcock, 1963) used the disruption of the telephone lines to symbolize Melanie Daniel's slide from confident socialite into female hysteria (Paglia, 1998: 78), so *The Living End* shows Jon's gay existence to be supported by little more than a crackling telephone connection. Jon vainly tries to maintain links with his gay heritage through various telephone booths but eventually has to accept defeat.

Therefore, the film's ending does not offer the romanticized nihilism of traditional road movie narratives such as *Thelma and Louise* or *Butch Cassidy and the Sundance Kid*. Despite having abandoned traditional subjectivity, glorious death is not granted to Araki's protagonists and instead there is only the arid dystopia of the California desert in which Jon and Luke attempt, and fail, to 'death fuck' on the highway roadside. What is so disturbing about Araki's ending is the denial of the cultural identifications which were so important to the heroes. Luke's romantic death does not happen and similarly Jon has abandoned his middle-class existence and will never regard his gay identity in the same way again. *The Living End* testifies to the loss of a coherent identity in the face of the pandemic. Like many queers struggling in the face of the pandemic – rejected by postmodern culture and fighting to maintain a coherent sense of identity in the midst of such ostracization – *The Living End* abandons Jon and Luke in the middle of the desert, isolated and removed from their previous cultural identifications.

Ga(y)zing at the Male Body

A dominant concern of Queer Cinema is an interrogation of the looks and gazes which structure cinema spectatorship. However, Queer Cinema (in accordance with its queer agenda) is not simply interested in replacing the traditional, heterocentrist gaze with a gay one – men gazing upon other men and openly fetishistic images of men's bodies – but instead interrogates the gaze of traditional cinema, forcing the spectator to question how his/her own sexual subjectivity is interpellated by traditional, narrative cinema.

Much 1970s film criticism was dominated by psychoanalytical theories which analysed cinematic spectatorship and the question of the 'gaze'. It is important to remember that the 'gaze' and the 'look' are not synonyms. While the 'look' is merely the action of the eye, the 'gaze' is associated with the phallus. As such, the 'look' is a literal exchange of vision while the 'gaze' is emblematic of power structures within patriarchal society.

Laura Mulvey's *very* famous essay 'Visual Pleasure and Narrative Cinema' has been an enormous influence in this field of scholarship. Indeed Mulvey's article has actually inspired a small library of feminist/ psychoanalytical criticism (see especially Rodowick, 1982; Stacey, 1987 and Gammon and Marshment, 1988) and even Mulvey herself has commented that 'Visual Pleasure' has taken on 'a life of its own' within film scholarship (1989: vi). In 'Visual Pleasure' Mulvey outlined the woman's position in traditional, narrative cinema as being one of 'to-be-looked-at-ness':

> The determining male gaze projects its phantasy on to the female figure which is styled accordingly. In their traditional exhibitionist role women are simultaneously looked at and displayed, with their appearance coded for strong visual and erotic impact so that they can be said to connote to-be-looked-at-ness.
>
> (1975: 27)

The dominant gaze in narrative cinema is male and is engineered through the three different looks operating in the process of film spectatorship. Firstly, there are the intra-diegetic looks between the film's characters, then there is the look of the camera as it records the filmic event and finally there is the look of the spectator at the filmic text itself. Hollywood usually attempts to disguise the latter two looks (camera and spectator) by minimising obtrusive camera angles so that the spectator is not distanced from the film text. The editing and cinematography conventions emphasize the diegetic looks between the characters so that the spectator is drawn into the cinematic world and Mirian Hansen aptly describes this as 'classical choreography' of the looks and gazes in traditional narrative films (1986: 11). Most importantly, these looks have a heterosexual male bias. The body which is usually offered for spectatorial pleasure and which is either fetishized or sadistically punished throughout the traditional narrative is the female body. According to Mulvey the woman's body signifies lack (castration). This can either be disavowed through fetishization (as in the films of Sternberg) or the woman can be sadistically punished (as in the films of Hitchcock).

Mulvey's article, however, largely ignores the question of the male body as spectacle (a point noted by Dyer, 1982; Neale, 1983 and MacKinnon, 1997). She summarizes the pleasure that a heterosexual, male spectator may gain from watching a male move-star as a form of regression to the mirror stage in which the child identifies with a more perfect, ideal ego:

> A male movie star's glamorous characteristics are thus not those of the erotic object of the gaze, but those of the more perfect, more complete, more powerful idea ego conceived in the original moment of recognition in front of the mirror.
>
> (1975: 28)

Paul Willemen, however, took issue with Mulvey's simplification of the pleasures which the male body affords to a male, heterosexually identified spectator. Willemen suggested that 'the two looks distinguished by Mulvey are in fact varieties of one single mechanism: the repression of homosexuality' (1994: 102, first published in 1976; see also Willemen, 1981). Identification and sexual object choice may not be as easily separated as Mulvey suggests. Willemen argued that the male spectator's narcissistic identification with the male hero is not necessarily 'a mere mediation in order to get at a desired woman' but that the gaze at the male hero may, in itself, provide considerable pleasure to the male spectator. Using the films of Anthony Mann as an example, Willemen argued that 'the viewer's experience is predicated on the pleasure of seeing the male exist, walk, talk, ride, move through or in cityscapes, landscapes or, more abstractly, history' (994: 103). Willemen then suggested that this 'fundamentally repressed homosexual looking' can evoke anxiety in the heterosexually identified male spectator and so the film's diegesis punishes the hero with ordeals of extreme sadism in which the hero's body is pummelled, bruised and beaten before rising victorious at the end. Hollywood action movies are the most extreme example of this. Where initial pleasure is gained from gazing upon the perfected body of Arnold Schwarzenegger or Jean Claude van Damme, this pleasure must then be 'paid for, in the diegesis by the mutilation or damaging of that body' (Willemen, ibid.).

Queer Cinema, however, exploded this issue. The homosexual voyeurism implicit in traditional cinematic spectatorship became explicit in Queer Cinema. Not only did Queer Cinema offer intra-diegetic looks of men gazing upon other men (the body which is offered for scopophilic pleasure, and either fetishized or sometimes sadistically punished, is very definitely male) but Queer Cinema also sought to explode the repressed homosexual voyeurism that could be found throughout mainstream Hollywood. Queer is not opposed to the dominant but draws its strength from the way it fissures from within. For that reason, Queer Cinema extravagantly parodied the iconography of contemporary Hollywood.

The most openly erotic film of Queer Cinema – certainly the film in which sumptuous male flesh is most often gratuitously displayed – is Araki's *The Living End*. Yet, as I have already pointed out, the *Living End* is indebted to Godard's *À Bout de Souffle*. Although *À Bout de Souffle* has been the subject of much critical study and has been praised for its examination of meta-narratives, its self reflexivity, its distanciation, restriction of spectatorial empathy and its examination of the medium of cinema itself, the implicit homo-voyeurism of the film has largely been ignored. One of the most striking scenes in *À Bout de Souffle* is the hotel room scene in which Michel and Patricia spend an afternoon together. The body which is offered for spectatorial pleasure is as much Michel's as Patricia's. Indeed, while Patricia is fully clothed, Michel is shirtless and even draws attention to his *Men's Health* style physique by stroking his own chiselled abs – at least three times during the scene.

As Susan Bordo has pointed out, it is still highly unusual to find a representation of a man touching himself in auto-erotic reverie (1999: 37) as the male body is always portrayed as a source of strength rather than sensual pleasure. Yet, the hotel room scene in *À Bout de Souffle* makes no pretence about displaying the strength of Michel's body but simply offers it for spectatorial pleasure.

Araki develops this with his typically cool irony. Throughout *The Living End*, both of the heroes' bodies are represented as candy stores of sexual delight instead of vehicles of masculine power. If there's the slightest opportunity of having a good fuck then Jon and Luke don't let the chance pass them by. Yet as the narrative progresses the traditional masculine displays of the Hollywood action/gangster film – the male body fighting and inflicting damage – actually become subsumed into Jon and Luke's lovemaking. That clichéd Hollywood image of masculinity – the pistol – becomes a virtual sex toy for Luke and when he's not trying to perform fellatio on the gun then he's using it to caress his own body. Indeed, in the sex scenes towards the end of the film, it's actually difficult to tell if Jon and Luke are fucking or trying to kill each other.

In the famous shower scene Jon actually chokes/strangles Luke during fucking while the film's climax represents Luke tying Jon up, fucking him and placing a gun in his own mouth. These are not merely vulgar references to the sex/death conceit of metaphysical literature or symbols of the threat of AIDS but are references to the homoerotic 'unquiet pleasure' (Willemen, 1994: 103) implicit in many action movies. Araki takes the implicit suggestion of Godard's *À Bout de Souffle* – that the hyper-masculine lead in the male spectator oriented gangster/action movie can be as much a source of erotic contemplation as the female body – and parodies it to a ludicrous extent. By structuring *The Living End* on so many levels of pastiche, Araki's eroticization of male bodies emphasizes the ubiquity of queerness. *The Living End* is not replacing the heterosexual male gaze of traditional cinema but exposing its repressed queer one.

In a similar vein, *My Own Private Idaho* offers the spectacle of the male body but on an even more disturbing level than the parodic eroticism of Araki. Throughout *Idaho* the spectator is forced to endure the extremely 'unquiet pleasure' of watching the male hero punished and beaten. In contrast with other Hollywood heroes, Mike represents a fragile body which is literally battered by the very elements of its environment (Arroyo, 1993: 73). Mike shivers are he huddles in doorways, vying for his latest tricks and, on some occasions, his body literally seems to collapse and he succumbs to his sleeping sickness (narcolepsy) which leaves him prostrate on the ground.

This, of course, can be read as a metaphor for queer oppression, but what *Idaho* is exploring, through the representation of Mike's body, is the 'unquiet pleasure' of pure sadism. The pleasure which the spectator gains from gazing upon Mike's youthful, vulnerable body echoes the guilty pleasure of Mike's closeted (presumably married) clients who need the release of pent-up homosexual desires but then often attack and hurt their 'rented' boys to appease their own guilt.

This (homo)erotophobia is emphasized in *Idaho*'s early scene in which an obese, middle-aged client – Walt – is on his knees sucking Mike's dick. After Mike has come (presumably in the man's mouth) Walt waddles away (with, it must be noted, great speed for someone of such vast girth) and locks himself in the bathroom. Walt thus echoes the actions of an ashamed child, locking himself away in a hidey-hole and unable to face Mike after what he has done. He then shoves the 'rent' money under the door. The spectator, however, is in the uncomfortable position of sharing Walt's uneasy pleasure. One of the most remarkable aspects of the fellatio scene in *Idaho* is that it represents a male body (Mike) in the convulsions of orgasm.

Orgasm is the joy of powerlessness. It is the shattering of the body's limits of sensual pleasure; the jouissance of the body losing all control because it is overwhelmed by the waves of pleasure pounding through every muscle group (see Bersani, 1987). Since the shattering effect of orgasm is one of absolute powerlessness, the male body is rarely represented in traditional cinema as overwhelmed by the throws of orgasmic pleasure. In traditional Hollywood the moaning and writhing of the female body always signifies the orgasm for both partners and when a male body is shown convulsing in orgasmic pleasure it is only ever to evoke humour (Bordo, 1999: 191).

Yet *Idaho* represents the very opposite. Mike is rendered powerless, shattered by his fifty dollar blowjob and, instead of the traditional cliché of fireworks symbolising orgasm, the film represents Mike's dream house crashing to the ground. Like the client Walt, the spectator is offered the image of Mike's orgasm for voyeuristic pleasure. Yet the guilty pleasure which the client/spectator has gained from Mike is then balanced by Mike's body being sadistically punished not only by the very elements but by its own ability to support itself. The voyeuristic pleasure is, to use Willemen's phrase, 'paid for'. *Idaho* interrogates the unquiet pleasure of mainstream cinema in which the spectator, like Walt, is guilty of enjoying the body of the male movie star and therefore needs to see this body punished by the narrative conclusion. The very pretty body of Mike is therefore quite literally smashed by the film's narrative.

Jarman's cinema, as I shall explore in a later chapter, develops these themes of queer masculinity in even more striking ways. Not only does Jarman represent passive male masochists (*Edward II*, *Sebastiane*) but he deliberately subverts gay stereotypes such as 'rough trade' and 'sugar daddies' (*Caravaggio*, *Last of England*), interrogates the traditional gaze of mainstream cinema and, like Araki and Van Sant, represents images of extremely violent sexuality.

Misogyny?

In its foregrounding of the male body, Queer Cinema has been accused of succumbing to clichéd gay male misogyny and Amy Taubin even argues that much of queer cinema is '*heedlessly* misogynistic' (1993: 178).

Yet it is too reductive to read a highly self referential film such as *The Living End* as representing women as clichéd stereotypes, the same as other mainstream films. The key point about *The Living End* is that its stereotypes are *so* extreme that they actually cross over into caricatures. The psycho lesbians who attempt to murder Jon are gross caricatures of all the psychie-dykes which homophobic Hollywood has been so heavily criticized for representing. In one of the funniest sequences in *The Living End*, the psychie-dykies chant (with suitable scorn) all the penis synonyms which strain to conflate penis with phallus: 'love truncheon', 'pussy plunger', 'baloney pony' and so on. The dykes then flourish a phallic gun but are unable to use the thing properly because one of them is then frightened by a snake in the bushes (very obvious metaphor) and has an hysterical breakdown. The point is that the scene employs hysterical phallic symbolism and exaggerates every negative stereotype of man hating, penis envying dykiness that there actually is. Of course it's ridiculously caricatured but, like every scene within *The Living End*, such images encourage highly self reflexive readings. Dismissing them as 'heedlessly misogynistic' is only possible if the spectator ignores the highly stylized, self-referential tone of the entire film. Indeed, as Glyn Davis argues one of the most interesting aspects of Araki's film-making is 'an emphasis on performance, which exposes the supposed 'naturalness' of everyday behaviour and identity as a sham' (Davis, 2004: 59).

In this respect, when accusing Queer Cinema of misogyny, it is important to remember that a key agenda of many of the films was questioning the concept of gender itself. Tom Kalin's *Swoon*, for example, opens with a luscious scene in which enigmatic drag queens glide across the screen with the elegance of New York socialites. Kalin insists that he featured those drag queens throughout his film because he 'wanted to gender fuck' and expose that 'gender is not innate, it's a performance' (quoted in Okewole, 1992: 36). These images of style and artifice, which expose gender as a performative effect, are then juxtaposed in the next scene with Leopold and Loeb's nude bodies. *Swoon*, therefore, sets up an immediate tension within its visual rhetoric. Although the body which is fetishized and offered for erotic contemplation is male, the gendered performance which dominates the screen is femininity. One of the subtextual themes of *Swoon* is the distinction between femininity as a masquerade and the sexed body, disrupting the assumed stable continuum of the body, sex and gender. Indeed *Swoon* actually challenges traditional dichotomies in which femininity is read as synonymous with the exhibitionist, hysterical body while masculinity is emblematic of the body which is a source of power, controlled by the intellect. In *Swoon* the opposite is the case. Leopold and Loeb, as the film's title suggests, are swooning, hysterical flappers who exist only for the sensual pleasures of their bodies. By contrast, their drag queen comrades represent elegant poise and control, the body contained within a stylised, gender masquerade, their cool intellect foregrounded.

In a similar vein, the queer film to have attracted even the attention of Judith Butler is Jennie Livingston's *Paris is Burning* which documents the 'balls' (dance parties) of Black and Hispanic drag queens in New York's Harlem. Butler argues that *Paris is Burning* shows the 'destabilization of gender itself, a destabilization that is denaturalizing and that calls into question the claims of normativity and originality by which gender and sexual oppression sometimes operate' (Butler, 1993: 128). While some critics may dismiss *Paris Is Burning* as a predatory documentary which exploits sad, pathetic creatures whose various attempts at drag evoke no form of transgression but merely an impotent reverence for the traditional gender binary, Butler argues otherwise and emphasizes that by 'doing' flawless femininity the drag queens in *Paris* are not simply paying homage to an essentialist or idealized femininity but are deconstructing the gender binary itself:

This is not an appropriation of dominant culture in order to remain subordinated by its terms, but an appropriation that seeks to make over the terms of domination, a making over which is itself a kind of agency, a power in and as discourse, in and as performance, which repeats in order to remake – and sometimes succeeds.

(1993: 137)

According to Butler, the thrill of *Paris* is how its characters demonstrate that gender is a performative effect. Indeed the saddest character in the documentary – Venus – is murdered because a client discovered that Venus's body was not conventionally sexed as female. Venus's 'drag' had been so utterly flawless that the discovery of the sexed body underneath inspired homophobic panic. Like Kalin's *Swoon*, *Paris Is Burning* teases gender away from the conventionally sexed body and represents sex and gender as subsisting in a tacit dynamism.

In chapter 5 I will argue that Jarman, although often criticized for extremely misogynistic images, can be read as attempting the same thing: the exposure of gender as a performative effect. Jarman's great screen icon – Tilda Swinton – is not represented as a female grotesque but as a character offering the Butlerian potential of destabilising the masculine feminine dichotomy and exposing all gender as imitative.

Representing AIDS in Queer Cinema

AIDS is why there is New Queer Cinema and it is what New Queer Cinema is about.

(Arroyo, 1993: 92)

Representing a microscopic virus is virtually impossible. Therefore many Hollywood representations of AIDS did not attempt to depict the virus but instead offered the horrific spectacle of a Person With AIDS (PWA). *Philadelphia*, for example, is one of Hollywood's most famous representations of a Person With AIDS and tells the story of Andy Becket who is fired from his law firm when his employers learn that he has AIDS. The film depicts Andy's legal battle to gain compensation for his unfair dismissal. However, *Philadelphia* is not really about Andy's (Tom Hanks) battle with AIDS but rather centres on the reaction of straight identified characters – most notably the homophobic lawyer Joe (Denzel Washington) – when they learn that Andy's body is infected. Indeed, the disappointing aspect of *Philadelphia* is that it rarely attempts to promote identification with Andy – the PWA. Instead the film is actually Joe's story: his initial revulsion at Andy's AIDS status, his battle with homophobia and his eventual understanding of the situation. Throughout the narrative Andy is simply something to be looked at – emphasized by the famous shirt-opening scene in the courtroom where Andy is asked to expose his lesion wracked torso to the jury. Andy is the abject AIDS victim whom the straight identified, HIV negative characters (and cinematic spectators) must learn to tolerate. In this sense *Philadelphia* is not an examination of Andy's battle with AIDS and how it affects his relationships or personal and mental health but is a political tract proclaiming that the straight identified majority should *tolerate* the infected, gay minority.

Queer Cinema attempted the opposite. The emphasis throughout the representations of the Queer New Wave is not on the infected body – something dehumanized and abject upon which the spectator gazes with pity – but instead featured the spectre of the pandemic as a subtextual theme. Queer Cinema, like early queer activism, was heavily influenced by the strategies of ACTUP which tried to inspire public understanding of the pandemic rather than a stigmatization of PWAs. The mantra of

ACTUP has always been 'Stop looking at us and start listening to us'. Therefore ACTUP attempted to break down the positive/negative boundary and the cultural prejudice of the abject, sick PWA body – the defining other for the normal, healthy body. One of the key agendas of ACTUP was to shift the emphasis from publicly identifying an infected victim – an HIV positive monster deserving pity – to a greater awareness of AIDS as a pandemic. ACTUP has encouraged a fight against 'AIDS the syndrome' not a prejudice against those infected.

AIDS, in this respect, has profoundly affected understandings of queer subjectivity. AIDS activism insisted that AIDS was not something which infected a minority but was a pandemic of universal importance. Therefore this politics also shook the foundations of a sexual identity. In the face of the AIDS pandemic, a sexual taxonomy becomes strangely archaic and in terms of sexual risk it would make more sense to think of sexuality in terms of what acts people engage in rather than with whom they do these acts.

Queer Cinema adopted the principles of ACTUP. Unlike earlier representations, the Queer New Wave (with the exception of *The Living End*) did not attempt to represent the PWA. Imaging a body infected by AIDS can only lead to dehumanising the person by focusing on how AIDS wracks the physical body (*Philadelphia*), or else it can trivialize the disease by representing it as a sexy, bohemian disease – the successor to 'consumption' (*Buddies*, *Les Nuits Fauves*). (These debates are explored in greater detail in the final chapter on AIDS.)

Therefore Queer Cinema, with the exception of *The Living End*, is not explicitly about Persons With AIDS. Instead most of the films represent the pandemic in a metaphoric fashion. Arroyo points out that in *Idaho*, the spectator may read 'Mike's narcolepsy as a displacement of AIDS' (1993: 79) and that his physical condition – pallor, emaciating, shivering – may 'contribute to the symptomatology' (ibid.). Unlike *Philadelphia*, however, the narcoleptic body of Mike is not offered as abject spectacle and, as I have argued already, this delicate and pretty body is an alternative, and discomforting, *objet désire* from the robust athleticism of Scott. Instead *Idaho* emphasizes how this body is crushed by its harsh environment – a metaphor for how the threat of AIDS is always present in every part of contemporary culture. Likewise the scenes on the open road, upon which

Mike is always collapsing and passing out, symbolize the queer subject stranded against the backdrop of AIDS – a background of desolation in which Mike loses identifications such as a sense of gay community or traditional family life.

Similarly Jarman's *Edward II* tries to assert the presence of AIDS without showing its possible effects on the body. Blood metaphors and red images feature in nearly every scene of *Edward* to assert the insidious presence of AIDS. Haynes's *Poison* offers a similar approach and its 'horror' section – a parody of 1950s horror flicks – is an obvious AIDS allegory with metaphors of AIDS as a leprosy-like disease. The films therefore attempt to represent AIDS as an ubiquitous threat rather than something which infects an abject minority.

The Living End, however, has been criticized for its sexy representation of Persons With AIDS. Jon and Luke are the HIV positive Bonnie and Clyde – gay outlaws whose HIV status allows them a raunchy, Bohemian existence. Yet, as I have discussed already, *The Living End* portrays the collapse of Jon's West Hollywood, middle-class, gay identity as testing HIV positive shatters Jon's assumptions about his future and his identity. Therefore, *The Living End* is not merely trying to eroticize the PWA but is attempting to show the effect of the virus on contemporary queer subjectivity. Indeed, one of the most disturbing scenes in *The Living End* is when Jon returns to the car to find that Luke has slashed his wrists and is examining his blood, amazed that his HIV positive blood looks so 'ordinary'. The scene asserts that AIDS is a blood-spread viral infection rather than the 'plague'-type condition which previous representations had suggested through their focus on the K S Lesions of a PWA. *The Living End* testifies to the isolation and loss of identity facing a PWA (symbolized, as in *Idaho*, by the omnipresent desert background) rather than focusing on the *possible* effects which the virus may have on the body.

In Chapter 8 I want to consider in greater detail how Jarman's cinema develops these themes. *Blue* escapes the bind of either representing AIDS metaphorically or else dehumanising the subjects through focusing on possible symptoms of the viral infection. However, it also manages to achieve the seemingly impossible by maintaining a sense of the physical body without actually representing it on screen.

Conclusion

Queer Cinema was more of a moment than a movement: an eclectic collection of films and videos which revised issues of queer subjectivity, history and spectatorship. José Arroyo raises an interesting point in this respect, relating to Jarman's films:

> Derek Jarman's work brings up interesting questions in relation to New Queer Cinema [...] Since there seems to be so much stylistic and thematic continuity in his oeuvre, what (aside from AIDS) makes *Edward II*, as opposed to his other movies, a New Queer Film?
>
> (1993: 95)

The following chapters will argue that Jarman, far from being the 'Godfather' of New Queer Cinema (Rich, 2000: 22) was, in fact, making 'queer' films long before the term was even coined. Even the AIDS pandemic can be seen to feature as a climactic symbol in work as early as *Caravaggio* (1986) in which Ranuccio and Michele's blood smearing connotes the blood-spread contagion. However, Arroyo also asserts that:

> Jarman, as we can see from his autobiographies, was very much influenced by the Gay Lib Movement [...] One can argue, though perhaps in an overly narrow auteurist sense, that this informs his representation of identity in *Edward*.
>
> (ibid.)

Although Arroyo is correct to suggest that Gay Lib politics fuel representations in *Edward II*, I want to argue that Jarman's status as 'queer' film-maker owes more to his representation of queer themes, such as an interrogation of sexual and gender identifications, the performativity of the body and how sexual desire is a solvent of identity, rather than to his explicit depiction of tendentious political rallies.

A collection of essays on queer film and video was published under the title *How Do I Look?* – a title of deliberate ambiguity which summarizes much of what I believe Jarman and Queer Cinema was trying to achieve. 'How Do I Look?' may, first of all, be read in an intransitive sense – how do queers look/appear to other people? Given the history of negative representation from mainstream cinema and the saccharine images of much gay identity politics films, how does the queer actually 'look' to the spectator? What *is* queer representation?

On the other hand, the second interpretation of 'How Do I Look?' is to read the verb in a transitive sense. How does the queer actually look at the images on the cinema screen? How is a queer spectator to react to the often disturbing images in queer cinema and what sort of cinematic experience are such images promoting?

Both these issues are at the forefront of the debates surrounding Queer Cinema and Derek Jarman. Theories of the gaze and cinema spectatorship; the representation of the sexed body; gender performativity and theories of postmodern, palimpsestic texts are, I shall argue, key issues within Jarman's cinema. Like the work of Haynes, Kalin and Araki, Jarman's films are not simply queer slogans or political tracts; films which have captured the political or cultural leitmotifs of the time. Instead these queer cinematic images encourage the spectator to reconsider his/her identifications within the matrix of gender, sex and sexuality.

3

MEN'S BODIES 1: ROUGH TRADE AND SUGAR DADDIES

Jarman's sexual politics are uncompromising. The subculture and sexuality his films participate in are not simply 'gay' or 'camp'. The films take on broad issues of sexual politics, particularly notions of masculinity.

(Mark Nash, 1985: 35)

The importance of the body in visual art cannot be over-emphasized. When we watch a film or gaze at a painting we are nearly always looking at bodies. Even the absence of the corporeal from the image – the sweeping panoramic view of a Western or the expanse of a landscape painting – still implies the body by its very absence because it is only the smallness of the physical body which allows the sweeping panorama or the landscape to attain such extreme dimensions (see Fuery, 2000: 76).

It is impossible to consider any form of culture without reference to the body. As Foucault has famously argued 'in every society, the body was in the grip of very strict powers, which imposed on it constraints, prohibitions or obligations' (1977: 136). The body was both the vehicle and symbol for the exercise of social power. Most importantly, Foucault has argued that the body placed on public display is the body subject to the power of the spectator's gaze. Foucault cites the architectural prison system of the panopticon as a metaphor.

A panopticon is a prison system composed of a peripheric ring of prison cells open to surveillance from a central warden's tower. The prisoners are continuously under surveillance from the warden but unable to see each other or return the warden's gaze. Eventually the prisoners internalize the sense of surveillance (they become aware that they are constantly being watched – even if the warden's tower is unoccupied) and learn to self-regulate their behaviour. Foucault points out that this system is a supreme form of discipline:

> In discipline, it is the subjects who have to be seen. Their visibility
> assures the hold of the power that is exercised over them. It is the fact
> of being constantly seen, of being able to be seen, that maintains the
> disciplined individual in his subjection.
>
> (1977: 187)

However, Foucault also explains that placing a body on display is not only
a means of exerting control over that body but a way of regimenting
desultory bodies (1977: 184). When bodies are placed on display, subject
to a spectatorial gaze, they can be objectified and arranged in a specific
hierarchy. As is evidenced in all beauty pageants, bodies on display are
regimented and ranked in order by the spectator's gaze.

The cinema is almost the perfect vehicle for Foucault's thesis.
Understandably, therefore it has been the concern of much feminist film
theory to criticize how the bodies which are objectified and classed in
cinematic economy have nearly always been female. Joan Copjec explains
that 'the panoptic gaze defines *perfectly* the situation of the woman under
patriarchy' (Copjec, 1989: 54). As can only be expected, therefore, male
bodies have been reluctant to be placed on cinematic display because to do
so robs them of patriarchal power. Like the prisoner in the panopticon, the
male body on display can be observed, objectified and regimented by
the gaze.

However, a possible exception to this is representing the male body in
activity so that the body can be regarded simply as a testament to male
strength rather than the disempowered object of the gaze. Richard Dyer
points out that even when a male body is represented in a relaxed pose it
always tenses its muscles to emphasize its strength and connote its
readiness for action (1982: 67). The male body is the body which does
something rather than the body which is simply looked at (see Neale,
1993). Therefore, there has been a history of the heroic male nude in
classical art and statuary, its defiant contropposto signifying strength and
fortitude (see Walter, 1978).

These next two chapters will argue that Jarman's cinema offers a challenge
to this formula. Developing the themes raised in the 'Queer Cinema' chapter

in the 'ga(y)zing at the male body' section, the next two chapters will argue that Jarman's films do not always permit the invisible, empowered gaze of the spectator to objectify, classify and regiment the bodies on the screen. Instead, Jarman's desultory bodies often actively refuse to be classified within traditional sexual taxonomies of gay or straight. This is emphasized continually by Jarman's cinematography which sometimes effectively blinds the spectator – often by a dazzling light shone directly into the camera – in order to prevent the regimenting gaze of cinematic spectatorship.

Secondly, these two chapters will argue that Jarman's representation of the male body is not simply erotic reverie, pandering to the libido of gay men. The male bodies in Jarman's cinema are too often dismissed as being little more than 'erotic shorthand' (Savage, 1991: 16) – tasty garcons fatales who spice up the narrative. Yet I want to argue that Jarman's representation of male bodies is not so much pandering to gay delectation as attempting to 'queer' various themes implicit in gay iconography. Jarman's male bodies not only interrogate notions of appropriate masculinity (his heroes are masochistic rather than actively dominant) but investigate cultural clichés which conflate specific bodies with specific sexualities. The result is that Jarman's films ask the spectator not only to reconsider how s/he looks at specific male bodies but also to question the very concept of the body as a prescription of sexuality and gender.

Rough Trade and Sugar Daddies: *Caravaggio*

The idea of the 'bit of rough trade' is practically a gay cliché or, what Alan Sinfield terms, a 'subcultural myth' (1998: 95). From Sir Stephen Spender and his working-class companion Jimmy Younger, to the novels of E. M. Forster and Alan Hollinghurst, to recent gay-themed films such as *Love and Death on Long Island* (dir: Kwietniowski, 1996) and *Gods and Monsters* (dir: Condon, 1998), the image of the older, upper-class gentleman savouring the delights of the young, working-class lad is ingrained in gay culture. The sugar daddy/rough trade relationship has become a standard trope of gay subculture.

In *The Wilde Century*, Alan Sinfield examines some of the factors which encouraged the popularity of this type of relationship. Firstly, Sinfield points out that the rough trade/sugar daddy relationship echoed pre-feminist heterosexual relations in that 'the social inferiority of the lower-class partner corresponded to the relative powerlessness of the heterosexual wife' (1994: 150). Secondly, Sinfield suggests that the sugar daddy/rough trade arrangement also mirrored the class-based structure of illicit heterosexual relations in the early twentieth century. It was relatively acceptable for a gentleman to have a mistress, provided she came from the lower classes. Society would excuse a gentleman messing around with street-girls or prostitutes but would not turn a blind eye to an affair with a lady of his own class (ibid.).

However, the main attraction of rough trade was not that these boys offered the possibility of echoing heterosexuality's class-based relations but that rough trade boys were straight identified. As Sinfield explains, gay was a middle-class concept and, in the early twentieth century, was not an identity category available to the lower classes. 'The lower-class boy might have same-sex experiences with others of his own class, but need not regard them as involving a queer identity – because, after all, it was leisure class men that had that' (ibid.: 145). The rough trade boys might well indulge in homosexual acts but, as Sinfield points out, would think 'of themselves as acting out of deference for money' (ibid.: 149).

Sinfield argues that claiming a gay identity was an option open only to the leisured classes – the middle or upper social echelons. Socio-economic factors were (and still are) a constriction on the parameters of identification. The lower classes had restricted mobility and access to particular forms of culture and, arguably, it is difficult to identify as 'gay' without having access to 'gay culture' within which to identify oneself. While 'homosexuality' denotes a sexual preference, a 'gay' identity connotes much more – such as how the subject organizes his life in terms of lifestyle and politics (McIntosh, 1997).

In the early to mid-twentieth century the professions (or cultural milieus) which tolerated homosexuality as an 'open secret' – the arts, theatre, the academy – were undeniably middle- or upper-class domains. Of course, Sinfield's research is not implying that claiming a gay identity was easy for leisured-class men. As the historian Hugh David has documented, middle/upper class men encountered great difficulties in trying to engage in same-sex activities (1997: 110). Nevertheless, gay identifications were, at least, 'accessible' to the middle/upper classes while they were not available to working-class men until a couple of decades ago.

However, Murray Healy, in his study of gay skinhead culture – *Gay Skins* (1996) – adds a further development to Sinfield's argument. Healy suggests that the exclusion of working-class men from homosexual identifications may not have been predicated *simply* upon social class constrictions. According to Healy 'the adoption of an identity is not solely dependent on access to a subculture' (1996: 17). Instead Healy argues that knowledge of identity categories (such as gay or lesbian) may be sufficient for a sense of identification as, after all, 'most people identify as gay, in their early teens, in isolation, before they have access to a scene or meet other homosexuals' (ibid.). Therefore, Healy stresses that there is an important distinction to be made between the history of gay *identities* and the history of gay *representations*. In other words, the exclusion of working-class lads from gay identifications may have been motivated by 'a drive for fantasy-preservation' (1996: 19) by those in the higher social echelons and, as such, is a representation rather than actual identity. The *image* of the straight, working-class lad was preserved by those in power because of its erotic potential. As Healy stresses, 'middle-class gay men who have invested in fantasies about sex with 'real' men (as the posh queens themselves phrased it, 'rough trade') would have all the greater investment in this. Working-class lads have to be kept straight' ibid.: 19).

There is, arguably, great erotic investment in the image of the straight identified man. Contemporary, American porn films often still demand that their 'stars' are straight identified. As John Mercer points out, gay porn 'frequently fetishizes the straight man as fantasy object' (2003: 286). Many porn narratives (see, for example, *Military Men* (1996)) represent straight identified men who turn to each other for a means of sexual release – due to the absence of women – rather than in an expression of gay desire (see Burston, 1995: 2 and Simpson, 1994: 132). Therefore, although Mandy Merck praises gay porn as a 'crucial affirmation of homosexual identity' (1993: 217) – and undoubtedly gay porn does acclaim homosexual acts as good fun rather than depraved buggery – it should be remembered that the sense of a gay identity is often erased from the narrative. As Mark Simpson summarizes, 'the 'gay porn video', then, depicts not gay men having gay sex but 'straight' men having gay sex (1994: 132). Porn films are therefore rarely set in gay bars of saunas (or any other gay identified space) but in settings of heterosexual frustration such as army barracks, navy ships or prison cells (1994: 133). In short, anywhere devoid of female flesh where the poor guys must 'make do' with superbly pumped-up pectorals, bugling biceps and lickably washboard abs. But they seem to, quite literally, rise to the challenge and 'take it like a man'.

Indeed, it is the very act of taking it 'like a man' which often gives porn its main erotic focus. Homosexuality was (and as Sedgwick (1993: 157) has argued still is) perceived within the matrix of effeminacy: the post Foucaultian trope of an 'interior androgyny, a hermaphroditism of the soul' (1978: 43). From the legacy of Oscar Wilde and the turbulence of his trial, the conflation of homosexuality and gender transitivity is another gay cliché. Sinfield points out that, after Wilde's public disgrace the image of the dandy – which previously had not been a semiotic of homosexuality but simply of upper-class laxity – was now ingrained in the public perception as the ultimate signifier of homosexuality (1993: 156). Foppishness or effeminacy became one of the key semiotics by which homosexuality could be deduced and so even lower-class men, such as Quinten Crisp, affected the Wildean effeteness. According to Crisp, homosexuals 'must, with every breath they draw, with every step they take, demonstrate that they are feminine' (1968: 21).

Rough trade, therefore, offered a supreme erotic fantasy. It was irrefutable, intransigent masculinity but yet still susceptible to the occasional erotic tussle from which the straight lad need not necessarily claim an identity. The leisured-class gay man could feel proud of the fact that he had persuaded this paragon of masculinity to partake of illicit pleasures. Therefore, what the eroticized image of rough trade actually did (and, arguably, in the plethora of contemporary gay porn videos unfortunately still does) was to strengthen *essentialist* perceptions of sexuality. The tough trade stereotype re-enforces the binaries of straight and gay and their corollaries of masculine and feminine. Rough trade was actually a defining other for the foppish, gay-identified Wildean type (Sinfield, 1993: 149). It strengthened essentialist notions of gender transitive homosexuality compared with masculine heterosexuality.

Essentialising Rough Trade Masculinity

This 'essentialising' of rough trade masculinity can be found in various gay novels, plays and films. One popular, contemporary example would be the work of the award winning novelist Alan Hollinghurst, a British writer whose gay-themed novels, *The Swimming Pool Library*, *The Folding Star*, *The Spell* and, most recently, *The Line of Beauty*, have achieved both commercial and critical success. Indeed *The Line of Beauty* was recently awarded the Booker Prize and was a very successful BBC TV production in 2006.

In his insightful analysis of Hollinghurst's novels, 'Desire as Nostalgia: the novels of Alan Hollinghurst', David Alderson points out that William Beckwith (the aristocratic narrator of Hollinghurst's *The Swimming Pool Library*) is only attracted to working-class men (2000: 32). Beckwith's boyfriend Arthur – a working-class, black man from East London – is attractive to Beckwith because he appears to represent an animalistic innocence, uncluttered by the regimes of Western culture. Alderson explains that 'Arthur appears to him ageless, inhabiting some realm beyond the processes of time, managing effortlessly, naturally to combine innocence *and* sexuality' (ibid.). Therefore, 'Arthur is idealised in his primitivism' because he embodies 'a condition beyond the western postlapsarian economy of sexual guilt and physical morality' (ibid.). Alderson concludes that Arthur represents a 'pre-cultural condition' (ibid.). In other words, Arthur is not interpellated by the regimes of sexual taxonomy which structure Western, bourgeois society and is therefore removed from the politics of gay identity and, more importantly, gay sexual shame. (Obviously, the politics of racial difference is also evident in this relationship. Arthur, like many other black men, represents 'the ontological reduction of the black man to his phallus' (Mercer, 1994: 174)).

Hollinghurst's *The Swimming Pool Library* represents the rough trade boys as essentialist, primitive masculinity. Therefore, it is hardly surprising that Beckwith perceives Arthur simply *as* his body. Beckwith only appraises Arthur in terms of his physical beauty, his drooling descriptions describing how he gains great pleasures from Arthur's 'high, plump buttocks', 'the ever-open softness of black lips; and the strange dryness of the knots of his pigtails which crackled as I rolled them between my fingers, and seemed both dead and half-erect' (Hollinghurst, 1988: 2-3). (Alderson points out that this theme is echoed in Hollinghurst's later work, *The Spell*, in its representation of 'that marginal Scudderite figure, Terry Badgett – whom Robin 'didn't really think of ...as being homosexual' (ibid. 44). This purely physical body, representing primitive innocence, is therefore, outside the constrictions of Western gay epistemology – especially the politics of gay sexual shame. Instead, the rough trade's sexuality represents animalistic needs. He represents utterly natural, unbridled sexuality. This, therefore, accords with Healy's argument that working-class boys were 'kept' straight by those in cultural power. The frisson of the working-class lad was the *fantasy* that this tough body, oozing a natural sexuality, was not constricted by the confines of sexual identifications and represented a natural or essentialist masculinity.

However, while writers such as Garland, Forster and Hollinghurst and filmmakers such as Pasolini, Eisenstein and Fassbinder may represent this erotic image of the 'bit of rough', Jarman attempts to interrogate or queer it. Jarman uses the stereotype of the rough trade to question how Western, bourgeois culture attempts to delineate sexuality and prescribe sexual desire to specific bodies. His work exposes the eroticism of rough trade – essentialist, masculine straightness – as being only a system of cultural representation or, to use Healy's term, an erotic fantasy. Throughout his films, Jarman is deliberately questioning/queering essentialist sexual and gender roles. His work consistently exposes sexual identity as a performative effect and asks the spectator to reconsider genders and sexualities. Although Jarman features images of rough trade bodies in many of his films, his queering of this gay cliché is best exemplified in one of his best known and more popular films: *Caravaggio*. The following analysis tries to show how *Caravaggio* not only questions the cliché of the rough trade lad as being simply his primitive, uncultured body but also interrogates how culture attempts to regiment desire and prescribe it to specific bodies. In doing so the chapter draws heavily upon the critical writing on *Caravaggio* by Timothy Murray and also Leo Bersani and Ulysee Dutoit. However, while Bersani and Dutoit offer close textual analysis of the film and Murray interrogates the cinematic gaze and questions sexual identification, my analysis hopes to further these critics' debates in specific relation to queer studies by examining how Jarman subverts the representation of the rough trade/sugar daddy cliché. The chapter will argue that Jarman, through his portrayal of the rough trade/sugar daddy relationship, is dramatising queer theory's assertion that desire cannot be regimented but instead is a powerful solvent of identities.

Caravaggio

Caravaggio was the closest Jarman ever came to making a traditional, narrative feature film. It tells the story of the Italian Renaissance artist Michelangelo di Caravaggio and the strange/queer relationship which he has with his model Ranuccio (played by Sean Bean) and the street urchin/prostitute Lena (played by Tilda Swinton). Caravaggio is called 'Michele' throughout the film and is acted by Dexter Fletcher as a youth and then by Nigel Terry as an adult.

Michele 'picks up' Ranuccio and Lena at a bare-knuckle boxing match and employs them both as models for his paintings. However, halfway through the film Lena is murdered. Michele is shown to be very distraught by Lena's death and Ranuccio is imprisoned as a prime suspect. Michele makes an elaborate deal with the Vatican (the promise of more paintings) in order to secure Ranuccio's release. However, at the film's climax, Ranuccio admits to having murdered Lena and, for reasons which the film does not make explicit, Michele slashes Ranuccio's throat.

Like Caravaggio's paintings, which are featured throughout the narrative, the film is not attempting to be historically accurate. Instead, Jarman employs his characteristic anachronism by including (among other things) calculators, motorbikes and typewriters throughout the film's diegesis. *Caravaggio* is clearly not trying to unearth the sexual politics/sexual identities of Italian Renaissance culture yet neither is it simply a ludic transposition of one set of modern signifiers into an historical setting. Instead, like most of Jarman's other features, *Caravaggio* should be described as palimpsestic in that it juxtaposes two distinct times and cultures, collapsing the intervening years. (A palimpsest is a manuscript from which some of the writings have been erased to make room for some more. In this sense a palimpsest is continually evolving and it is impossible to speak of an 'original' palimpsest.) Jarman's images create this palimpsestic effect by evoking a landslide of semiotic meaning with signifiers radically producing a whole new range of signifieds. The image does not simply show the insertion of an anachronistic sign into a specific period but prises open the chain of signification itself.

Politically, this palimpsest allows Jarman to fuse his contemporary queer politics with historical formations. As James Tweedie explains, 'resistance has a history, the film suggests, though that history may remain obscured by centuries of accumulated discourses' (2003: 381). By including anachronistic details in an historical setting, Jarman combines 'the retrospective gaze of history and the prospective gaze of contemporary queer movements' (2003: 381). Therefore, Jarman is able 'to use' Caravaggio's life story as a vehicle for examining contemporary sexual politics (see Bersani and Dutoit, 1999: 8), especially the circumscription of sexual desire to specific bodies. In particular, Jarman examines the essentialist, straight masculinity of the rough trade body.

In the early scenes of *Caravaggio* Michele appears to conform to the rough trade myth. The film represents the tough, street-wise rent-boy Michele Caravaggio who, like all hustlers, is straight-identified. (Mark Simpson describes the 'hustler' as 'a straight boy who lives by offering his body to gay men, but takes this as an affirmation of his heterosexuality' (1994: 159)). Michele is an image of street-wise, tough masculinity and this is emphasized by Jarman employing one of the dominant techniques of Hollywood representation: juxtaposition. In an early scene Michele is juxtaposed with an effeminate boy who is posing for one of his tableaux. The femmey boy is a virtual parody of the Crispian homosexual – not only in his voice but also in his rouged cheeks – and forms a defining other for Michele's rough-trade masculinity. The femmey boy then remarks that young Michele is 'well-fixed' by having recently secured the Cardinal as his patron. Michele replies that he has an easy time of it because the Cardinal wants 'fuck all' – a few 'cheap thrills'. The implication is that, for Michele, sexual 'thrills' are indeed simply 'fuck all' – just another activity offered for money. Michele does not claim an identity from an activity that he simply uses to gain some cash.

Yet, unlike the other scenes in the film, this scene has a camp quality, not least because of the femmey boy who breaks from his classical pose and starts whining (in a stereotypical London gay accent) that Michele is 'well fixed'. Like later scenes in the film (see below), this scene challenges spectators' expectations and warns that identities may not be as fixed as the spectator may believe. Jarman is deliberately caricaturing the conflation between gender performance and sexuality. This scene presages the two major themes which Jarman will be examining in *Caravaggio*: that sexual desire cannot be conscripted to sex or gender performance and that the eroticized image of 'straight' rough trade may be no more than an 'image'.

Therefore, despite this superficial conformity to the rough trade stereotype, Jarman's Michele actually disrupts or queers one of the main factors in the eroticism of the rough trade body. Dr. Page's lover in Garland's *The Heart in Exile*, or the boys whom William Beckwith adores in Hollinghurst's *The Swimming Pool Library*, simply *are* their bodies. The masculine semiotics of their bodies form the key element of their beauty. They are not attractive because of their education in the arts or sciences but instead offer only a supremely masculine, rough trade body.

However, *Caravaggio*'s images deliberately prevent Michele from being reduced to a mere object of rough-trade desire. This is especially evident in the scene where young Michele is filmed with a revolving camera – an unusual cinematic technique, especially for Jarman. This revolving camera technique was famously employed by Laura Mulvey and Peter Wollen in their film *Riddle of the Sphinx* which featured a recurrent 360° pan of the camera in order to challenge, if not even impede, the traditional cinematic gaze. As Mary Ann Doane suggests, this circular movement 'effects a continual displacement of the gaze which 'catches' the woman's body only accidentally, momentarily, refusing to hold or fix her in a frame' (1987: 34).

This revolving camera technique is used in the scene when young Michele has brought his 'client' (a stereotypical old pervert with the comb-over from hell) back to his rooms. The spectator anticipates a salaciously voyeuristic scene in which the camera offers the 'client's' gaze at the body that he has 'bought' for a few hours' entertainment. Yet in this scene the bodies revolve around a pivoting camera which varies the depth of focus as well as offering unstable angles (see Murray, 1993: 156). The result is that the spectator is unable to identify with the client's point of view. Michele's body is not caught by the camera and held within its frame. The scene therefore prevents the objectification of Michele's body. It impedes the gaze of the spectator and challenges the fetishization of the traditional rough trade object of desire. It forbids the reduction of Michele simply to the eroticized spectacle of his body.

This is further emphasized by the film's narrative in which Michele becomes the protégé of the Cardinal. In contrast to traditional rough trade/sugar daddy relationships, young Michele is not supported by the church/Cardinal because his body is so desirable but because of his artistic talent. The church/Cardinal funds Michele because of his artistic vision and ability to produce devotional art for the established church. However, one of the most interesting aspects about young Michele is the way he conflates selling his art with selling his body. As David Gardner points out, when Michele is hustling on the street, he is not painting simply to pass the time but is using his art as a means of 'laundering' the gaze of his clients. The 'art patron' uses the pretext of the painting to approach Michele (Gardner, 1996: 48). Therefore, when Michele is with his client/art patron he demands payment for his body because he is 'an art object and very, very expensive'.

Traditional (or rather – elitist) perceptions of 'Art' insist that the artist is some sort of visionary or seer who makes a 'finely honed distillation of his experience' (Sinfield, 1998: 87). This Art is then nurtured by perspicacious critics until eventually it is appreciated widely and taught as part of a university syllabus. Yet Jarman's representation of young Michele deliberately confuses this issue. When Michele sells his physical body along with his art, it raises the question: what is the art object? What is the 'finely honed distillation of experience'? What offers the sense of transcendence – the timeless artwork or the physical body?

When young Michele becomes the Cardinal's protégé, this is further emphasized. During the Cardinal's pompous lectures, Michele barely stifles his yawns and the voiceover of his internal monologue describes his boredom. He has a supreme indifference to cultural knowledge, class, science and all of the arts, including his own. At one point Michele simply requests the return of his confiscated, illegal knife as payment for one of his paintings. The knife is an important symbol throughout the film. Its power is one of physical threat as it is used to penetrate bodies, both Michele's and Ranuccio's, while eventually being used to slash Ranuccio's throat in the film's climax. Yet it is also used to paint when Michele jabs it into his painting and traces an arc across the canvas. The knife, therefore, symbolizes a dominant theme in the film: the tension between art (which, especially in the case of Christian art, is supposed to evoke a sense of transcendence beyond the physical) and the rough, earthly body. Young Michele is the artist, patronized by the church because of his visionary, transcendent art but he is also physically rough – an uncultured body with little interest in the arts or sciences. Jarman's representation of Michele therefore questions the cliché of the 'bit of rough trade' as being simply his body. The idea of the artist as a visionary or seer is subverted while the status of the rough trade stereotype is elevated. The erotic frisson of young Michele is his animalistic innocence combined with his artistic vision, the tension, as in Caravaggio's paintings between body and spirit. As Bersani and Dutoit point out, Caravaggio's actual paintings often inspired public outcry because his models for Christ and the Madonna were too obviously just street rats and common whores. 'It is as if they were proclaiming that the subject on the other side of their represented bodies is nothing but that: *their bodies*' (1999: 48). Indeed, Caravaggio's art disturbs the Christian theology which dictates that the Word precedes the body. Rather than a sense of the Word made Flesh, there is an overwhelming sense of the earthly or physical in Caravaggio's images and this is symbolized throughout the film by the body of young Michele himself. Although patronized for his artistic vision, it is Michele's body which is foregrounded.

However, although *Caravaggio* questions the cliché of the rough trade figure as being simply his body, the film also challenges the idea of this body as straight-identified. As Timothy Murray argues, an interesting issue in *Caravaggio* is that the film 'attests to the difficulty of mapping homosexual praxis, whether textual, sexual or visual, from the omniscient stand-point of an *essential* identity' (1993: 141). It shows that sexual identity cannot be delineated simply by sexual object choice, gender performativity or by sex.

Homosexual, homosocial or queer?

One of the most striking elements of *Caravaggio* is that Michele's sense of sexual identification changes as he grows older. From the straight-identified, rough trade hustler, Michele grows up to become openly gay identified. His rise to middle-class status (he becomes a respected painter) seems to allow him a more open sense of gay identification. In this respect the film exposes the image of working-class, straight masculinity as being nothing more than a system of erotic representations rather than an essential identity.

This fluidity of identification is symbolized by the way the film charts the progression in time, showing the transition from young Michele (played by Dexter Fletcher) to older Michele (played by Nigel Terry). Firstly, the spectator is shown young Michele painting while wearing a black hat. This is followed by a scene which shows adult Michele sitting in a tavern wearing the same hat. The only semiotic which identifies Nigel Terry as playing the same character as Dexter Fletcher (only now a bit older) is the black hat. Jarman's use of this cinematic convention in *Caravaggio* thus highlights the fact that the spectator is asked to judge a character's identity simply because of a piece of clothing. Moreover, while young Michele was initially represented as a straight identified hustler, older Michele is shown to 'cruise' Ranuccio in the tavern in a fashion which is reminiscent of gay men 'out on the pull'. Michele's companion Davide simply remarks that 'You won't get anywhere with him'. The camera locks the spectator into identification with Michele by first showing him, then the object of his gaze and then his reaction. The image suggests that the roles of rough trade and sugar daddy are not fixed but merely systems of representation where the positions can shift. Michele is now the middle-class, successful painter (who is openly gay identified) while Ranuccio is the bit of rough trade.

Understandably, given this cruising scene, the spectator's expectation is for a gay romance to blossom between Michele and Ranuccio. Yet this doesn't happen. Nowhere does the film represent sexual activity (other than a soft kiss) actually taking place between the two men. The relationship that ensues is certainly not one of traditional gay sugar daddy/rough trade patronage. The inclusion of Lena in the narrative, for whom Michele seems to have a distinct passion, muddles the issue of homoerotic desire. At one level, Lena's triangulation of the relationship between Michele and Ranuccio invites us to read it as homosocial – the term made famous by Eve Sedgwick (drawing upon the theories of

Irigaray (1985: 170) – which describes 'social bonds between persons of the same sex' (1985: 1) – as much as homosexual. Sedgwick has explored the representation of homosociality in classic literary texts, arguing that in many cases we find an erotic triangle in which the 'bond that links the two rivals is as intense and potent as the bond that links either of the rivals to the beloved' (1985: 21). Initially, this appears to be the case in *Caravaggio*. Michele and Ranuccio are often as closely knit in their rivalry as they are in their desire for Lena (see discussion below). Yet homosociality is an insufficient term to describe the characters' relationship as this triangle shifts on yet another axis in which Lena's fevered lovemaking with Ranuccio has been fuelled by her jealousy of Michele's attentions for Ranuccio. Likewise, Michele's and Ranuccio's passions for each other seem to be at their most intense when they are also vying for Lena's attention.

Looks and Gazes

These erotic tangles are conveyed through the diegetic gazes of the film. Lynne Tilman points out that 'the male characters are as much fixed by Lena's gaze as they are by each other's and she is by theirs' (1987: 22). For example, in the scene where Michele gives Lena a ballgown and then kisses her, the out-of-focus Ranuccio watches in the background. Lena and Michele then both look at Ranuccio and then there is a shot of Ranuccio looking at them. This could certainly suggest a homosocial triangulation. As Tilman points out, when 'Caravaggio first approaches Ranuccio, Lena is there, and what could have been a close-up of Ranuccio alone as looked at by Caravaggio is a medium shot of Ranuccio and Lena as looked at by him' (1987: 22). Such a reading emphasizes how the different positions can permutate. However, Tilman has conveniently ignored the fact that the first representation of Ranuccio is through Michele's gaze, offering him to the spectator as erotic object within the conventional paradigms of romance cinematography. There is no doubt that the initial desire expressed is homosexual. Yet this desire does not develop as the spectator would imagine. Instead we find a 'queer' erotic triangle between Michele, Ranuccio and Lena. How do we classify the passion which is uniting these three bodies?

It is in effect impossible to offer a determinate reading of the film's climax in which Michele slits Ranuccio's throat after he has admitted to killing Lena. A feminist reading could suggest justifiably that Michele is unable to love a man who displays such violence against women. Another reading may suggest that Michele's love for Ranuccio can only exist in a pathologically sadomasochistic matrix and this is certainly emphasized by the earlier fight scene in which Ranuccio stabs Michele who reciprocates by smearing his blood across Ranuccio's face. Both stabbing scenes are preceded by Ranuccio's wicked grin as if in anticipation of the pleasure of sexualized violence. These scenes not only allude to the erotic connection between sex and death (see Dollimore, 1995) (the *petite mort* of the orgasm) but are arguably metaphors for the 'money shot' – a term describing the splatter of fluids in porn films which testifies that the spectator gets 'value for money' and actually sees an orgasm. This image is echoed at the end of the film when Ranuccio falls limp into Michele's arms and, in a scene bristling with AIDS overtones, smears his blood across Michele's face.

All these readings are possible. The point is that the narrative offers neither a 'gay romance' nor a 'homosocial triangle'. It deliberately confuses issues of love, sexuality and sexual identification. How do we delineate Michele's sexual identification and his relationship with Lena and Ranuccio? In many ways the film illuminates the theories of both Sedgwick (1990: 85) and Dollimore (2001: 35) who have argued that desire has the power to unfix identities which previously had seemed very stable. Dollimore has actually argued that, far from being Foucault's 'reverse discourse' (1978: 43) in which minority sexual identities can gain a power in self-recognition and articulation, sexual 'identity politics might be in part a defence against the instabilities and difficulties of desire itself (2001: 32). *Caravaggio* attests to the power (and danger) of desire to dissolve sexual identities and, ultimately, render its subjects unclassifiable.

Challenging Specatorship

The film's cinematography seems to demand above all that the spectator should not attempt to make reductive readings of its images – especially the rough trade body and his sexuality. On a number of occasions, Jarman employs his favourite 'trick' of momentarily blinding the spectator by shining a dazzling light directly into the camera. When, for example, Michele is first painting Ranuccio he throws him gold coins as payment for his modelling. Ranuccio, because he is wearing only a loin-cloth with no pockets, stuffs the gold coins in his mouth. When Michele pays Ranuccio his final gold coin he places it within his own lips – thus forcing Ranuccio to remove the coin in the action of a 'profane kiss' (O'Pray, 1996: 150). The scene implies the start of same-sex passion between Ranuccio and Michele. Immediately preceding this seduction scene, however, the spectator has been dazzled by Jerusaleme (Michele's assistant) shining a light-reflecting panel into the camera. The spectator is momentarily blinded by the light.

Caravaggio, Jarman, 1986

This 'blinding' image serves as a warning for what is to come, suggesting that a reductive reading of the passion between Michele and Ranuccio by the spectator will lead only to confusion and blindness. And indeed, although the seduction scene suggests the start of same-sex passion between Michele and Ranuccio, the next scene represents fevered, heterosexual love-making between Ranuccio and Lena.

The visual motif linking these two scenes, however, is the gold coins which, having first been used by Michele as a means of seducing Ranuccio, then become toys of heterosexual foreplay between Ranuccio and Lena. Later in the film these very same coins are used in Michele's death scene to cover his dead eyes, simultaneously looking like gaping, wide eyes yet testifying to blindness. One of the themes implied by such imagery is 'blindness' or, at least, an inability to focus on a specific image. What is a symbol of homosexual seduction in one scene shifts to become a token of heterosexual love-making in another before finally becoming dead, un-seeing eyes. Like the blinding light shone directly into the camera, Jarman is deliberately dazzling his spectator and preventing him/her from making reductive readings.

Caravaggio, Jarman, 1986

This 'blinding light' image is employed later in Lena's death scene in which her body floats on the river in a pastiche of Millais's *Death of Ophelia* (1852). The sun reflects off the water and renders everything dazzling gold.

The image queers the meaning of Millais's *Ophelia* which imprisoned the woman's body within the gaze of traditional patriarchy. Firstly, Millais's painting testified to the myth of the woman as hysterical, uncontrollable and eventually suicidal body (see Showalter, 1985: 90-1), thus emphasising the traditional Western dichotomy of man as intellect, woman as only her uncontrollable body (see Spelman, 1982). Secondly, the image offers the stillness of death: a traditional romantic tope which represents the woman's body as transfixed, motionless and vulnerable to the gaze of the male spectator. In *Caravaggio,* however, the death of Lena represents a body that is indistinguishable. Lena's body is unrecognizable, even to the point of being ungendered. The blinding image prevents the spectator's gaze from focusing upon the woman's body and fetishizing the image in accordance with traditional homocentric, scopophilic pleasures.

All of these scenes emphasize that the film will constantly challenge the spectator's right to 'fix' specific bodies within ocular prescriptions. This is most aggressively emphasized in a scene after Lena's death where Michele uses her dead body as a model for another painting. Like all of *Caravaggio*'s painting scenes, there is an air of bristling sexuality about this image. Michele is shirtless, his skin moist and glistening with sweat, and he almost pants as if sexually heated while he smears his thick, impasto paint onto the canvas. The scene sets up many levels of 'looking' in which Michele gazes (in accordance with the *Ophelia* traditions) upon Lena's dead body while the spectator gazes upon Michele's shirtless, sexually heated torso. Yet this erotic trope of gazes is shattered when Michele turns to the camera and curses the spectator: 'God curse you!' Although on a narrative level this testifies to Michele's rage for Lena's murder, it is yet another Jarmanesque challenge to the spectator's gaze.

Therefore, the power of *Caravaggio* is the way it confuses or queers traditional sexual dynamics of not only traditional gay sugar daddy/rough trade patronage but of homosociality and homosexuality. As Timothy Murray argues, the film:

challenges its reader to reflect on, rather than avoid, this fluid slide between homosocial and the homosexual. That is, *Caravaggio* displays how easily alternative (homosexual) modes of socialization find themselves fused with homophobic and misogynistic (homosocial) traditions. The film's sometimes-contradictory slide between homosocial and homosexual relations illustrates the instability of any 'gay male political identity'.

(1993: 134)

Spectators who hoped *Caravaggio* would be a 'gay romance' would be very disappointed. The film, as symbolized by the rough trade, *originally,* straight-identified body of young Michele, consistently exposes the concepts of straightness or homosexuality as being merely representations. *Caravaggio* testifies to the impossibility of fixing desire within the traditional praxis of sexual identity politics. The film quite deliberately 'blinds' the spectator, interrogating his/her right to classify the filmic images, and shows the futility of attempting to map sexuality and sexual desires. The body of Michele testifies to the representation of the rough trade icon as being simply another form of erotic re-presentation and not the essence of intransigent, straight masculinity.

The film's climax therefore offers an ironic twist. The straight-identified, rough trade Ranuccio who, throughout the film had insisted that he was only flirting with Michele because he wanted Michele's money, finally admits to having killed Lena because he didn't want Lena blocking his affection for Michele. In his final words, Ranuccio claims to have murdered Lena because he loved Michele. The scene shows that Ranuccio – the straight identified hustler – is driven by homosexual passion while the gay-identified, middle-class gentleman is animated by his desire for Lena. *Caravaggio*, therefore, not only forces a reconsideration of how we delineate desire and attempt to map it onto specific bodies, but asks the spectator to reconsider the clichéd image of the middle-class gay gentleman with his straight-identified bit of rough trade.

4

MEN'S BODIES 2:
THE MASOCHISTIC HERO

The male masochist dominates Jarman's cinema. From Sebastian to Caravaggio, to King Edward to Wittgenstein, Jarman has created unconventional heroes who not only seem to amble aimlessly through their days but derive a masochistic pleasure from their tortures. Yet this representation is not simply coded eroticism – a chance to show prostrate, submissive male bodies – but an examination of the very issue of masochism itself and the way it is culturally linked to submission, passivity and femininity. Jarman's masochistic heroes not only question the concept of masochism as 'feminine' but expose the conflict between sexual shame, pride and its relation to masochism.

Although masochism has culturally been linked to the female body, the original word was coined by sexologist Richard von Krafft-Ebing because of the behaviour of a male patient, Leopold von Sacher-Masoch (1965). Sacher-Masoch, like Sade, was an aristocratic writer whose novels, especially *Venus in Furs*, illuminated the specific sexual pleasures which we now term 'masochism'.

What exactly is masochism? This is certainly a question which is easier to pose than to answer. Indeed theorising masochism seemed to stump even Freud who wrote extensively about the subject in several of his essays including 'A Child is Being Beaten' (1919) and 'The Economic Problem in Masochism' (1924) without seeming to arrive at any firm conclusion. In his 'Economic Problem in Masochism' Freud begins the essay with the rather tenuous argument that the masochist wants to be treated like 'a naughty child' (1961: 162). He suggests this because so many masochistic fantasies consist of being 'gagged, bound, painfully beaten, whipped, in some way maltreated, forced into unconditional obedience, dirtied and debased' (ibid.). However, as Anita Phillips points out, 'parents do not, in general, bind and gag, whip or painfully beat, dirty or debase their children, in response to acts of naughtiness – and never did' (Phillips, 1998: 29). Masochistic fantasies therefore do not remind us of our childhood unless, of course, they are referring to schoolyard bullying. Freud maintains this theory to the essay's conclusion when he asserts that masochism serves no function and is, in fact, potentially dangerous for the human subject. The key problem is that, throughout the essay, Freud has ignored the fact that sexual pleasure is central to the masochist. Without this factor the masochist is simply someone who accepts pain and humiliation for no other reason than auto-destructive pathology.

The other problem with Freud's theory on masochism is the way he outlines three different types of masochism but then proceeds to confuse the areas in his further elaboration. According to Freud, the three main types of masochism are: 'erotogenic', 'moral' and 'feminine'. 'Erotogenic' is the corporeal pleasure-in-pain masochism; the clichéd sexual image of the whips and chains. By contrast, the moral masochist seeks to have his/her ego pummelled. However, Freud described the ego as 'first and foremost a bodily ego' (1961: 26) which would therefore suggest that moral masochism is also related to corporeal sensations and that an overlap is implied between the two. Thirdly, Freud's writings posit 'feminine masochism' as the most common but proceeds only to describe male patients who suffer from it. Freud reads this as a male pathology as the 'feminine masochist' positions himself as a woman:

> If one has an opportunity of studying cases in which the masochistic phantasies have been especially richly elaborated, one quickly discovers that they place the subject in a characteristically female situation.
>
> (1961: 162)

However, the problem which patriarchal culture has with male masochism is the way it violates the gender divide. While female masochism is 'an accepted – *indeed a requisite* – element of 'normal' female subjectivity' (Silverman, 1992: 189), the male masochist 'radiates a negativity inimical to the social order' (206). The male masochist violates the gender boundaries and descends into the dark realm of femininity as, in patriarchal culture, 'being victimized is synonymous with being female' (Studlar, 1988: 19).

The male masochist is problematic for the contemporary gender binary in various ways. Firstly, he places his body continuously on display. Masochists, whether being beaten physically or morally, require it to be done to them in the sight of witnesses. They need an external agency to do something to them. Secondly, this exposes the myth of the autotelic masculine subject. In this respect, the male masochist is a dangerously queer specimen distressing cultural paradigms of masculinity and femininity. He is the body to be gazed upon, he is the body of passivity and he is the body exposing that his subjectivity comes from the Other. He must therefore be controlled and safely re-inscribed back into acceptability.

One of the avenues which has existed to sanitize masochism for public consumption has been religion – especially the dominant Western tradition of Christianity. Masochism is, and always has been, readily compatible with Christian ideology. The belief that Christians should endure 'pain' in the earthly life of flesh in order to receive the 'pleasure' of eternal salvation is essentially the masochistic trope of pleasure in pain. Christians also theatrically prostrate their sacrificial subjectivity in the face of the symbolic order by claiming that their meaning comes from an external force or spiritual 'Other'. Christians will often cite that they are simply 'performing God's will', thus signifying a rejection of phallic autonomy which, without the façade of the established church, would be a dangerously emasculating activity.

Apart from Christ himself, the Christian masochist to have dominated artistic representation has been St. Sebastian. It is strange that this very minor saint, who holds only a tiny role in both Christian history and theology, should have inspired artists such as Tintoretto, Perugino and Titian and writers such as Wilde, Pater and Proust. St. Sebastian, however, is beautifully emblematic, almost to the point of caricature, of the pleasure/pain dichotomy of Christian martyrdom. His body may be wracked with arrows – blood streaming from the wounds – but his face is uplifted to heaven, transcending the pain in a moment of serene bliss.

Even more remarkable is Sebastian's status as 'the patron saint of homosexual men' (Kaye, 1996: 86). In almost all his various guises, St. Sebastian has maintained a 'subculturally resonant homoerotic role' (ibid.: 88). His beautiful body, impaled with arrows as he is tied to a pillar or post, has offered homoerotic frissons from the sweet devoutness of Perugino to Pierre and Gilles's kitschy portrayal of a Bel-Ami style Sebastian complete with collagen buffed lips.

There are various reasons for Sebastian's exaltation as a gay icon. As I explained in Chapter 1, latter twentieth century gay politics was obsessed with the issue of 'gay identity'. 'Gay' did not simply describe someone who indulged in specific acts but signalled an identity which was laced together under the banner of oppression. The ethnic style politics of Gay Lib was united by a mythic sense of homogeneity in the face of oppression. St. Sebastian is almost the perfect cover-boy for this politics. Historically, the saint was isolated in a soldier's camp but yet chose to bravely reveal an 'essential' self. He is therefore a beautiful symbol of homosexuality as identity rather than a collection of perverse acts. Not only is he a figure whose sexual identity seems to be a matter of essentialist expression rather than a performance of sexual acts, but he is the oppressed, slaughtered gay martyr (see Kaye, 1996: 91).

Artistically, Sebastian is also the perfect iconoclast. He testifies to the covert kinkiness of hardcore religion; as Kaye summarizes, Sebastian reveals 'religious ecstasy as an erotic put-on' (1996: 86). In all his artistic guises, Sebastian asserts the pleasures of being fucked – albeit metaphoric arrow fucks. These arrow fucks inspire supreme ecstasy, comparable only with Bernini's sculpture *The Ecstasy of St. Theresa*. Sebastian's beautiful eyes are raised to heaven in sublime ex-stasis as his limits of sensual excess explode in supreme masochistic pleasure.

Jarman, however, reworks or queers this famous gay myth. Firstly, Jarman's Sebastian offers a sexuality which, at best, can be described as ambiguous but definitely not 'gay'. Secondly, he exemplifies the queer potential of male masochism which disrupts the gender parameters of masculinity and femininity, shattering the established binary of a masochistic, passive body which is gazed at and a sadistic, controlling body which has the right to gaze.

Throughout *Sebastiane*, Sebastian's body is represented as object of the gaze. Although there is a fleeting glimpse of Sebastian at the Emperor's party, the first main image of the queer martyr is in the soldiers' camp when Sebastian is having his morning shower. 'Sword and sandal' epics have always celebrated the nearly nude male body, and understandably, have been cited as homoerotic – not only because there is so much male flesh on display but because the narrative of these films is often similar to the 'buddy movie'. Yet the difference between the exposed flesh of, say, Steve Reeves' as compared to Jarman's Sebastian is that the former exposes his body in order to display his body's power, a testament to his masculine power and authority. In *Sebastiane*, by contrast, Sebastian's body is first offered to the camera's gaze while he is standing under the shower. There is no evidence of his body's power and, indeed, throughout the film Sebastian refuses to engage in any physical activity, even sparring practice. While showering, Sebastian's passive body is offered to the gaze of the camera which is usually also Severus's gaze.

As feminist film criticism has argued, to control the gaze is to be in the masculine, dominant position (Mulvey, 1975; Kaplan, 1983). For obvious reasons, this is why so much feminist criticism has condemned heterosexual pornography for blatantly objectifying the woman's body and then packaging it as a commodity. However, as Linda Williams, has correctly argued:

> Gay, lesbian and bisexual pornographies presented an even greater challenge to this oversimplified Lacanian formula. For gay porn could not be reduced, as it would seem the Canadian feminists did try to reduce it, to an aggressive male gaze at a feminized object.
>
> (1993: 56)

Firstly, gay porn removes the problem of power imbalance being attributed *automatically* to differently sexed bodies as the participants are all men. Secondly, gay porn, more than any other representation testifies that activities such as 'offering oneself' and 'inviting the gaze' are far from passive activities but are very active traits. Indeed John Mercer employs the term 'power bottom' (2003: 286) to describe a character type in gay porn who not only asserts a pleasure in being fucked but who, more importantly, orchestrates the entire seduction through offering his penetrable, supposedly 'passive' body to the active top. As Susan Bordo emphasizes, "passive' hardly describes what's going on when one person offers himself or herself to another. Inviting, receiving, responding – these are active behaviours too, and rather thrilling ones' (1999: 190).

We see a similar trope at work in *Sebastiane*. While Sebastian appears to be an utterly passive character, who submits to his tortures at Severus's hands, the question of who is manipulating whom comes under consideration. It should always be remembered that although the objectified body is bearing the weight of the gaze, the subject who is doing the gazing is often mesmerized, unable to do anything except stare. This is evident when Severus gazes upon Sebastian showering and is shown to be transfixed – even unable to continue writing his diary – because of the sight of Sebastian's body.

The narrative develops this theme using the metaphor of 'soldierly' passivity in which Sebastian refuses to fight and is punished by Severus (he whips Sebastian) for his disobedience. The film sexualizes this activity through the editing which juxtaposes Sebastian's flagellation with the other soldiers drooling over a painting of a female nude. When they hear Sebastian being whipped in the other room, one of the soldiers describes the activity (in Latin) as Severus 'really bashing his meat tonight'. The striking issue is that Sebastian does not seem to find these torturous activities disagreeable. In fact, the very opposite is the case. The final scene shows Sebastian's execution, as he is impaled with arrows, in the traditional slow motion of cinematic eroticism. A close-up of Sebastian's face shows erotic pleasure as he is penetrated each time with an arrow. Jarman's original script (thankfully not the filmed version) makes this scene even more explicit:

> The soldiers fire arrows one by one. One of the arrows goes through Sebastian's neck. It is sexual and ecstatic for Sebastian. He has a hard-on.
>
> (quoted in Peake, 1999: 544)

Arguably, this is what Sebastian has longed for throughout the film: the unadulterated masochistic pleasure of utter subjugation. Sebastian has manipulated and controlled Severus to finally achieve his sexual aims.

Therefore, describing Severus as 'sadistic' is not entirely accurate. Severus's original pleasures (from watching Sebastian in the shower to Adrian and Anthony making love) were simply voyeuristic. Sebastian, on the other hand, has an entirely different sexual agenda as evidenced by the voyeuristic sequence in which both Severus and Sebastian watch Adrian and Anthony's lovemaking. In this censor's nightmare scene, Severus watches the tender yet, as Rowland Wymer points out, very bland (2005: 42), lovemaking between Adrian and Anthony. Although Severus is aroused by watching Adrian and Anthony's smooching, Sebastian, who is also present on a nearby rock, seems to have supreme indifference to the boys' lovemaking. Then, when Severus attempts to seduce Sebastian by requesting that he help him to remove his armour, Sebastian refuses. This is not simply the rejection of Severus's body but Sebastian's desire for greater masochistic pleasure, anticipating that refusal of Severus's advances will incite more delicious punishment. Therefore, it is not really Severus who extracts sadistic pleasures from humiliating Sebastian but the queer martyr himself who demands ever increasing masochistic thrills and orchestrates the events to ensure that he gets them. As Anita Phillips summarizes 'the masochist is a conscious manipulator, not a victim' (1998: 19).

What is remarkable about *Sebastiane* is that the film testifies to the impossibility of suggesting that there is a watertight binary of controlling, sadistic gaze and passive, masochistic gazed at. Passive hardly describes the way Sebastian has manipulated and controlled Severus throughout the narrative, eventually forcing the soldier to lose all self control and smash every item of furniture in an act of frenzy while begging Sebastian to 'love' him. Indeed, an obvious comparison can be drawn with Bunuel's film *Belle de Jour* which opens with what appears to be a sadistic beating of Severine. (The heroine's name is the feminine version of Sacher-Masoch's masochistic hero Severin in his novel *Venus in Furs*.) *Belle de Jour*, however, swiftly cuts to an image which reveals that this beating was only a daydream of Severine's. Throughout the rest of the film, Severine's active masochism is emphasized, especially in the final scene where she is shown to have complete control over her husband (Fuery, 2000: 11). Although a feminist reading could argue that Severine offers the classic fantasies of a woman who has *internalized* and eroticized her oppression with contemporary culture and is simply enacting masochistic fantasies for the male gaze as masochism is, after all, 'an accepted – indeed a requisite – element of 'normal' female subjectivity, providing a crucial mechanism for eroticizing lack and

subordination' (Silverman, 1992: 189), this contestation cannot arise in
Sebastiane though, when the two bodies represented are both male. The
idea of control vacillates precariously between Sebastian and Severus.
Who is actually manipulating or controlling whom? What Sebastian does,
is to testify to the false dichotomy of masculinity being synonymous
with activity and sadistic control while masochism is synonymous with
passivity and femininity.

The second intriguing aspect of Jarman's representation of the gay
martyr is that Sebastian's sexuality cannot, from the film's narrative, be
described as 'gay'. Sebastian rejects the advances of Severus by telling him
(in Latin) that he shall never have him. The meaning is, at best, ambiguous.
Sebastian is either rejecting all same-sex sexual activity or he may simply
have a problem with Severus but be quite agreeable to erotic tussles with
some other man.

This ambiguity is conveyed through the cinematography as, from the
start of the film, Sebastian is positioned as object of desire rather than
homosexual subject. For example, during the shower scene, Sebastian is
enjoying his own soapy flesh in an image not dissimilar to the famous
opening sequence of masturbatory delight in Brian de Palma's *grand guignol*
horror *Carrie*. In both cases the pleasure is autoerotic. The voice-over
reveals Sebastian's ribald morning prayer to his god which proclaims that
not only the sun rises but the 'scarlet cock' as well. This is not being acted
for the pleasure of Severus's gaze (the spectator's gaze) but for Sebastian's
own autoerotic pleasure.

In this sense, Jarman's representation of St. Sebastian is, to use
Kristeva's pun, a "soulosexual' (1987: 78). The character typifies the auto-
erotic, masochistic pleasures of Christianity. Jarman emphasizes this in a
pastiche of the Narcissus pose in which Sebastian lounges on a rock while
peering down at his reflection in the water. This scene is juxtaposed with
the other soldiers exchanging bawdy jokes while playing piggy-in-the-
middle in the water and so inflects the image, yet again, with sexuality.
Sebastian, in stark contrast to his bawdy companions, rests meditatively
on the rock and offers praise to the beauty of his god's body. The camera,
however, cuts from Sebastian to his pool reflection showing that there is
no god's body in evidence in this sequence, only Sebastian's narcissistic,
'soulosexual' pleasure. Sebastian's continual lauding of his god's beautiful

body is always juxtaposed with the visual image of Sebastian either enjoying his own flesh or narcissistically gazing upon his own reflection.

It is interesting to note that Brian de Palma – a director renowned for his pastiches of visual art – used St. Sebastian as a dominant image in *Carrie*. When Carrie White is locked in the closet by her lunatic mother, she lights a candle held by a statue of St. Sebastian and, in the film's climax, when Carrie uses her telekinetic powers to impale her perverted mother with the kitchen knives, Mrs. White's body assumes the classic martyred pose of St. Sebastian. St. Sebastian, in de Palma's film, is a metaphor for suppressed sexuality which is then perverted by the reins of religion (see Kaye, 1996: 104).

Arguably Jarman's film offers a similar although less didactic image. Despite the film's chronology (1976), Sebastian is one of Jarman's queerest characters. Not only is Sebastian's sexuality unclassifiable, ranging from what can only be described as auto-eroticism to the most extreme sexual masochism, he also demonstrates that masculinity is not necessarily synonymous with activity and femininity with passivity. As Kaja Silverman points out, masochism not only 'subverts many of the binary oppositions upon which the social order rests' (1992: 187) (such as pleasure and pain) but it is also 'incompatible with the *pretensions* of masculinity' (ibid.: 198, my emphasis) and therefore upsets gender dichotomies. However, this trope of male masochism and its relation to queer sexuality is further developed in Jarman's later feature, *Edward II*.

Shame and Masochism

'Queer' is still a slippery term. In citing non-normative gender and/or sexuality as its defining concept, so many people are able to situate themselves on the trendy queer continuum. Queer has already become a baggy monster which has recently ballooned to include the phenomenon of the 'straight queer'. But as both Butler (1993: 226) and Sedgwick (1993b: 4) have pointed out, queer remains a volatile, bristling category precisely because it can never be removed from all those years of shame. That is why the concept of the 'straight queer' is a cultural as well as linguistic oxymoron. Until someone knows what it is like to hear the word as an insult, often accompanied by a fist in the face or a knee in the stomach, then there is little point in (re)claiming it. Queer derives its force because its bearer has had to fight through all the years of shame to gain a pride in the word.

In this respect 'queer' unites shame and pride in an uneasy alliance. Pride is not simply a matter of inverting shame. The subject does not simply reclaim 'queer' from the homophobes and suddenly develop a great pride in it. The volatility of pride is that it cannot be stripped of its underside – shame. The two always jostle for dominance within the queer subject.

Shame, as can only be expected, has always enjoyed a fraternity with masochism. The prime example has always been Christianity which is virtually predicated upon masochistic shame. According to Christian ideology, we are all unworthy sinners and, conveniently for the established church, we seem to continue sinning again and again. We must therefore prostrate ourselves in our quest for forgiveness.

It is important, in this respect, to clarify the difference between 'shame' and 'guilt' which, although often used as synonyms, are very different. Guilt is transitive and external to the subject. In courts of law the defendant 'pleads' guilty because he 'did it'. He is guilty of a particular crime. Guilt is something which the subject can acknowledge and, in doing so, can distance him or herself from the performance which is 'guilt'. Within our judicial system a subject can then expunge his guilt through disciplinary proceedings (our usual means being a fine or a term of imprisonment) and will then be thought to have paid his debt to society. He will have cleared his guilt, atoned from the wrongful deed he has committed and then no longer be guilty.

Shame, however, is entirely different. As Steve Connor summarizes, 'guilt relates to actions, shame to being' (2001 219). Shame cannot be separated from the subject; shame *is* the subject:

You cannot embrace, or identify, or acknowledge your shame, because you are proximally inundated in it: your 'you'-ness is swallowed up by its 'it'-ness. The ashamed person cannot identify with is shame, because he is identical with it.

(Connor, 2001: 219)

Although Connor doesn't use the term 'performative' in his description of shame, the idea of performativity is appropriate to this debate (see Sedgwick, 1993b: 5). Shame, like all performative effects, is also an *identity* effect. To *feel* shame is *to be* ashamed.

To use a hypothetical but very possible example: a flamboyant queer may well sashay past a bunch of homophobes loitering on the street corner. One of these homophobes may offer an utterance which is not so much constative as performative: 'queer!' (The choice of whether or not to adorn this utterance with a four letter expletive would be left to the harasser's own personal discretion.) This is a performative utterance because it constitutes an identity effect for the harassed queer. This identity effect can, of course, only come about through the interpellation of witnesses. The homophobe must be fairly confident that his colleagues share his disgust of queers as his performative utterance demands tacit social agreement. If he were in the company of people all sporting OutRage T-shirts then his performative utterance would be pointless.

Nevertheless, the homophobe's insult is a performative utterance conferring upon the queer an identity effect. Firstly, this is an identity of non-normative sexuality. Secondly, and more importantly, this is an identity of shame. In performatively declaring someone 'queer' the homophobe has made the queer experience shame; shame for not conforming to normative standards – either gender or sexual or, more probably, a conflation of the two – and has declared that the queer subject must exist outside his field of normativity. While this is an immediate ontological effect – flooding with shame usually elicits an immediate physical response in facial capillary dilation – it also imparts an identity-effect because being ashamed of his sexuality is an identificatory characteristic for the queer. It has been the agenda of queer politics to try and excise this shame, to separate the signifier 'queer' from its signified 'shame'. Although this theme is implicit in much of Jarman's cinema, the film to address the issue explicitly is *Edward II* which analyses the relationship of shame and pride and its equation with masochism.

In an early scene of *Edward II*, King Edward is unable to make love to Isabella and, in one of the film's most frightening images, smashes his head against the wall until blood pours from his forehead. Colin MacCabe has described this scene as demonstrating how 'Edward's passion for

Gaveston [is] a consequence of his inability to be roused by the queen's body' (1991: 12-13). MacCabe's reading, however, is problematic for two reasons. Firstly, it pathologizes homosexuality in a petty folk-constructionist way and suggests that Edward is simply turning to men for sexual thrills because he can't perform for Isabella. Secondly, MacCabe's reading ignores the film's narrative which has shown that Edward's desire for Gaveston predated his marriage to Isabella and certainly did not seem to impede his siring Prince Edward. In the film there has also been at least one romantic scene between Edward and Gaveston before the Isabella/Edward scene which MacCabe describes.

Yet what is most interesting about this scene is the masochistic way Edward physically punishes himself - pounding his head against the brick wall until blood gushes forth. It's as if King Edward has declared himself guilty and deserving of punishment and physical punishments – beatings, flagellations – have historically been the main method of atoning for guilt.

It is here that the relationship between shame and guilt becomes important. Guilt refers to a specific deed while shame refers to identity. Edward's masochism is not an expression of his shame but an attempt to transform it into guilt which is qualifiable and can be expunged. Christianity revolves on this continuous metamorphosis of shame into guilt. Christians are fundamentally unworthy which is why they continuously sin. Yet this sin can be atoned for (prayer, fasting, penance) and so Christians' shame at being flawed and weak is *transcribed* into the more acceptable, treatable form of 'guilt' through masochism. This is the basis of the Christian calendar and certainly goes some way to explaining why Christianity is such a popular religion.

King Edward tries to do the same thing and turn his shame into tangible guilt. He appears to punish himself for what seems to be a single act: failing to be aroused by Isabella. He finds himself guilty of failing to perform sexually. Yet what makes the scene so shocking is that his allocated self-punishment seems too excessive for one simple act. Isabella watches her husband's self mutilation with a mixture of horror and amazement. The scene shows Edward's attempts to transcribe queer shame into guilt and expunge the one act through masochism.

King Edward's masochism is exemplified throughout the film by the representation of his body. On most occasions Edward offers a spectacle of supreme passivity and usually waits for something to be done to him. He then usually weeps and whimpers as, for example, when he is coerced into signing Gaveston's dismissal and cries like a baby while he is cajoled in the language normally used to appease a child: 'Come, come now'. Indeed, throughout the film, Edward's body is coded in a particularly masochistic way. While all attempts are made to ensure that Isabella's gender performance remains the spectacular object of the gaze (see Chapter 5), it is Edward's body which competes with Isabella to dominate the spectator's affections. The camera consistently offers lingering close-ups of Edward's body – both his pained expression and his gleaming torso. Yet Edward is rarely represented during activity and when he is, such as the gym scene, its main purpose is to parody gay gym culture and transform the King's body into erotic spectacle.

One of the most striking aspects of Edward's body is the extreme pallor of his skin, resembling at times the translucency of a Leonardo da Vinci chiaroscuro, notably his *Virgin of the Rocks*. As Patrick Fuery has argued:

> The close-up of luminous skin to signify feminine beauty (Ingrid Bergmann in *Casablanca*, Greta Garbo in *Camille*) would seem to be a form of film spectacle which demands so much of the body that it is tortured (too pale, too smooth, too readily demonstrative of pain) and there certainly is a level at which this is a product of the power structures of the phallocularized gaze.
>
> (2000: 83-4)

We see this in the close-ups of Edward's extraordinarily pale skin which, unlike Isabella's, does not offer the defence of seamless make-up. Isabella's heavily made-up appearance resists the subjugation of the gaze in that her skin becomes more than human, more perfect, more impenetrable. Edward's appearance, by contrast, is always one of intense vulnerability. His pale skin looks so fragile and is marked by faint, blond freckles glittering across his cheeks and shoulders. This skin often becomes stained with slimy tears as he cries about losing Gaveston and whines about how unfair his life is. It is a body almost demanding to be subjugated.

As Foucault has pointed out, the spectacle of the body being punished was a key factor in early disciplining procedures and the exercise of power (1991: 25-6). The publicly punished (tortured) body of the condemned offered the spectacle of power and control to the spectators as the condemned man could be beaten, whipped or even quartered as a vehicle for displaying the judicial control of the state. Yet, as Foucault charted, public punishment/torture often failed to elicit the desired result. The condemned subject, utterly disempowered through beatings and other public tortures, often assumed the status of a hero (1991: 61). This condemned body, stripped of all power – prostrate and helpless – often commanded more respect and attention than the powerful force which was subjugating it. The spectacle of public discipline was, therefore, unsuccessful as the prostrate body, ironically, attained an heroic status.

Edward II, Jarman, 1991

However, as Foucault points out, there remains a trace of the public performance of torture in modern culture. The cinema is certainly one such trace as many cinematic spectacles, often action or horror films, represent bodies being tortured by other more powerful bodies. This is evident in *Edward II* where King Edward is represented as the body crushed and overpowered by the state. The film can be (and often is) read simply as a political tract – an allegory of how Thatcherite politics conspire to squash the queer victim. Edward is a queer martyr who is punished and victimized. Yet he readily submits to his subjugation believing, as Steve

Connor argues, that 'male shame, like male masochism is general, has a crudely and traditionally heroic aspect' (2001: 224). It is only in utter debasement that the hero can achieve true exaltation.

Yet although Edward battles the external conflict of politics and state he constantly fights an internal battle with his queer shame. While he originally tried, unsuccessfully, to transform it into guilt and then expunge it through masochistic punishment, he later tries to invert shame into its corollary of pride by flaunting his relationship with Gaveston. Therefore, the Royal Court's discontent is not so much Edward and Gaveston's relationship as such – Edward has sired an heir, remains married and is basically functioning as a token figurehead – but the public demonstration of their affection. Edward lavishes gifts upon Gaveston and elevates his base status by conferring titles.

Edward's problem is the tension which exists between shame and pride. Shame cannot simply be inverted like a sundial and turned into pride. No amount of reclamation of the signifier 'queer' can ever separate it from its connotations of shame. By attempting to glorify his shamed actions, the stigmatized subject can deflect shame – but only in a fleeting, momentary fashion. Shame cannot simply be inverted and turned into pride but instead the two must exist together in a tacit dynamism as one cannot have any meaning without the other.

However, the victorious ending of *Edward II* represents one character who has managed to attain a queer pride through shame. When King Edward emerges from his dungeon cell, he finds Prince Edward, in almost full drag, dancing on top of a cage which holds the dusty and decrepit looking Isabella and Mortimer. Where King Edward failed to attain a true pride in his queer status, it is Prince Edward who offers a vision of queer pride premised upon shame.

Throughout the film, King Edward attempted to deflect shame by flaunting his relationship with Gaveston but it has been Prince Edward who, throughout the narrative, has fought an internal battle of queer shame versus pride. This has been symbolized by Prince Edward's infatuation with military toys (guns, tanks, terrorist style balaclava masks) which seem to be strange toys for such an effeminate child. These toys, however, represent the internal battle taking place in the child's head as he wrestled with his internal desire to experiment with gender performance against the external heteronormatizing influence of Isabella and Mortimer. (I discuss the representation of 'queer' Prince Edward in greater detail in Chapter 7.) It is little Prince Edward who is the actual queer hero of *Edward II*, having overcome his own internal battles and finally achieved a sense of pride through queer shame.

Note

Chapter 4: 'Rough Trade and Sugar Daddies' was previously published as 'Queering a Gay Cliche: The Rough Trade/Sugar Daddy Relationship in Derek Jarman's *Caravaggio*', *Paragraph*, 2005: 28(3). I am grateful to Edinburgh University Press for the permission to reprint.

5

WOMEN'S BODIES 1: THE QUEER PERFORMANCE OF TILDA SWINTON

Many critics have noted – only quickly to ignore or rationalise – Jarman's depiction of women, particularly in *Edward II*, where the most objectionable moment appears to be when Isabella kills Kent by biting into his neck. While it is not helpful to label Jarman a misogynist, his depiction of women is neither peripheral to his work nor something to be simply explained away in order to maintain Jarman's films as good objects.

(Biga, 1996: 21)

Tilda Swinton [...] the most important figure in Jarman's films.

(Wymer, 2005: 105)

Gay male misogyny has become a cliché. Gay themed novels, films and plays often delight in representing grotesque, abject women; female monsters who are wedged into the narrative for no other reason than to strengthen the subjectivity of the text's gay heroes. These monstrous, heterosexual women are used to bolster gay male subjectivity in two ways. Firstly, these female monsters provide a defining other. The female grotesque, juxtaposed with gay lovers, prettifies or exalts gay love. The gay lovers are beautiful, sexy and vibrant while the female monster – emblematic of heterosexuality – is dour, ugly if not even downright repulsive. Secondly, these women are often used as a site of convenient transcription for everything that the gay male subjectivity of the text's heroes cannot accept about itself. Dana Heller, writing about the novels of David Leavitt, explains how:

Leavitt's insistence on women's abject presence in a text that has no difficulty affirming homoerotic openness seems to indicate that no gay male character need assume a role analogous to woman's subordinate role so long as 'real' biological women remain formally positioned to absorb the fear, rage, victimization, loneliness and rejection that homosexual men are, of course, also vulnerable to in homophobic culture.

(1995: 158)

According to Heller, the woman's body simply becomes a convenient dumping ground – an abject sponge. Critics have read Jarman's films as prime examples of gay male misogyny (Bersani and Dutoit, 1999: 17; Peake, 1999: 37). In this chapter, however, I want to argue that Jarman's representation of his beloved screen icon – the wonderful Tilda Swinton – is never simply 'gay male misogyny'. Focusing on Swinton's performance as icy queen Isabella in *Edward II*, but referencing many of her other Jarman roles, I wish to argue that these films' queer status is greatly indebted to the performances of Swinton, especially given that many of her performances question the sex, gender, sexuality continuum and offer the potential of making *Gender Trouble*.

Camp Isabella

'Don't you ever tire [...] of all this campery? [...] Mae West is dead.'
(quoted in Mars-Jones, 1983: 7)

One of the most striking issues about Swinton's performances in Jarman's cinema is her ability to portray such widely differing roles. She moves seamlessly from performances of extreme seriousness which are some of the most unsettling in Jarman's canon (the bride in *The Last of England*, Lena in *Caravaggio*) to performances of high camp (Lady Ottoline Morrell in *Wittgenstein*) and, most remarkably, a performance in which she manages to combine both (Queen Isabella in *Edward II*). Indeed, one of the most visually spectacular elements in *Edward II* is the campiness of Isabella who, in the same vein as Tallulah Bankhead, Gloria Swanson, Raquel Welch and Mae West (arguably the most revered camp icon of all - see Hamilton, 1995), offers an image of excessive, theatrical femininity. She is over-the-top; she is artificial; she is camp.

However, before analysing the representation of Isabella it is important to try and discern what camp is and, more importantly, what it is trying to achieve. There have been innumerable attempts to describe camp but most of this writing has simply offered long lists of persons, object of activities that the writer considers to be camp (Blachford, 1981; Babuscio, 1984; Dyer 1992). The problem is that although everyone has heard of the word 'camp' – and it is certainly one of the most overused words in popular criticism – it is notoriously difficult to theorize. Its etymology is also unclear as it is thought to either stem from the French *se camper* (to strike a pose) or the old English *kemp* meaning uncouth or an affront to decency (Meyer, 1994: 75).

One of the first to attempt to theorize camp was Susan Sontag who, in her now infamous, 'Notes on Camp' argued that, 'Camp is a certain mode of aestheticism. It is one way of seeing the world as an aesthetic phenomenon. That way, the way of Camp, is not in terms of beauty but *in terms of the degree of artifice, of stylization* (Sontag, 1982: 106, my emphasis). Sontag views camp as a mode of representation structured around 'artifice' and 'stylization'. Yet although this is a useful starting point, it doesn't really clarify how camp is different from parody or even irony.

Therefore, Sontag's essay has been criticized by many theorists and has now become a 'vilified talisman' (Medhurst, 19997: 280) in much queer studies. D.A. Miller, for example, writes of Sontag's 'phobic de-homosexualisation of camp' (1993: 212) because she plucked camp from its gay roots in order to give it an intellectual validity, while Moe Meyer criticizes Sontag's essay for describing 'camp trace' (1994: 5). According to Meyer, camp is 'the total body of performative practices and strategies used to enact a queer identity' (1994: 5). Andy Medhurst develops this argument even further and, in his deliciously campy essay on camp, insists that camp is the exclusive property of gay men (1997). Women or straight men, it seems, have no claims to the sensibility of camp. Indeed Medhurst concludes his essay with the gloriously campy rant that camp is 'ours, all ours, just ours, and the time has come to bring it back home' (1997: 291).

This raises two important questions. Firstly, if Sontag's essay is wrong and camp is *not* merely a way of representing something in terms of artifice and stylization, then what actually is camp? What area of consideration has she ignored in her analysis? Secondly, why do so many critics insist that camp is a gay male preserve? What is it about camp that is supposed to make it essentially gay?

To address the first issue, one of the key areas missing from Sontag's analysis was the question of gender. Camp, if it is to maintain a specificity which distinguishes it from other forms of irony or parody, must be structured around gender. In other words, camp is an ironic performance of gender: it is gender which camp represents in terms of artifice or stylization. This is not to suggest that gender parody is the sole constituent of camp but rather that camp must maintain an ironic representation of gender if it is to preserve its status as camp rather than simply irony or kitsch. Therefore, a camp representation or performance will draw attention to gender roles as actually being gender roles. In camp, both masculinity and femininity, through hyperbole, exaggeration, parody or irony, are represented as constructs or performances.

However, why should this be important to gay men? In his study of sexual discrimination in schools, Parker noted that homophobia is not the main problem in schoolyard bullying. Instead the problem is often effeminophobia – the fear of effeminacy:

> In the case of the boys at Coleridge, in calling someone a 'poof', pupils were not implying that certain individuals were in fact gay. Rather this term and others like it (i.e. fag, faggot, queer) were implicitly conceptualized in terms of gender as opposed to sexuality, and therefore constituted some kind of gender-structured generic, meaning 'non-masculine' or effeminate.
>
> (Parker, 1996: 150; see also Pascoe, 2005)

As Parker's study of Coleridge school affirms, homosexuality is still perceived as a gender based semiotic, the post-Foucaultian trope of an 'interior androgyny, a hermaphroditism of the soul' (Foucault, 1998: 43). In other words, homosexuality is thought to be signified by gender transitivity or what we now term 'effeminacy'. In this respect, when an eleven year old schoolboy calls his colleague a 'queer' he is not suggesting that another eleven year old is sexually gay but simply that the boy is non-conforming to dominant ideas of masculinity and, perhaps, is not good at sports or likes performing arts or music. Therefore, from as early as the school playground, everyone learns that being labelled 'gay' is dependant upon gender performance. In dealing with this, gay men either focus upon 'passing' for straight and concentrate on constructing a masculine performance or they emulate a 'camp' performance and flaunt exaggerated feminine signifiers. (Quentin Crisp is one of the most famous examples of a gay man employing this strategy of defensive offensiveness.) Yet both the 'straight acting' gay or the effeminate queen do so because they are aware of the cultural perception of sexuality and gender as collapsible categories. Therefore, if gay men are forced to master the art of constructing/self-policing their gender signifiers, they will take great pleasure from a text that exposes gender as a 'doing' or a construction. For this reason gay men have enjoyed camp performances by stars such as Tallulah Bankhead, Racquel Welch, Joan Collins and, I would add to this, Tilda Swinton as Isabella or Ottoline Morrell, as these women's campiness demonstrates the artifice and imitative quality of femininity and unmasks gender roles as being roles. A camp representation reveals all gender as being a construct.

Sadly, camp is now thought of as dated. Mark Simpson emphasizes the decrepit nature of camp sensibility by writing that 'as disco had not been invented yet – there being no gays to sniff poppers and whoop it up in bell bottoms – the pitiful homosexual's only solace was singing along to Judy Garland's 'The Man That Got Away' and, of course, 'Over the Rainbow' (Simpson, 1999: 2)'.

However, is camp really so dated? The theories of gender performativity, which have largely underpinned queer theory, are undoubtedly similar to camp's attempt to 'render gender a question of aesthetics' (Dollimore, 1991: 311) or expose the 'artifices attendant on the construction of images of what is natural' (Dyer, 1993: 42). Although Butler rarely uses the word 'camp' in her writing, David Bergman praises her work for having 'done the most to revise the academic standing of camp and to suggest its politically subversive potential' (1993: 11). In other words, camp has the ability to make *Gender Trouble*.

In *Edward II* Isabella is ridiculously glamorous. She appears in a different *couture* dress in every single scene and Swinton's acting style has a flamboyance and over-the-topness which could be dismissed as 'hammy' if the actor were not the highly respected Tilda Swinton. Bette Talvacchia succinctly describes Isabella as 'a self conscious parody of Hollywood glamour' (Talvacchia, 1993: 119) while Jarman himself points out that, in one shot Swinton 'really is chairman of the board of Pepsi Cola! [...] Joan Crawford!' (in O'Pray, 1991: 12).

Indeed, as if following the mantra of Andrew Lloyd Webber's heroine in *Evita*, who sings 'they need to adore me, so Christian Dior me', Isabella wears an excessively glamorous gown in every scene. From Dior to Givenchy to Chanel, Isabella is always attired in the finest of *haute couture*.

Edward II, Jarman, 1991

Yet 'parody of Hollywood glamour' is too light a term to describe the representation of Isabella. She is not simply parodying Hollywood glamour but moving into the most excessive realm of camp. Why, for example, wear one strand of pearls when, in one scene, a Chanel-clad Isabella shows how to have neck and wrists swathed in them? Although Coco Chanel advised her ladies to inject a little humour or self-parody into their wardrobe by wearing cheap costume jewellery with their *couture* dresses (see Gray, 1981), Isabella is surely taking the advice a little too far.

Also, this glamour is rendered all the more artificial by its incongruous setting against Edward's dungeon-like castle as Isabella's opulence is always framed by looming, moisture-dripping walls. Yet despite such a bleak *mise-en-scène*, Isabella, in one gorgeously camp image, struts around the gloom of Edward's castle in the totally unnecessary sunglasses and headscarf while dressed in Dior's finery.

Edward II, Jarman, 1991

Similarly, *Wittgenstein*'s Ottoline Morrell appears 'in a succession of pink, green, and scarlet hats and boas made of ostrich feathers' (Wymer, 2005: 162) looking, as Wymer suggests, like a parody of Carmen Miranda.

Yet is this more than simply fun? Is camp political? Judith Butler certainly sees it as such and suggests that it has radical and subversive potential. In praising camp, Butler describes how a local gay restaurant closes for vacation and the owners put out a sign, explaining that 'she's overworked and needs a rest' (Butler, 1999: 156). This *rather* mediocre example of gay campiness inspires Butler to develop some rather elaborate theories: 'This very gay appropriation of the feminine works to multiply possible sites of application of the term, to reveal the arbitrary relation between signifier and signified, and to describe and mobilize the sign' (Butler, 1999: 156). For Butler, this tired example of gay campiness draws attention to the arbitrary nature of gender – separating signifier from signified – and as such is an implicitly political action. Butler argues that this camp gesture is not an appropriation of the feminine but instead exposes how femininity itself is a construct (1999: 156).

Edward II, Jarman, 1991

On the other hand, according to Leo Bersani, Butler is writing 'heavy stuff for some silly and familiar campiness' (1995: 48). In contrast to Butler, Bersani asserts that camp is not radical in any way as it simply parodies or exaggerates existing gender binaries and therefore remains within the controlling regime of those categories:

More exactly, resignification cannot destroy; it merely presents to the dominant culture spectacles of politically impotent disrespect. Is this truly subversive, and, more fundamentally, what does subversive mean? [...] It is, in any case, extremely doubtful that resignification, or redeployment, or hyperbolic miming, will ever overthrow anything.

(ibid.: 51)

Edward II, Jarman, 1991

Arguably, Bersani is correct. There may be some who read the representation of Isabella as illuminating Butler's theories but it is equally possible to read her simply as silly, camp excess – a recent version of *Sunset Boulevard*'s Norma Desmond or *Dynasty*'s Alexis Carrington-Colby-Dexter.

However, this is where the famously androgynous body of Swinton and her command of Brechtian acting style deserve consideration. In all Jarman's representations of Swinton there is a marked tension between Swinton's body and her gender performance. Indeed it is Swinton's curiously amorphous body and her distinction as an actor which ensure that her performance cannot be dismissed as being merely a little light campiness.

Camping up Brecht

In her phenomenally influential essay 'Visual Pleasure and Narrative Cinema', Laura Mulvey outlined the position of the female body in classical cinema in which the woman connotes 'to-be-looked-at-ness' (Mulvey, 1975). The pleasure which the (heterosexual male) spectator gains from a classical, narrative film is the re-enforcement of constructed beliefs of man as active, desiring subject and woman as passive object. However, when the gaze of the film is a queer one, the question of woman's to-be-looked-at-ness is inflected differently. David Hawkes points out that 'in Jarman's work, the fetishised body is always male' and that Jarman's cinema 'challenges the definitions of sexuality and gender roles which have defined classical cinema' (1996: 105).

This 'challenge' to conventional definitions of sexuality and gender roles is very much in evidence in *Edward II*. Although the fetishized body in the film is undeniably male – Edward and Gaveston flaunt their bodies in vests and T-shirts while Gaveston is even represented nude – it is Isabella's feminine stylization or feminine masquerade that dominates the screen. Isabella sparkles throughout the film. All the traditional Hollywood conventions of representing the female body are employed to the point of extreme parody. Isabella is often framed in doorways and she herself often pauses, standing as still as an artist's model, in order to give the spectator time to adore her appearance. As Kate Chedgzoy summarizes, 'all aspects of the *mise-en-scène* conspire to make Isabella the spectacular object of the gaze whenever she is on screen' (1995: 209).

It is here that Mary Ann Doane's influential theory of 'feminine masquerade' (1991) is illuminating. Drawing upon Joan Riviere's famous argument that womanliness and masquerade 'are the same thing' (Riviere, 1986: 38), Doane claimed that femininity was synonymous with wearing a masquerade which disguised woman's essential lack. Femininity was a performance enacted for the audience of men. As Lacan has suggested, women, paradoxically, are made to 'be' the phallus or 'embody' the phallus:

'Paradoxical as this formulation might seem, it is in order to be the phallus, that is, the signifier of the desire of the Other, that the woman will reject an essential part of her femininity, notably all its attributes through masquerade'

(1985; 84). In simpler terms, women simply pretend to be what they lack: the phallus. As Judith Butler argues, it is in '"appearing as being" the phallus that women are compelled to [...] masquerade' (1999: 60). 'Womanliness' or, to use the more popular term, 'femininity' is a mask; something which women 'do'. This theory of masquerade has been hugely important for feminist visual arts criticism on two levels. Firstly, it emphasizes patriarchal power in which women are forced to engineer a specific representation of femininity in accordance with man's desires. Secondly, and more importantly, it exposes femininity as a performative effect. It reveals a gap between the body of woman and her disguise of femininity.

In his superb essay, 'Masquerade or Drag? Bette Davis and the Ambiguities of Gender', Martin Shingler argued that Hollywood icon Bette Davis, throughout her long and varied screen career, 'exploited the ironies and ambiguities of gender' (1995: 181) and that, on occasions, her 'masquerade of femininity comes remarkably close to that of female impersonation, to drag' (ibid.: 185). According to Shingler, Davis's exaggerated feminine masquerade is not just bad acting, as some myopic reviewers interpreted her performances as being, but a deliberate attempt to deconstruct essentialist ideas of gender. Indeed 'like the drag queen, Davis holds femininity up to ridicule, highlighting its unnaturalness (constructedness) and demonstrating that femininity is no more than a mask, one which either sex may assume' (ibid.: 186).

Arguably, a similar strategy is at work in Swinton's performances, especially Isabella. While Isabella's exaggerated femininity sparkles across the screen, there is a continuous distance evoked between Swinton the actor and the feminine masquerade which she is obviously 'doing' on screen. As Michael O'Pray points out, 'Brechtian acting theory – the notion that a distinction between the actor and his or her role must be enforced – has been particularly influential on Swinton's approach' (1996: 162). Indeed, Swinton herself has insisted that she has chosen to act only roles that subvert femininity and offer an iconoclastic deconstruction of gender (see Goodman, 1990: 219). In short, Swinton is trying to reveal that 'there is no gender identity behind the expressions of gender, that identity is performatively constituted by the very 'expressions' that are said to be its results' (Butler, 1999: 33). O'Pray therefore suggests that the scene in *The Last of England* where the Bride (Swinton) tears up her wedding dress, can be read as 'the behaviour of Swinton the actress towards the role of the bride' (1996: 163).

This distinction between Swinton the actor and her feminine masquerade as Isabella is particularly evident in one of *Edward II*'s queerest images. In this scene Isabella, despite being attired in yet another *Dynasty*-esque evening gown, is engaged in target practice. Although *Edward II* is based upon a Marlowe text, and in Renaissance England it was not uncommon for women of birth to engage in shooting or hunting, it was highly unlikely that they did so while attired in full evening dress. It should also be noted that Jarman's deliberate anachronism makes Isabella much more indebted to the traditions of Classical Hollywood glamour than Renaissance nobility and, in Classical Hollywood, the ability to shoot is a clichéd symbol of masculinity. Therefore, the target practice scene bristles with a tension between the body of Swinton the actor, her excessive female masquerade and the cinematic cliché of her masculine activity.

However, while O'Pray may argue that this scene illuminates Brecht's 'making strange' effect, I should simply describe it as camp. Like Brecht's *Verfremdungseffekte*, which makes the image appear strange and opens a critical distance for the spectator, the use of camp exposes the image as constructed and artificial. Whether we term Isabella's target practice scene – in which an overdressed, camp woman, acting in a soap opera-ish fashion – Brechtian or camp, both open a critical distance and force the spectator to re-evaluate the semiotic. Swinton plays the scene campily in order to expose a critical distance between Swinton the actor and the superimposed masquerade of femininity. Swinton is, of course, famous for her androgyny and this has been exploited to full effect in her theatrical performance *Man to Man* and her film portrayal of the sex-changing hero(ine) in Sally Potter's *Orlando*. This line of argument, however, is not intended to essentialize the body. As Butler has emphasized, it is impossible to say if there is 'a "physical" body prior to the perceptually perceived body' (1999: 146). Instead, I am arguing that Swinton's performance attempts to create a distance between the film character/role and the actor Swinton beneath the masquerade.

This deconstruction of gender dynamics is made very explicit in one of Swinton's most famous images in *Caravaggio* – indeed this is almost an iconic Swinton image given that it has been reproduced in so many books on Jarman's cinema. In this scene Lena (Swinton) gazes at her own reflection in a hand-held mirror, referencing the tradition in classical art of representing the female body looking at herself in the mirror, thus asserting that this body is complicit in the art of making herself into something 'to-be-looked-at'. However, after admiring her appearance, Lena then turns away from the mirror and gazes directly into the camera as if demanding, 'What are you looking at?' Swinton's gaze at the spectator asserts that this is not a clichéd image of femininity, but a performance deliberately drawing attention to the construction of femininity, and then proceeds to question the spectator's assumed right to judge and classify the body on display. A similar technique is also employed, although in a much less confrontational way, in *Wittgenstein*, where Ottoline Morrell is reading one of Wittgenstein's letters while dressed in her Carmen Miranda-style extravagance, but momentarily pauses from the reading to make an ironic, sideways glance into the camera. This ironic aside asserts that Ottoline Morrell is not simply a camp spectacle adding a dash of comic relief to the film but is a deliberate interrogation of gender performativity. Swinton is not playing a character that is simply to be laughed at but a role which is caricaturing, like a drag artist, traditional gender scripts.

Throughout Swinton's performances in Jarman's cinema there is a constant tension at work between feminine gender – as stylization and spectacle – and Swinton the actor beneath the performance. Whether we term this Brechtian alienation, camp or, as Shingler may argue, 'drag', it facilitates a queering of the presumed stable continuum of sex and gender.

Is Isabella a defining other or abject sponge?

Some critics might argue, on the other hand, that Isabella's campiness is merely the creation of a convenient defining other. Jarman simply represents this camp, excessive woman so that Gaveston and Edward can define their masculinity against her – a standard trope in much contemporary gay film and literature. Indeed much contemporary gay film often uses the female other as a foil against which the gay male leads can define their masculinity and therefore not be read as effeminate. In *Edward II* though, this is certainly not the case. Jarman does not flinch from giving both Edward and Gaveston scenes of hysterical, body convulsing emotion. Edward, on several occasions, weeps and sobs while Gaveston is shown howling like a demented animal after he has been banished.

In traditional Hollywood cinema it is (nearly) always the female body that is uncontrolled and hysterical. Hollywood exploits this to the crudest level during sex scenes when the woman's writhing and moaning signifies the orgasm for both sexual partners (Bordo, 1999: 191). When, occasionally, a man is shown in the throws of orgasm it frequently evokes only humour as in Al Pacino's wailings in *Frankie and Johnny*. Of course, Hollywood's males have the potential for excessive emotion in terms of violence and aggression but this is always used to attain something within the narrative. The bodies that collapse, break-down and sob uncontrollably are always female or else male bodies that are feminized and deviant such as the villains'.

One of the most excessive issues of femininity is hysteria, which has conventionally been linked to the female body. Hysteria stems from the Greek word for womb – 'hysteron' – and was originally thought to be a random wandering of the womb throughout the body. One solution was thought to be vile-smelling salts which would drive the wandering womb back down into its proper place. Lacan, elaborating the work of Freud and his famous case of the hysterical Dora, argued that hysteria comes from an inability to reconcile one's gender with the sexed body. 'What is Dora saying through her neurosis? What is the woman-hysteric saying? Her question is this – What is it to be a woman?' (1993: 175). Stephen Heath elaborates Lacan's theory by suggesting that hysteria is: 'A problem of sexual identity in phallic terms: the hysteric is unsure as to being a woman or man' so that the female hysteric is 'in trouble with her position as a woman, simultaneously resisting and accepting the given signs, the given order' (1982: 46). Unable to 'cope' with her position as 'a woman', the female hysteric manifests the classic symptoms and rebels against phallocentric society through screaming, screeching, kicking and biting.

We should imagine that Jarman's Isabella offered the perfect foil for this. Given her excessive femininity and its disjunction with Swinton's androgynous body, there would be ample opportunity for her to suffer the gender-based confusion of an hysteric. Yet Isabella is always icy. She is James Bond cool. In many ways she represents the autotelic, sense-dead subject of the masculine ideal. Despite appearing to be nothing but a stylishly feminine masquerade, Isabella has a methodical, analytical mind. This is most evident in the scene where Edward attacks Isabella while she is being fitted for another of her sumptuous gowns. Using the strength of his male body, Edward overpowers Isabella by grabbing the back of her neck and pushing her forward into subservience. When the King departs, Isabella drops to her knees, hurt and frightened. Yet throughout the entire scene, Isabella retains a cool dignity. It is the King who is frenzied and even hysterical. Jarman does not offer the abject spectacle of feminine hysteria. It would be possible to have Isabella scream and howl like an animal yet, throughout the film, it is the male bodies who are shown overwhelmed in paroxysms of emotions. This is markedly different from the representation of gay love seen in recent gay romances such as *Trick* and *Broadway Damage*. In the formula of conventional love stories, boy must meet boy, boy must lose boy and boy must regain his lover again or else find Oprah Winfrey-style 'inner strength' and move on with his life. During the scene of loss there must be pain and tears yet this will risk feminizing the male hero. One solution has been to transcribe this onto the female friend who becomes hysterical over the slightest thing. In *Trick*, Katherine screeches in a diner because there is no cheese on the 'goddamn fucking fries' while in *Broadway Damage* Myra has a nervous breakdown over the most clichéd of feminine phobias: finding a mouse in her bedroom.

Jarman doesn't employ this strategy and the pain of Edward and Gaveston's break-up is shown to be very real and very excessive for both of them. Indeed *Edward II* can be read as offering a queer resignification of the Cartesian head/body split. As Elizabeth Spelman has famously pointed out there has traditionally been a gendered dichotomy between the head or intellect, which has always been construed as masculine, and the 'vulgar, beguiling body' (1982: 113) that has historically been feminine. In *Edward II*, we see the opposite. Edward and Gaveston are simply their physical bodies – weak, vacillating and oriented only towards pleasures of the flesh. By contrast,

Isabella is represented as not even having a traditionally gendered body but is shown to be a cunning, manipulative, analytical mind working behind the disguise of feminine masquerade to challenge the power structures within the film's narrative.

Abjection and the Female Vampire

The scene in *Edward II* which has provoked the greatest accusations of misogyny, is Isabella's blood slurping, vampire-style murder of Kent when she literally shreds Kent's jugular with her teeth. Although the accusations of misogyny are understandable, this scene needs to be analyzed within the context of the theories about the female vampire and, most importantly, Kristeva's writings on abjection.

In *Powers of Horror*, Kristeva explained her now much overused theory of 'the abject' as something which must be 'jettisoned from the 'symbolic system' […] what escapes that social rationality, that logical order on which a social aggregate is based' (1980: 65). The abject is something that disturbs borders and boundaries. It is therefore something which threatens identity because 'abjection is above all ambiguity' (ibid.: 9). The abject is neither good nor evil, neither subject nor object. We are both repelled and nauseated by it yet also attracted and intrigued. Its power lies in the way it threatens to collapse meaning, to dissolve the firm and safe boundaries of the symbolic order. Abjection, however, holds a special relationship with the woman's body. According to Kristeva, the boy child, 'having been the mother, will turn it into an abject' (ibid.: 13). This continues throughout patriarchal society as the female body is always the body that is relegated to the status of the abject. The female body is transgressive of borders and boundaries: it leaks, not only in excremental ways but also through menstruation. It is the body which is penetrable and becomes impregnated. It then changes shape, horrifically swelling and distending as it gestates.

In *Edward II*, the abject body is not represented as female but male. Kent becomes the leaky, feminized body that is violently penetrated by Isabella's fangs. His body convulses as Isabella's teeth sink into his flesh. Then, as Kent's body is penetrated, it leaks, splattering blood all over its smart suit. Little Prince Edward gazes upon the horrific scene with the classic mixture of revulsion and intrigue which abjection inspires and, after tentatively dipping his fingers into the pool of blood, licks the fluid. The spectators, as they have done on numerous previous occasions, identify with the young Prince Edward who, throughout the film, has played a chorus-like role in that it is often his point of view of innocent surprise which the spectator is invited to share.

Yet Prince Edward's reaction to Isabella's vampirism echoes the pleasures which Isabella has offered queer spectators throughout the narrative. The spectator is simultaneously repelled by her and yet curiously drawn to her. Throughout the film she has sparkled on the screen unlike the dull Edward or slimy Gaveston. There is something marvellously liberating about her character and her development into a female vampire is not so markedly different from the effect she was achieving through being a camp spectacle. Like camp, the female vampire questions hegemonic gender and sexual roles. As Barbara Creed has argued, 'the female Dracula is masculinized; she is an active, predatory seducer' (1993: 63). Indeed, there is a queer edginess or dynamism to the female vampire as contradictory, non-normative gender tensions subsist within her body. She is not only coherent with camp sensibilities in that 'she appears to be "normal" by society's standards….and yet she is not' (Weiss, 1992; 91) but she disturbs the boundaries of masculine and feminine and unites them in a fluctuating tension. As Christopher Craft suggests, the female vampire challenges:

> the easy separation of the masculine and the feminine. Luring at first with an inviting orifice, a promise of red softness, but delivering instead a piercing bone, the vampire mouth fuses and confuses […] the gender-based categories of the penetrating and the receptive. With its soft flesh barred by hard bone, its red crossed by white, this mouth compels opposites and contrasts into a frightening unity.
>
> (1984: 109)

In short, the female vampire is a queer creature. She disturbs boundaries of gender, sex, sexuality and social propriety by disrupting the continuum between female subjectivity, femininity and sexuality.

Although Creed may argue, therefore, that the female vampire is abject

(1993: 61), vampiric Isabella is not comparable with Dana Heller's description of woman's 'abject presence' (1995: 158) in gay literature. The vampiric Isabella is glorious in the way she transgresses and violates borders and boundaries, not only of the body but also of gender roles, and is certainly not a revolting spectacle that must be abjected to the margins. By contrast, recent gay romances – notably *Trick* – have cruelly used the abject female body as a convenient other. During *Trick*'s pick-up scene between Marc and Gabriel, which takes place on a subway train, the gaze of the scene is a gay male one. It is Marc's body which is represented in slow motion so that the spectator can take pleasure in his luxurious gait and the lines and ellipsis of his exquisite musculature. The camera locks the spectator into Gabriel's point of view and drools over Marc while he feigns sleep on the train. There is only one other gaze in the subway and this comes from a dour *hausfrau* – a most unattractive beastie and caricature of Middle American conservatism – who admonishes the cruise between Gabriel and Marc. This woman's body is set in stark contrast with the boys'. They are young, beautiful and lithely muscled while she is middle aged and obese. The image exalts beautiful gay sexuality while denigrating ugly heterosexuality through a cruelly caricatured image of feminine excess. Jarman certainly doesn't offer this reassuring fantasy in *Edward II*. If Isabella is a vampire then, like all female Draculas, she is elegant and bewitching and, in some shots, she is breathtaking. By contrast, the one character that is often ugly, even monstrous, is Gaveston, as seen especially in the shot where he is 'a chattering, evil incubus' (Jarman, quoted in O'Pray, 1991: 10) on the throne – a gargoyle from a Bosch or Fusselli painting.

The body of Isabella, on the other hand, is not offered as an abject, revolting spectacle; a defining other for the gay, sexy beauty of Edward or Gaveston but as something glorious to behold.

Returning to the issue of camp and gay male adoration of Hollywood female artifice, I agree with Brett Farmer (2000: 145) who argues that the camp celebration of the excessive female body is not so much misogyny as queer exaltation. It celebrates images of female vampires, ageing, over-the-top women and sexually voracious monsters 'precisely because of its denaturalizing and disorganizational dynamics' in which a 'female grotesque transgress(es) and confound(s) all manner of social conventions from notions of gender propriety and decorum to received dictates about erotic desirability and appropriate sexual relationality' (Farmer, 2000: 146-7).

Edward II, Jarman, 1991

Queer Isabella?

Edward II represents a politics founded on sexual inequality. Jarman himself was perfectly happy to have his film read as a political slogan, exemplified by the printed script which subordinated the Marlowe text to the huge queer slogans on every page. However, the film earns the status of 'queer' through its representation of camp, gender dissonant and eventually monstrous Isabella as much as it does through its portrayal of Edward and Gaveston's political struggle to find love in the midst of heteronormative oppression. Alan Sinfield suggests that 'the masculine/feminine binary was a historical wrong-turn in western culture; it would be better if we could do without all that' (1998: 110). *Edward II* not only exposes the idea of gender as a cultural construct but also redistributes the characteristics that usually delineate the rigid dichotomy in mainstream film texts. Who is actually masculine or feminine in *Edward II*? Who is the objectified, feminized body or the active, masculine subject? As Sinfield suggests (ibid.: 110) masculinity and femininity are cultural constructs that help maintain the rigid sex-gender grid of heterosexuality. *Edward II*, especially in its representation of Isabella, challenges this idea.

Is the representation of Isabella simply another example of gay male misogyny? Arguably not, when we consider that Isabella dominates the screen and is not simply a convenient dumping ground for everything which gay masculinity cannot accept about itself. In *Edward II*, Isabella queerly disrupts gender dichotomies; a vibrant character who actively interrogates the sex-gender continuum, the scaffold of heterosexuality. *Edward II* does not represent the reassuring image of pretty, gay love juxtaposed with the monstrous, heterosexual woman. Instead the film offers an altogether more queer interrogation of cultural, social and gender identifications and, in doing so, asks the spectator to reconsider the cliché of gay male misogyny.

6

WOMEN'S BODIES 2: SUBLIME FEMINITY

While Jarman may represent monstrous femininity which, as I have argued, should not be dismissed as clichéd gay male misogyny but read as an interrogation of gender roles, many of his other films seem to display a marked rejection of femininity altogether. *The Angelic Conversation*, for example, although inspired by Shakespeare's Sonnets, omits the Dark Lady who appears in the later sonnets. Tracy Biga suggests that Jarman's rejection of femininity represents:

> a yearning for a state characterized by the absence of the father and the absence of the differentiation of gender, a state before the metonymies of the middle give birth to a metaphoric totalization; a pre-Oedipal state where the motor of linear narration – the conflict between desire and the law – does not apply.
>
> (1996: 22)

Biga suggests that Jarman's apparent misogyny is a veiled representation of a longing for the pre-Oedipal state or, to use Kristeva's term, 'the semiotic chora'.

Like the theories of the abject, Kristeva's writings on the semiotic chora have often been misinterpreted. Kristeva argues that the semiotic chora is a time of pre-Oedipal bliss when the child is fused with the mother. In this way it is a reworking of Lacan's theories preceding the mirror stage. Kristeva, however, makes it clear that the semiotic chora is a dimension of language and not, as it is often incorrectly described, as something outside language. Sarah Edge summarizes the Kristevan semiotic chora as a 'pre-symbolic sense of self in which the mother of the imaginary (feminine), and feelings associated with her, are central and compelling rather than peripheral and debased' (2000: 269).

According to Kristeva, this memory of the semiotic chora does not simply disappear but is merely kept under control by the symbolic order. Kristeva argues that the subject can gain access to the semiotic chora through music, poetry, expressive use of colour or any alternative medium of expression not constrained by the symbolic use of language. Yet this is a typical Kristevan 'double bind' in that the chora is only thinkable within the symbolic order which, paradoxically, it is attempting to undercut.

Is something like this happening in various films of Jarman's but especially *The Angelic Conversation*? Is this 'cinema of small gestures' an attempt to return to the bliss of the semiotic chora? The look of the film is virtually a fast-action slide show and the film pulses with a steady, hypnotic rhythm. It has a loose 'narrative': the two boys are separated at the start, then they offer themselves to an arrogant, indifferent King and then finally, after wrestling, they are together. However, the power of the film does not come from its narrative but from its curiously hypnotic and calming rhythm. The film's coherency is maintained through its use of colour, its visual rhythms and the continuous pulse of the slide-show scenes. It is almost as if the film operates on a different level from symbolic meaning.

As Biga suggests, the film is about a pre-Oedipal love; a love which is uninflected by the law of the father and the tyranny of gender. For evidence, she cites the Shakespearian Sonnet used in *The Angelic Conversation* which suggests that love can only thrive in this pre-Oedipal state:

Love is too young to know what conscience is
Yet who knows not conscience is born of love?

(Sonnet 151)

This reading accords with much of the academic scholarship on the Sonnets which situates them within the matrix of pre-Oedipal love. C.S. Lewis, for example, concludes an analysis of whether or not the Sonnets represent homosexual desire by suggesting that 'the love is, in the end, so simply and entirely love that our cadres are thrown away and we cease to ask what kind' (quoted in Dover Wilson, 1966: xvi). Shakespeare is 'expressing simply love, the quintessence of all loves whether exotic, parental, filial, amicable, or feudal' (ibid.).

However, Jarman's quotation of the Sonnets, which can, in their original form, be read as expressing ungendered, pre-Oedipal love, is not really sufficient evidence to defend against the accusations of Jarman's misogyny by suggesting that the film is a veiled longing for the pre-Oedipal state. Instead, it is more important to look at the construction of *The Angelic Conversation* itself which can be seen to deliberately circumvent the issue of misogyny which is implicit in Shakespeare's own Sonnets.

In this respect, it is important to note how scholars have read the Sonnets, especially in relation to the question of homosexuality and misogyny. J.W. Lever offers the traditional reading which is, unfortunately, still used in many British secondary schools. Lever suggests that the sonnets offer a 'sustained exploration of the theme of friendship' (quoted in Dover Wilson, 1966: xiv). This reading can, at best, be described as naïve and is reminiscent of the Victorian standards of studying Shakespeare which often involved brutal editing of the texts so as to remove all the frightfully obscene puns. C.S. Lewis, by contrast, offers a more insightful reading which, at least, takes into account the intense language of lovers which colours the Sonnets:

The precise mode of love which the poet declares for the Man remains obscure. His language is too lover-like for that of ordinary male friendships: and though the claims of friendship are sometimes put very high in, say, the 'Arcadia', I have found no real parallel to such language between friends in sixteenth-century literature. Yet, on the other hand, this does not seem to be the poetry of full-blown pederasty. Shakespeare, and indeed Shakespeare's age, did nothing by halves. If he had intended in these sonnets to be the poet of pederasty, I think he would have left us in no doubt [...] a whole train mythological perversities, would have blazed across the page. The incessant demand that the Man should marry and found a family would seem to be inconsistent (or so I suppose – it is a question for psychologists) with a real homosexual passion. It is not even very obviously consistent with normal friendship. It is indeed hard to think of any real situation in which it would be natural. What man in the whole world, except a father or a potential father-in-law, cares

whether any other man gets married? Thus the emotion in the
Sonnets refuses to fit into our pigeon-hole.

(quoted in Dover Wilson, 1966: xv)

Lewis offers a reading grounded in common sense although his suggestion
that Shakespeare did not do anything by halves and therefore would have
flaunted the language of 'pederasty' across the page is blithely ignoring
the fact that to do so would have certainly risked imprisonment or judicial
punishment. Although the label 'homosexual' did not exist in
Shakespeare's day (Sinfield, 1994b: 18), homosexual acts were not to be
widely publicized.

However, in recent years the most famous reading of the Sonnets has
been offered by Eve Sedgwick who uses them as an illumination of her
thesis of homosociality. Sedgwick has argued that the Sonnets should be
read as akin to Greek homosocial desire rather than our present knowledge
of homosexuality:

The Sonnets present a male-male love that, like the love of the
Greeks, is set firmly within a structure of institutionalized social
relations that are carried out via women: marriage, name, family,
loyalty to progenitors and posterity, all depend on the youth's making
a particular use of women that is not, in that abstract, seen as
opposing, denying or detracting from his bond to the speaker.

(1985: 35)

The love of a man for another man was laudable because only another
man could embody analogous praiseworthy, masculine elements. Sedgwick
argues that the Sonnets represent 'a desire to consolidate partnership with
authoritative males in and through the bodies of females' (1985: 38).

When the relationship in the Sonnets becomes triadic, with the
inclusion of the Dark Lady, a distinct erotic element enters the scenario.
In one of her most striking descriptions ever, Sedgwick notes that 'the
Dark Lady is, for the most part, perceptible only as a pair of eyes and a
vagina' (1985: 36). Indeed, in Sonnet 129, Shakespeare implies lust for
the Dark Lady and there is a stark contrast between the terms of
violence associated with lust and the elevated, highly esteemed

homosocial love experienced earlier for the young man.

> The expense of spirit in a waste of shame
> Is lust in action; and till action, lust
> Is perjur'd, murderous, bloody, full of blame
> Savage, extreme, rude, cruel, not to trust;
> Enjoy'd no sooner, but despised straight;
> Past reason hunted; and no sooner had,
> Past reason hated, as a swallow'd bait
>
> (Sonnet 129)

In the following Sonnet Shakespeare writes of the Dark Lady in a way distinctly lacking the elevated beauty of the homosocial love for the young man:

> My mistress's eyes are nothing like the sun
> Coral is far more red than her lips' red:
> If snow be white, why then her breasts are dun
> If hairs be wires, black wires grow on her head
>
> (Sonnet 130)

Later, in Sonnet 151, the speaker writes of how the Dark Lady gives him an erection as 'flesh staies no farther reason/ But rising at thy name doth point out thee'. If this is compared with the famous 'Shall I compare thee to a summer's day?' (Sonnet 18) the misogyny implicit in homosocial desire becomes apparent. Women are deserving of lust and carnal desire but are not worthy of the exalted love reserved for homosociality. Indeed Sedgwick notes that there is a 'devastating thoroughness with which the Sonnets record and thematize misogyny and gynephobia' (1985: 33).

However, in *The Angelic Conversation*, Jarman makes the speaker's voice a woman's. Dame Judi Dench reads the Sonnets in her impeccable English accent while the camera fetishizes the male bodies of the lovers. The traditional filmic formula is therefore reversed as the lovers become the objects of the gaze while the woman has the voice and the power to look. It is important to note that Judi Dench is not used as the voice of one of the lovers addressing the other. Instead her voice is completely dissociated from the action and the desire represented on screen. By doing so the film avoids the misogyny implicit in homosociality. Where Greek homosociality saw the woman as unworthy of the exalted love, which should be shared only with another man, but perfectly capable of physical displays of sexuality and child bearing, the film reverses this. Now, physical sexual affection is the experience shared between the men while the woman is the privileged viewer. The sexually charged image of the Dark Lady does not appear in *The Angelic Conversation* but is subsumed into the representation of one of the lovers. Jarman writes that 'Philip in his black dinner suit and black fan becomes the Dark Lady of the sonnets' (1987: 143). In this respect the lovers can be read as representing both homosocial, Greek love and the more carnal desire traditionally experienced for a woman. Although it may be argued that the female voice of the speaker is excluded from the action, it should be noted that the female speaker has a position of elevated power which the sonnets themselves never awarded to the Dark Lady.

However, returning again to Kristeva's theories about the female body and the 'chora' we can find some illumination of Jarman's enigmatic film. Kristeva points out that although the female body is often deemed abject – the body from which the child must split in order to become autonomous – there is also the sublime female body or the body of the semiotic chora which masculine sexuality can then later accept as an object of love. In *The Angelic Conversation* we see only the femininity of the sublime. The female voice is coterminous with the environment enveloping the lovers and, arguably, the final scenes, which Jarman describes as ending in the garden, can be read as representing the semiotic chora. One of the lovers presses flower blossoms to his lips while the other basks in a shimmering pool. The sequence melts from one image to the other until the images appear to fuse and the individual identities of the lovers have disappeared. Even more than the rest of the film, these scenes progress in terms of visually poetic rhythms. Yet if this signals a return to the chora it is important to remember that the chora can only be understood within the patriarchal symbolic order that it attempts to challenge. It is here that the universally recognized feminine symbols of flowers and water in this scene are important. Are they something which offer a difference within the matrix of language and meaning but yet are only discernible within the symbolic itself? One of the lovers is enveloped in the shimmering pool while the other presses the blossom to his lips as if drinking the flowers. The hazy, blurred effect of the editing dissolves the bodies into their environment in which symbolic difference collapses.

Steven Dillon's recent study of Jarman's films, *Derek Jarman and Lyric Film: The Mirror and the Sea,* argues that Jarman's films should be read in the tradition of lyric cinema, because his 'images speak figuratively rather than declaratively' (2004: 4), and points out that two recurring motifs in Jarman's cinema are the mirror and the sea. The mirror has traditionally been read in two ways: as a symbol of narcissism and therefore representative of homoerotic models of desire (see Dyer, 1990: 67) or, in accordance with French feminism, notably Irigaray, as emblematic of the 'patriarchal attempt to focus, order and rule' (Dillon, 2004: 50). By contrast Irigaray praises the image of the sea as representing fluidity or formlessness – something beyond the control of patriarchy (1991). Yet as Dillon points out, Jarman simultaneously occupies both positions throughout his cinema:

> Jarman's films, in certain respects, take the side of French feminists such as Hélène Cixous and Irigaray, in that he might be said to write, cinematically, a kind of *écriture feminine* against the law, against the patriarchy. Yet, as a man, he necessarily also inhabits a position of power and control of ideological focus rather than dispersal. Hence the pivotal images of the mirror and the sea: the mirror that Irigaray rejects, and the sea that she invokes.
>
> (2004: 51)

Indeed at some points the two motifs blend in Jarman's images of narcissism (Sebastian and King Edward gazing upon their reflections in pools of water) representing the masculine symbol of the mirror dissolving into the fluid, formless ocean. Arguably a similar blurring of gendered symbols is occurring at the end of *The Angelic Conversation* in which one of the lovers is enveloped in the shimmering pool while the other presses the flower blossom to his lips.

The Angelic Conversation is therefore achieving a very queer resignification of homosociality. Homosociality actually seems to become a part of the homosexuality against which it normally defines itself and where homosexuality has historically been the defining other of homosociality it now becomes its natural consequence. Likewise, the misogyny implicit in homosociality collapses under the elision of homosexual and homosocial relations. The female body is not featured in the film at all, yet the final bliss of the film signifies a return to the semiotic chora of pre-Oedipal love.

CS Lewis, therefore, offered a particularly insightful suggestion when he argued that the emotion of the Sonnets 'refuses to fit into our pigeon-holes'. Although the term did not exist in his time of writing, Lewis is surely describing something which we would now term 'queer'. Through rejecting the conventional paradigms of homosociality and the limiting labels of sexuality, Jarman's re-presentation of the Sonnets is offering the queer sense of edginess which destabilizes the supposedly immutable boundaries and does not fit into 'pigeon-holes'.

There will, however, always be critics who label Jarman's work as 'misogynist', if only because it is a convenient description and one which has conventionally been attributed to gay men. It's certainly easier to cite 'gay male misogyny' than argue, as I have been doing in these two chapters, that Jarman is trying to offer a queering of gender and sexual roles. Yet I believe it is too simplistic to read Jarman's unique images as mere clichés of gay male misogyny. Is Tilda Swinton, who is arguably, 'the most important figure in Jarman's films' (Wymer, 2005: 105), to be viewed as little more than a camp joke or a defining other? Likewise is Jarman's rejection of traditional ideas of femininity as found in Shakespeare's Sonnets and a deliberate attempt to elide the boundaries of homosociality and homosexuality a standard image of gay male misogyny? Jarman's images are often not 'pretty' and rarely 'straight-forward' but, like all of his unique representations, his portrayal of femininity is challenging and difficult but, most importantly, very queer.

Note

Chapter 6: 'The Queer Performance of Tilda Swinton' was published in an abridged form as 'The Queer Performance of Tilda Swinton in Derek Jarman's *Edward II*: Gay Male Misogyny Reconsidered', *Sexualities*, 2003: 6 (3-4). I am grateful to Sage for permission to reprint.

7

THE LEGACY OF JEAN GENET ON FILM

Jarman's work is illuminated by the world Genet revealed.

(David Gardner, 1996: 39)

Derek Jarman has occupied a new cultural space [...] a Saint Genet.

(Colin MacCabe, 1991: 14)

Jean Genet has always been one of the *enfants terribles* of gay literature and opinion is still divided about his work. Are his writings transgressive and challenging or are they simply the erotic ramblings of a self-loathing homosexual? Genet continuously conflates homosexuality with the criminal underworld, represents straight-identified men as the *only* desirable sexual partners and even links homosexuality directly with betrayal. It could be argued that love does not exist in the world of Jean Genet, just frenzied fucking in the bushes. These motifs of Genet's writing not only fuel accusations of self loathing but make his work incompatible with the political ideals of Gay Liberation.

As can only be expected, critics offer diametrically opposed readings of Genet. Some describe Genet's work as 'poison' (Lilly, 1995: 104) which 'provides invaluable ammunition to those who would impose their own heterosexual norm upon society' (Thody, 1969: 72). Other critics such as Bersani (1995), Sinfield (1994; 1998) and Manning (1999) view Genet's work as artistically and politically important in that it not only challenges the label 'homosexual' but the very idea of sexual scripts. Is Genet's writing the eroticization of internalized oppression and self-loathing (Lilly, 1993) or is it, as I shall term, 'proto-queer' in its reclamation and inversion of homophobic insults? Or is Genet's writing going even further and trying to achieve what Bersani terms a 'meta-transgressive *dépassement* of the field of transgressive possibility itself' (1999: 163)?

More importantly, is Jarman's cinema simply (as Mark Nash described Queer Cinema in general as being) 'the world of Genet and existentialism translated and updated' (1994: 100)? A world which represents the queer as outsider, pariah or criminal; where the queer – role model of homosexual angst – must accept the life script foisted upon him and live his role to its fullest; where the underworld of society is eroticized; where sex is incompatible with love and where betrayal is an intricate part of homosexuality. What are the links thematically and artistically between the world of Genet (as illuminated by his film *Un Chant D'Amour* and film adaptations of his novels) and the cinema of Jarman?

On a superficial level Jarman's connections with Genet are numerous. Like Genet, Jarman has held a certain 'bad-boy' reputation by refusing to pander to popular gay taste through 'negative' representations of queers, his eroticization of criminality and his representation of violent sexuality. There are obvious Genetesque pastiches to be found in all of Jarman's films such as the wrestling scene in *The Last of England*, the sadistic images in *The Garden* and the prison-like (*Chant d'Amour*) setting in *Edward II*. However, Jarman's cinema is not so much interested in merely quoting Genet but adapting and developing his political and artistic themes.

This chapter will attempt to explore the relationship between Genet and Jarman. It will argue that Genet's work is 'proto-queer' and that his writings posit many of the theories which 'queer' would mobilize several decades later. The chapter will argue that Genet's most salient themes – the rejection of a 'gay identity' and the deployment of negative, queer imagery – are indeed appropriated by Jarman but are developed in unusual and striking ways.

Identity Politics: Gay Community versus Queer Nation

Why are there so few gay identified men in Genet's work? One of the most remarkable aspects of Genet's world is that it represents a considerable amount of 'same-sex sexual activity' but this is nearly always enacted by straight identified men. With the exception of the 'Queen' type (for example, Divine in *Our Lady of the Flowers*), most of Genet's men – and certainly those who exert an erotic attraction – are straight identified. In *Querelle de Brest*, Genet the narrator even interjects to clarify that:

Indeed, neither Mario nor any of the chief characters in this book
(with the exception of Lieutenant Seblon, but then Seblon is not in
the book) is a real homosexual.

(1990: 73)

Exactly what does Genet consider is a 'real' homosexual? If his straight
identified characters don't claim an identity from their specific sexual
activities, then what exactly constitutes homosexuality in Genet's view? Is he
referring to some innate essence, some essentialist core which constitutes
homosexuality? Or do his writings actually challenge the very idea of 'real'
homosexuality? Is *Querelle de Brest* exposing the constructionist, proto-queer
view that there might be much homosexual behaviour but that very few
people are willing to claim an identity effect from the activity?

For critics who write from a strong Gay Liberationist standpoint,
Genet's refusal to label specific characters (especially those who exert an
erotic attraction) as homosexual is a sign of self-loathing and oppression.
A critic such as Mark Lilly, for example, finds Genet's work 'morally
repulsive' (1993: 90), 'grotesque' (ibid.: 104) and political 'poison' (ibid.).
Lilly, however, writes from a stolidly Gay Lib perspective and even
dedicates his book to 'all those militant activists in the lesbian and gay
community' (ibid.: dedication). As can only be expected, Lilly's criticism is
coloured by the politics of Second Wave Gay Liberation which argued for
the political necessity of establishing an identifiable and quantifiable gay
community. According to Lilly, Genet's eroticization of criminality and
the straight identified man is emblematic of self-loathing. The
homosexual's longing for straight identified men is 'of course a kind of
self-contempt because, by definition, it places gay men themselves outside
the group of the desirable' (Lilly, 1993b: 216). However, it is exactly these
issues of 'definition' and being 'outside the group' which, I should argue,
are the very points of Genet's writing. Certainly, in an interview, Genet
explained his concept of homosexuality as being:

a man who, by his very nature is out of step with the world, who
refuses to enter into the system that organizes the entire world. The homosexual
rejects that, denies that, shatters that whether he wants to or not.

(quoted in White, 1993: 197, my emphasis)

In contrast to Lilly, I should argue that Genet is describing what could be termed proto-queer theory. For Genet, a homosexual is 'out of step' with society and 'refuses to enter into the system that organizes the entire world'. Far from trying to belong to a specific group – a quantifiable minority – which would only be assimilated back into the dominant regime, Genet's work is trying to overthrow the very categories of sexual taxonomy themselves. Accepting the label 'gay' or 'homosexual' is simply a means of re-inscribing the subject back into the social scripts. It allows the dominant to circumscribe the subject within a convenient appellation so that the 'gay' subject can be located within society. Although the 'gay' identified subject attains a recognized position it is still a socially registered position – a position controlled by the rubrics of conventional society. For Genet, therefore, the 'homosexual' cannot and *should not* be assimilated into society. By refusing to crystallize sexual subjectivity into clearly delineated categories, the Genetesque 'homosexual' is resistant of social absorption. As Michael Warner has famously emphasized 'queer gets a critical edge by defining itself against the normal rather than the heterosexual' (1993: xxvi). Far from pleading for tolerance and acceptance, Genet's work can be read as attempting to prise open the sexual labels and expose them as being simply a system of normative regulations. Instead of begging for a safe enclave within society, queer Genet tried to overthrow the interpellating power of society itself.

This is a different reading of Genet's straight identified men (who all fuck with other men) from Lilly's theory of self-oppression. Perhaps what we find in Genet is the exposure of identity effects as being simply 'effects'. The dissolution of essentialist identity and the rendering of sexual taxonomies as merely imposed labels. This can be seen in Genet's most famous character Querelle who, despite his unfortunate name, is vehemently straight identified. Yet this heterosexually proclaimed man asserts a pleasure in being fucked both by Nono and Mario.

The best film adaptation of *Querelle de Brest* (and arguably of *any* Genet novel) is Fassbinder's *Querelle* – a film which has almost been canonized within gay culture. Its imagery (notably the white-vested sailor) has been parodied in various examples of gay film, art and advertising, most recently Jean Paul Gaultier's advertisement for 'Le Male' aftershave – an advertisement which not only quotes from the narrative of *Querelle* but mobilizes very queer themes, especially Butler's theory of gender as a performative effect.

Querelle is a full-length colour film which features an impressive cast, including Brad Davis, Jeanne Moreau and Franco Nero. In keeping with Fassbinder's obsession with Hollywood, the film has the appearance of a Sirk or Minnelli melodrama. The action is shot entirely within a studio set and no attempt is made to imbue this setting with a sense of naturalism.

Querelle, Fassbinder, 1982

Querelle also features unrealistic, expressionist/Sirkian colour schemes, dialogue which echoes the stylized, campy feel of 1950s melodramas and moments when the action is deliberately stalled either by a voice-over interjection or through a tableau-like scene. The film is set in the shipping port of Brest and tells the story of (anti)hero Querelle, a sailor who also makes some pocket money smuggling opium. His brother Robert (acted by Hanno Poschl) is having an affair with Lysianne who, together with her husband Nono, runs the Feria bar – a favoured haunt of sailors. One of the rules of the Feria bar is that its customers have to play dice with Big Nono. If they win they can have their pick of the Feria's whores but, if they lose, Nono gets to fuck them. Querelle plays dice with Nono and loses *deliberately* by cheating. He then gets fucked by Nono and thus begins Querelle's obsession with playing the 'passive' role during homosexual intercourse. This vehemently straight identified character will also be fucked again by Nono and also by Mario (chief of police).

The most striking aspect of *Querelle* is its frank representation of sexual activity. Querelle the sailor is a queer creature who not only fucks Lysianne but equally enjoys being fucked by Mario and Nono. Richard Dyer argues that 'it is possible to treat *Querelle* as an abstraction of the erotics of power' (1990: 91). For Dyer, the film examines the question of power in fucking – 'the person who fucks is powerful and the person who is fucked is powerless' (ibid.: 92). Dyer asserts that Querelle's pleasure in being fucked is 'the pleasure of humiliation' (ibid.). Querelle is debased; buggered by Nono's big cock. Dyer's detailed analysis of *Querelle* therefore leads him to the conclusion that Querelle's 'pleasure/humiliation can only be that if homosexual acts are accepted as indeed inferior and degrading in comparison to heterosexual ones' (96). Being fucked gives pleasure to Querelle but it is the pleasure of abject humiliation. Indeed, 'in *Querelle* the self is annihilated through the internalization of heterosexual norms' (ibid.: 96).

However, it is possible to offer a different reading from Dyer's. Firstly, the Nono/Querelle fucking scene does not delineate the question of power as clearly as Dyer suggests. Nono is shown to be so overwhelmed by the physical sensation of fucking that he is rendered as powerless as Querelle. Both of them experience the shattering effect of having their bodies' limits of sensual excess exploded. They both experience the self-annihilation of orgasm and, after the act, both slump into the nirvana of post-coital exhaustion. The question of 'who is doing what to whom' becomes redundant as both sexual partners are shattered by the turbulence of sensual excess. Being penetrated is not necessarily commensurate with abdicating power. Indeed as Gregory Woods emphasizes, 'abdication is itself a sign of real power' (1999: 276) and, arguably, Genet is saying that 'only real men can do it' (ibid).

This question of 'the erotics of power' (Dyer, 1990: 91) is echoed throughout the film by the myriad of framing diegetic gazes. It is not a question of the person doing the gazing as being powerful but of the person being 'gazed at' who is the controller of the other's gaze. For example, the early scenes of the film show Seblon mesmerized by Querelle's body and unable to stop gazing upon him. As Stephen Shaviro asserts, Querelle demonstrates that 'voyeurism cannot be celebrated as a state of sadistic mastery' (1993: 169) but as 'a passion of powerlessness' (ibid.)

This is further emphasized by the ironic use of shot/reverse shots throughout the film in which one character is always framed by the gaze of another who in turn is framed by someone else's gaze. The film offers a Sadian trope of interpellating gazes in which every character is in turn objectified by the gaze of another character. Who is actually controlling the gaze in *Querelle*? (I consider this in greater detail in the final section of this chapter.)

Querelle's 'passivity' is further questioned by the scene in which Querelle realises that he loves Gil. The voice-over states that Querelle must 'give up his passivity' and become the active partner. For Querelle this loss of passivity actually signifies vulnerability. While being sexually passive represented supreme indifference, even autotelic insouciance, becoming an active suitor would signify the vulnerability of succumbing to desire: 'thus, being desired, while himself not experiencing desire, invests Querelle with an aura of intense erotic power' (Shaviro, 1993: 173).

Therefore, the equation of power/powerlessness is removed from the film's images. Querelle's pleasure in being fucked is not the pleasure of humiliation because his passivity bestows him with a sense of empowerment. Instead, being fucked is simply the self-shattering pleasure of sensual excess. This queries Dyer's assertion that *Querelle* represents the debasement of homosexual fucking rendered through the 'internalization' of heterosexual supremacy. If 'Querelle's pleasure/ humiliation depends upon the real power relations of society' (Dyer, 1990: 96) then the film's rejection of those power relations (the hyperbolic diegetic gazes, the inversion of sexual activity versus passivity) negates the humiliation of homosexual fucking. Asserting a pleasure in being fucked is shown to be 'actively powerless' while the person who desires to fuck is consumed by his passion and therefore more powerless than his passive partner. The binary between exalted heterosexual norms and the debasement of homosexuality is brought into question by queer Querelle.

Therefore, I should argue that Genet's interest in representing straight identified men who fuck with other men is not simply the erotic reveries of a self-loathing homosexual. Nor is Querelle's acceptance of passive homosexuality the masochistic pleasure of subjugation or humiliation. Instead Querelle's discovery of new sexual gymnastics is Genet's attempt to overthrow the entire system of sexual subjectivity. Far from re-enforcing the hetero/homo hierarchy, Genet's world removes the hierarchy altogether. Instead of straining to establish a quantifiable homosexual minority, Genet attempts to overthrow the entire social matrix which condenses sexual activity into specific identities. In fact, none of the characters in Genet's novels are 'real homosexuals' because in Genet's world the very system which labels sexual subjects dissolves as easily as Querelle's heterosexual identity. Sexual identifications can simply evaporate with the throw of Nono's dice.

Jarman, however, develops Genet's concern with sexual identity politics. At first glance there would appear to be an ambivalence in Jarman's cinema. His films seem to waver between emphasizing the importance of Gay Lib identity politics and Queer's rejection of the confines of identity. *Caravaggio*, for example, as I have argued already, exposes the failure of sexual labels to delineate sexual subjectivity. The triadic relationship between Michele, Rannucio and Lena cannot be condensed into conventional terms. On the other hand, this seems to be in stark contrast with films like *The Garden* or *The Angelic Conversation* and Bersani and Dutoit even describe *Edward II* as 'a gay and lesbian rally' (1999: 18).

It is indeed very possible to read *Edward II* as a political rally, particularly if we consider the jarring scene where the OutRage protesters rush in to protect Edward. Arguably the film is straining to represent the Gay Lib rally mentality which argued for the political benefit of making visible a quantifiable minority. In a similar vein, *The Garden* sets up a tendentious argument between gay life and 'heterosoc' in which one is exalted/martyred while the other is denigrated. Yet reducing Jarman's films to the status of a gay rally is problematic and I want to refute these readings by arguing that Jarman's cinema has more in common with Genet's representation of the queer who fissures society from within rather than challenging the dominant by establishing a distinct minority.

Firstly, it is important to remember that none of Jarman's characters (with the possible exception of Wittgenstein) can be gay identified as they all exist in a period when the term itself had not been invented. What Jarman does, however, in all his films is to cloud the representation of the historical period with anachronism. Jim Ellis suggests that this makes Jarman's films emblematic of what could be termed 'queer' rather than 'gay' period films (1999: 290). Ellis points out that Jarman's approach is not 'archaeological' but 'genealogical' (ibid.: 299) and that Jarman's cinema is in stark contrast with the traditional period film – which sought to represent a specific era in painstaking detail – such as *Chariots of Fire* or the Merchant-Ivory 'heritage' films. By contrast, Jarman's films collapse period settings with contemporary society.

Yet it is too simplistic to argue that Jarman merely wants to locate gays in history. Instead, a better description of Jarman's films would be to describe them as palimpsestic (see Chapter 4). For example, *Caravaggio* features a striking scene in which the art critic Baglione is writing his scathing review of Michele's latest show. On one level, the image is simply anachronistic because it shows the critic writing on an early twentieth century typewriter while wallowing in his bath. Yet the image is also a pastiche of David's painting *Death of Marat* (1793) – a neo-classical painting which represented the famous leader cooling his eczematous skin condition by soaking in his bathtub. What is often overlooked, however, is that David's *Death of Marat* is exemplary of '*neo*-classicism', signalling a return to classical restraint and simplicity. The painting rejects complicated foreshortening, excessive colour and includes only the necessary details to convey meaning. Marat's musculature has the classical dignity of Greek sculpture imbuing the picture with a serene nobility, despite the degrading subject matter of a dead man slumped in a bathtub.

Therefore, when featured in *Caravaggio*, this image has the effect of collapsing the intervening years. The typewriter is early twentieth century while the image is a pastiche of David's painting which itself quotes from classical art. The image is not so much the jarring intrusion of one anachronistic detail into a specific period but the blurring of all the intervening years. Like a palimpsest, the image has evolved through the years; each era imposing a new set of signifiers upon it. It expands the matrix of reception demonstrating that there is no postal service of meaning. It cannot simply be inscribed nor circumscribed by the signifier/signified dichotomy itself but instead there is a landslide of semiotic signification with signifieds becoming signifiers and attaching a whole new range of signifieds. The image does not simply show the insertion of an anachronistic sign into a specific period but prises open the chain of signification itself.

Caravaggio, Jarman, 1986

Therefore, when 'homosexuality' is represented in this slide of signification it does not simply become anachronistic 'gayness' stuck into a period setting. Representing same-sex passion in an historical setting is not simply the political exercise of showing that there were famous 'queers' in the cultural/historical landscape. Instead, Jarman's films offer the altogether more queer potential of exposing the institutionalized repression of dissident sexual desire throughout history. The focus is upon the homophobic landscape of English history, rather than simply trying to prove that 'gay' icons existed in our past.

The Angelic Conversation, for example, is not simply staging a gay reading of the Sonnets. Instead the Sonnets provide an oblique or jarring commentary on the film's action. The exaltation of ungendered love, expressed in the voiceover, contrasts with the images of burning cars, the ever-oppressive radar and even the wrestling of the two boys. The overriding image is of the oppression of the physical environment clashing with the lyricism of the poetry. What can be described as 'gay' images of the boys making love, contrasts with the homosociality of the Sonnets and when Philip is featured with his dark suit and fan he also becomes the Dark Lady of the Sonnets as well as being the young man. The effect is to reshuffle the signification of the original text. The film gathers together the various meanings attributed to the original texts and, like a palimpsest, reveals their progression through the different eras.

Yet as both Arroyo (1993) and Bersani and Dutoit (1999) have argued, *Edward II* appears to challenge this argument. The inclusion of OutRage protesters seems to insist on the anachronistic inclusion of gay men within a previous era. This scene, more than any other in Jarman's cinema, has been read as establishing his insistence on identity politics and Arroyo, quite understandably, asks what actually makes *Edward II* a queer film (1993: 95)?

However, what *Edward II* makes very clear is that rally-style politics do *not* work. Gaveston is beaten to a bloody pulp while Edward is dethroned and imprisoned (although his subsequent execution is represented only as a nightmare). Rally style politics only succeed in placing a minority against a majority and that can only have limited success. Queer, therefore, argued for the mobility of identity effects. From its inception, Queer established itself as being in reaction to identity politics. The character who achieves this in *Edward II* is the real hero of the film – little Prince Edward.

In one superbly queer scene, Prince Edward is framed by his glamorous mother, attired in yet another gorgeous designer gown, while he is wearing a balaclava and carrying a toy machine gun. These symbols of violence are juxtaposed with his fluffy dressing gown. As in other Isabella/Prince Edward images in the film (such as the vampiric communion they share after Isabella's murder of Kent) the boy's closeness to his mother is emphasized. Like other representations of Prince Edward, this queer image suggests the deconstructive potential sought by Queer. Prince

Edward is not opposed to the dominant but fissures it from within. He is embraced by the dominant but yet reshuffles its parameters. As I have argued earlier, the boy's obsession with violence is symbolic of his internal battle with queer shame which he finally transcends to achieve a sense of queer pride. One of the queerest factors is the boy's effeminacy juxtaposed with his obsession with violence, making him a strange, even unintelligible, subject – a boy whose obsessions are both make-up *and* machine guns. Therefore the victorious ending, showing Prince Edward dancing on the cage, testifies not to Isabella and Mortimer's defeat but to their sense of exhaustion, expressed by their fossilized appearances. Prince Edward is a subject who seems to have moved beyond their comprehension because he cannot be situated within the hetero/homo binary. It is therefore Isabella and Mortimer who are located within the identificatory prison, symbolized by the cage, while Prince Edward dances on top of it. What Prince Edward demonstrates is the radical potential of queer for destabilizing the regime of normal and exposing it simply as a system of coercive representations.

Edward II, Jarman, 1991

In a similar vein, *The Garden* is another Jarman film which can also be read as a gay rally. Unlike *Edward II*, it exalts gay love by representing two beautiful male lovers who are sadistically tortured by heterosoc. Yet *The Garden*'s ending is not simply an image of the lovers together but an alternative 'last supper' in which the lovers, Tilda Swinton, Jody Graber and an older man share a silent communion together: an image celebrating the non-nuclear family. Thatcherite politics did not so much try to establish a binary between homosexual and heterosexual but between queer and normal. And 'normal', for conservative politics, has always been signified by 'the family'. Politicians have only to offer the explanation that they 'do this for our wives and children' to secure a public acceptance of their argument. Likewise, people in political power always desire to be photographed against a background of their loving, 'normal' family. Conservative politics tried to establish 'queer' as a threat to family and home and, by implication, normal decency.

Therefore, the emphasis throughout *The Garden* is not so much about the persecution of the male lovers as a focus upon the fear and hatred of difference. Throughout the film, various socially sanctioned institutions (church, military) terrorize and assault those who do not conform. In an early scene Tilda Swinton represents a Madonna-style figure, cradling a child on her lap, who is assaulted by hack photographers. As in the other scenes of *The Garden* this sequence is a political allegory veiled by the Christian story. While the Bible's Madonna was mother of Christ and (especially within Catholicism) an important figure in Christian worship, she was technically a single mother who not only bore a child out of wedlock but gave birth to him in a stable. If Thatcherite politics cited the 'queer' as being the main assault on family decency, then single mothers were not far behind in the criticism. Yet what makes this sequence very striking is Swinton's characteristic stare into the camera, thus promoting, as O'Pray suggests, 'the spectator's identification with the unseen attackers' (1996: 180). This glare (by now an almost iconic Swinton action in Jarman's cinema) into the camera shatters the spectator's sense of invisibility and his/her sense of identification with the traditional gaze of the film. Swinton's belligerent gaze forces the spectator to address how (s)he is viewing the images and question whether (s)he has the right to gaze upon these images and classify them in a traditional way. In a similar *Garden* scene, a stalking camera approaches Spring and Jody Graber who can be read as representing Joseph and the young Jesus. Joseph (Spring) holds his hands up in defence, trying to block the camera's lens and, in a later night time scene when the camera returns again, Joseph tries to block its gaze by covering the lens with his hands. Like Jarman's other films this sequence employs his key technique of shining a light directly into the camera's lens, this drawing attention to the mechanism of spectatorship, not only making the spectator aware of his/her position as voyeur but challenging his/her ability to quantify the film's characters.

The overall effect of this is to impede traditional cinematic identification and reject the qualifying and quantifying gaze of the spectator. In this respect, far from being political tracts which seek to establish a quantifiable minority group, Jarman's films seek to destabilize the limiting confines of identity and challenge images delineating specific sexual subjectivity. But what political effect does this have? What does the image achieve by challenging the confines of identity? In order to answer this, I want to return to Genet and address the theme which Bersani describes as a 'meta-transgressive dépassement of the field of transgressive possibility itself' (1995: 163).

The Politics of 'Inside/Out' and 'Narrative Transcendence'

The world of Genet is the world of the criminal. Genet himself spent most of his youth and adult life in prison for crimes which ranged from stealing to assault and certainly the image of the 'thief' is as synonymous with Genet as the image of the tortured homosexual.

Mark Lilly makes the remarkable claim that Genet became a criminal because it strengthened his masculinity:

> Genet burgles as a way of 'freeing' himself from that 'faggotry' which he himself, having internalized society's values, sees as unmasculine. The thief is one of the 'manly' types and as long as Genet steals he has a good chance of evading the 'queer' insult.
>
> (1993: 98)

This is certainly a possible, but not very probable, explanation. Surely being a thief, which leads only to years of imprisonment, is a rather over-zealous way of 'evading the queer insult'? Are there not less difficult ways of establishing masculinity which don't result in languishing in prison? Lilly's description also trivializes Genet by reducing him to a petty obsession in which Genet – the paranoid fag – must contest his queerness at all costs.

The writer to challenge these type of readings of Genet was the philosopher Jean-Paul Sartre whose *Saint Genet* probably did most to elevate Genet's status within literary and artistic circles. For Sartre, Genet's criminality was exemplary of existentialist philosophy which argued that it is impossible to attain universal, incontrovertible knowledge. There is no transcendent truth. There is only existence and this existence is shaped by certain social variables such as family, education and religion. The existential subject must accept what society has accorded him and then inhabit it to the full. Therefore existentialism revolves on a tension between accepting the subjectivity which is foisted upon us by external variables and then developing this subjectivity through our own personal choices. To reject the life-script which society has imposed upon the subject is an example of what Sartre termed 'bad faith'.

In this respect, Genet can be viewed as a Sartrean existential hero. As Sartre argues 'he had to make himself become the other that he already was for the others' (1979: 14). In simpler terms, Genet lived out fully the subjectivity which society had accorded him. Society designated Genet a criminal because of his homosexuality so then Genet really did become a total criminal. As Richard Dyer summarizes, 'the existentialist hero, Genet, is the one who fully accepts this social designation and lives it out defiantly' (1990: 83).

However, queer theory offers the potential of reading Genet as something other than an 'existentialist hero'. Genet's fascination with society's underworld is not an attempt to live out, to its fullest potential, what society has imposed upon the subject but instead may be read as an attempt to invert societal norms through 'subversive shuffling' (Gardner, 1996: 38) and turn everything inside/out. All things despised – crime, homosexuality, betrayal – become exalted in Genet's oeuvre. Society imposed homophobic terms of shame upon Genet but Genet re-appropriated these terms and 'embracing the conditions of repression, discovered strength through abjection' (Sinfield, 1994: 196); a veritable cover-boy of queer transgression.

It is here that critical disagreement arises about Genet. Mark Lilly, in contrast to Sinfield, reads nothing transgressive about Genet and instead argues that 'the extent of Genet's self-oppression, and his having internalized the homophobic values of the surrounding culture, can hardly be doubted' (1993: 90). According to Lilly, Genet is simply eroticising his oppression and wallowing in it.

These contradictory readings of Genet can be applied to Genet's short, silent film: *Un Chant d'Amour* and both readings can be argued to have validity. Is *Chant* attempting to 'turn that prison inside out and expose society to the terms of his (Genet's) prison aesthetic' (Gardner, 1996: 38) or is it the eroticization of oppression; the self-hatred of a pitiful fag?

Set in a dank prison, *Chant* chronicles a warden spying on various prisoners. The film then moves into a sequence of chiaroscuro lit images which show men making love and then finally shows sequences of two of the prisoners, outside the prison, playing and making love in a woodland setting. Interspersed between the sequences are shots of a garland of flowers being swung between two prison windows.

Chant is a difficult film to read, not least because of its unconventional editing. It is impossible to say if the chiaroscuro sequence and the woodland sequence are the daydreams of the warden or of one of the prisoners. It would, for example, be possible to interpret the woodland sequence as the daydream of the dark-skinned prisoner. Yet on at least one occasion the woodland sequence is not preceded by a shot of the prisoner (thus establishing that it will be his reverie) but by a shot of the guard. On the other hand, the chiaroscuro sequence cannot be claimed as the erotic daydream of the guard because it is preceded a couple of times by the swinging garland of flowers.

Critics have argued that these dream sequences (woodland and chiaroscuro scenes) show the queerly liberating effect of being in prison: 'imprisoned, one is somehow freer to love' (Gardner, 19965: 38). (This interpretation, of course, is dependant upon reading the chiaroscuro sequences as the reveries of the prisoner.) Arguably Genet is showing that, while the position of the homosexual was oppressed in free society, the confinement of prison, ironically, gave homosexual encounters a certain validity. Imprisoned, homosexual intimacy was allowed to blossom so that being incarcerated could really become a woodland frolic or a passionate chiaroscuro sequence.

One of the dominant images in *Chant* is the cell wall – the symbol of confinement. Yet this wall is not simply a division between the prisoners but is a fetish for homoerotics. The dark-skinned prisoner places his cheek in longing to the wall and he exhales smoke through a straw while the younger prisoner then inhales this smoke – a crude metaphor for fellatio. This passionate exchange would not be possible if the men were not in prison. It is only through their oppression, their confinement, that these men are able to exchange such electric passion.

Un Chant d'Amour, Genet, 1950

Chant, however, is referenced throughout Jarman's cinema but especially in the iconography of *Edward II*. Like *Chant*'s prison cells, Edward's castle is dark and claustrophobic and the walls even appear to be dank with moisture. The *mise-en-scène* always conveys a sense of the characters constrained or even imprisoned by the castle walls and in one scene even reed-thin Isabella teeters down a corridor in her high heels, barely able to squeeze through the narrow space. Similarly, when Edward and Gaveston are assailed by Mortimer or the chorus of nobility, they are nearly always confined to a small space, constricted by looming, stone walls.

However, in one of the film's most famous scenes, the *mise-en-scène* conveys an entirely different impression. In what I shall call the 'Annie Lennox Sequence', Edward and Gaveston enjoy a final dance – before Gaveston is to be banished to France – to the accompaniment of Diva Annie Lennox singing Cole Porter's *Everytime we say Goodbye*. What links the scene most decisively to *Chant* is the sense of the lovers transcending the dank gloom of the prison like setting while Lennox, in a pastiche of the action of *Chant*'s dark-skinned prisoner, even presses her cheek to the stone wall as she sings.

Edward II, Jarman, 1991

Like *Chant* this sequence demonstrates a transcendence of imprisoned gloom as Edward and Gaveston dance together, lit beatifically by a single spotlight. This spotlight is not simply a visual pun on the cabaret status of Cole Porter's song but irradiates the lovers and elevates them out of the bleak confines of the room. What is most touching about the scene is the way Edward and Gaveston seem to create something special, almost magical, in the midst of the castle's oppression. The scene is also remarkably chaste with a sense of innocent playfulness displayed by both

Edward and Gaveston, dressed in baggy pyjamas which downplay the eroticism of their bodies. The sequence is also remarkable for representing one of the few close-ups in the film as, during Lennox's cadenza, Edward and Gaveston kiss. The majority of shots throughout the film are medium shots, taking in the claustrophobic castle walls and the tableau style representation of the characters. The close-up of Edward and Gaveston's kiss, by contrast, becomes the focus of the entire screen and momentarily frees the characters from the castle confines, the expression of their love transcending, momentarily, their environment.

This *Chant*-esque theme is further elaborated in the final sequences where Edward is imprisoned in the castle dungeon with Lightborn as his gaoler. As Gardner suggests, 'prison is a privileged space of desire in *Edward II*' as, in prison, a sense of mutual understanding, a chaste, platonic love, blossoms between Edward and Lightborn. Therefore, although imprisoning Edward is supposed to be a punishment for his transgression, the space of the prison ironically allows Edward the love he was not permitted to share with Gaveston.

Therefore, both Genet and Jarman are attempting to turn everything inside/out. Both artists are representing spaces of traditional oppression but showing that queer love, in the midst of this oppression, can have the effect of freeing the subject from his confines. Yet both Genet and Jarman move one stage further in their attempt to overthrow the dominant order as for both artists the re-appropriation and re-deployment of terms of abuse is a key facet of their work. Genet makes this particularly evident throughout his oeuvre by representing everything which society designates 'ugly' as special and beautiful. As Richard Dyer (1990: 570 points out, some of the scenes in *Chant* are particularly repulsive – such as a shot of a prisoner picking dirt out of his big toe. Yet for Genet this stomach-churning image is a representation of masculine beauty. Genet is therefore attempting to turn conventional society inside/out and achieve a redeployment of terms of beauty and ugliness.

However, Jarman's cinema draws upon this theme of redeployment in many of his films but must obviously in *The Garden* where it is the salient motif. The film uses Jarman's garden at Dungeness as a metaphor for queer love. This Dungeness garden received considerable praise from gardening experts not only because it managed to cultivate flowers in its acidic, seaside environment but for the way it produced such strange 'queer' plants. Indeed, plants which other gardeners would weed out, such as sea kale, became the main objects of beauty in Jarman's garden. This garden, therefore, produced something unconventionally beautiful in the midst of oppression and this metaphor for queer love obviously thrilled Jarman so much that he dedicated much of *The Garden* to sumptuous shots of the Dungeness garden in full bloom.

What *The Garden* attempts to do, in the legacy of Genet, is redeploy the dominant terms. Every term of abuse which would normally be used against 'queers' is, in the film, shown to be more applicable to the straight-identified. Jarman's male lovers are a tender, loving couple while those who oppress them are vindictive, cruel, ugly, perverted and sadistic. Indeed, in various shocking scenes we see the lovers abused by the establishments of conventional society. In one horrific scene they are tarred and feathered by military-style figures – characters that can be read as representing the police authorities. Tony Peake argues that the sequence represents the unnecessary and cruel perversion of innocence:

> Tilda Swinton plucks a chicken, an act redolent of a simple and warm domesticity. There is a pillow fight. Feathers fly, but again the act is innocent. Then the gay lovers are tarred and feathered. Now the feathers represent repression: innocence has been perverted.
>
> (1999: 459)

In a similar scene, the lovers are harassed by leering thugs dressed in Santa Claus suits who bellow the carol *God Rest You Merry Gentlemen* at the sleeping lovers. The singing of the carol connects the thugs to the established church and indeed the lead singer tries to perform the carol with the elevated, Anglican tones of an Evensong Cantor. Yet, paradoxically, while the thugs are emulating church authority, they are dressed in the secular costume of Santa Claus. The traditional Santa Claus look – red suit, black boots and white beard – was invented by Coca Cola because the costume echoed the colours of the brand logo. This paradox is further emphasized by the Santas holding commercial Christmas presents such as mobile phones and video cameras. In this respect the sequence represents feigned Christianity as nothing more than an established means of condemning those who do not conform. What both scenes attempt to do is subvert the dominant binary system of representations so that everything traditionally deemed ugly and disgusting is shown to be beautiful while everything established as good and true is shown to be false.

The Garden, Jarman, 1990

However, does a redeployment of the terms of beauty and ugliness really present any challenge to the dominant? How transgressive is the shuffling of cultural boundaries? Therefore I want to argue that Jarman, like Genet, is not merely trying to redeploy terms of abuse but is trying to achieve what Bersani terms a 'meta-transgressive *dépassement*'.

Meta-transgressive *dépassement*

Bersani disputes readings of Genet which see his work as attempting an ironic redeployment of cultural norms because that would still leave 'Genet socially positioned' (1995: 161). Instead Bersani argues that:

Genet's use of his culture's dominant terms (especially its ethical and sexual categories) are designed not to rework or to subvert those terms, but to exploit their potential for erasing cultural relationality itself (that is, the very preconditions for subversive repositionings and defiant repetitions).

(1995: 153)

This is a complicated argument which suggests that Genet is not interested in redeploying the social agendas which formulate subjectivity but instead is trying to move beyond those very social life scripts themselves. Bersani argues that Genet is trying to achieve 'a kind of meta-transgressive *dépassement* of the field of transgressive possibility itself' (1995: 163). In simpler terms, Bersani is suggesting that Genet is not simply trying to reclaim all homophobic terms of abuse and redeploy them proudly but instead is rejecting the very cultural paradigms which have positioned him as a criminal and pariah.

This is an interesting philosophy but what does it actually mean for a subject to achieve this 'meta-transgressive *dépassement*' in which, for example, the term 'evil' is no longer defined against 'good'? As Sinfield argues 'this would be a remarkable achievement, since conventionally evil is defined against good and transgression is limited by the boundary that it would cross' (1998: 133). What Bersani seems to be describing is a subject impervious to social interpellation. What this actually could be is hard to imagine. Surely we only understand our subjectivity through the interpellation of, what Althusser termed, the Ideological State Apparatuses such as church, family and education? If we topple off the edge of the ideological chart we would surely become a sort of non-entity, a non-person.

Therefore, what we find in both Genet and Jarman is a fevered introspection in which their heroes often turn away from society and retreat into a narcissistic hermeticism. To take Genet's oeuvre first, many of his characters are narcissistically self-obsessed and their intense fascination is their own physicality and their bodies. In *Chant* some of the prisoners are auto-erotic, finding great pleasure in their *own* bodies, and even the famous scene of the prisoner placing his cheek in longing against the wall can be read as a pastiche of Cocteau's *Orphée* where Jean Marais presses his check to his own reflection in an image of narcissistic, self adoration. Likewise, in *Querelle*, Seblon describes Querelle's 'great passion' as being his 'own body in repose. It is as if he is reflecting himself in his own image'. Seblon quite accurately cites Querelle as narcissistic and therefore, when Querelle eventually does become attracted to someone else – the murderer Gil - it is because, as the film's voiceover tells us, Querelle saw in Gil a 'foetal Querelle': another version of himself.

Yet what makes Querelle such an interesting film is the way it actually (de)constructs subjectivity. The traditional diegetic gazes of the film, which establish character subjectivity within the narrative, are employed in an ironic, attenuated fashion. *Querelle* undermines the filmic gazes not through an alternative regime of cinematic shots but by parodying the traditional Hollywood shot/reverse shot formula to such an extreme. In *Querelle*, every character is looking at someone else in circuit like fashion. One shot is framed by another shot of someone looking at the first shot which, in turn, is framed by another shot of someone else looking. In one Feria bar scene, for example, Querelle's body is beautifully framed and offered for spectatorial pleasure. This then cuts to a shot of Mario looking at Querelle and then to a shot of Lysianne looking at them both in the mirror. Indeed throughout the film there are various shots of Lysianne looking at reflected images thus undermining the authenticity of the image itself. To quote the title of the final film of Fassbinder's favourite director, Douglas Sirk, *Querelle* is an obvious *Imitation of Life*.

This is emphasized by one of the most curious elements in the film: the diegetic narrative often does not match the visual images. We are continuously told, by both voice-over and film characters, that Querelle and his brother are 'very much alike'. Yet visually they are not at all similar. Likewise, Querelle falls in love with Gil – in whom, the narrative tells us, he sees himself 'reflected' – but Gil is played by the same actor who plays Querelle's brother who is not even remotely similar looking to Querelle. Therefore the film offers a tension between what the visual image shows and what the diegetic narrative declares. We are told that Querelle is 'like' his brother and Gil but yet there is absolutely no visual similarity. The result of this is a destabilization of the power of the cinematic gaze and the dominance of the image. Subjectivity is created not by the right to see others but by the objectification of being seen by others (Sartre, 1966). In

Querelle, however, the looks of the film are exaggerated to such an extent (every character is looking at everyone else ad infinitum) that establishing subjectivity becomes problematic.

This superb Fassbinder film accords beautifully with Bersani's reading of Genet which cites the core of his work as being the 'meta-transgressive *dépassement*' of the social world itself. Fassbinder is showing that Querelle doesn't actually exist, which is why he breezes through the film and escapes without punishment for the murders he has committed. How can Querelle define himself when the dominant force of the look doesn't exist in the film? In whose gaze is Querelle defining himself when he is caught in a vortex of reciprocal looks by a group of idiots who don't even seem to see what they're actually looking at? Every character seems to think that Querelle and his brother are so 'alike' but yet there's no visual similarity at all. This explains the seemingly silly ending when Lysianne reads the cards and declares that she made a mistake: Robert doesn't have a brother. It's not just that Lysianne has gone mad but that, throughout the film, Querelle himself has not been an interpellated subject.

This theme is echoed in Jarman's cinema although he revises it in various ways. A dominant image in Jarman's work is of two male lovers who seem to exist outside of temporal society (*The Angelic Conversation*, *The Garden*). Yet while Fassbinder employs conventional Hollywood cinematography in *Querelle* but parodies it – albeit subtly – to emphasize Genet's theme, Jarman's cinema is less influenced by Hollywood and more painterly in appearance. Therefore, while Fassbinder's *Querelle* suggests that Querelle has attained Genet's *dépassement* of society through its cinematography and editing, Jarman delights in simply representing his male lovers who are physically distant from the constrictions of normal society. For example, in *The Garden*, the stillness of the lovers is often set in contrast to the hysteria of the other characters such as in the bathhouse scene where the lovers remain aloof, serene, while the other characters are all screeching and laughing in a maniacal fashion. In a similar sequence, *The Garden*'s lovers are set against images of the Gay Pride parade in the 'Think Pink' number. The sexualized frenzy of the parade and the up-beat tempo of the show tune, campily lip-synched by Jessica Martin, all contrast with the stillness of the lovers. Likewise the lovers, at the start of the film, wash each other's hair, loosely echoing the Baptism of Christ, as represented in devotional paintings such as *The Baptism of Christ* (1450s, Piero della Francesca), in which all time stood still as Christ rose from the water and God declared that he was his son.

Yet although Jarman may represent images which suggest this *dépassement* achieved by queer love, the spectator's identification with the lovers is restricted. In Jarman's cinema the spectator is rarely invited into the reciprocal gazes of the lovers. For example, in *Edward II* when Gaveston is first re-united with Edward, their meeting is filmed frontally and they almost appear to perform for a static camera. Indeed, very surprisingly for a 'lovers-reunion scene', there are no shot/reverse shots between Edward and Gaveston.

Edward II, Jarman, 1991

However, what makes *Edward II* such an uneasy ride for a gay identified spectator is that the shot/reverse shot is later employed – but only between Edward and Isabella. In Isabella's introductory scene the spectator has a shot of Isabella – hair flowing and looking prettier and less austere than she will later – attempting to make love to her husband. This shot of Isabella is then succeeded by an eyeline match shot from Isabella's point of view showing her indifferent husband, uninspired by her attentions, lying on the bed below her. The film then cuts back to Isabella's reaction and shows her pain at the physical rejection she has suffered. This is the first time in the film when spectatorial identification has been encouraged but, strangely, it is with Isabella rather than Edward.

Bersani and Dutoit, therefore, have problems with *Edward II* (1999: 16). Certainly the lovers seem – when they are together – to have transcended the claustrophobic oppression of the castle and when Edward is with Gaveston he is 'bathed in a bright, clean light which makes Edward's reddish-blonde hair shine like a halo' (Arroyo, 1993: 84). By contrast, when Gaveston is gone, Edward is 'lit in earth tones, brown, ambers, yellow. Sometimes they are dispersed, undulating rays cast over his body which have a slight blurring effect, as if he were underwater' (Arroyo, ibid.). Therefore the lovers together are supremely happy. But as Bersani and Dutoit ask (1999: 16), Edward and Gaveston may have transcended the oppression of the castle but into what? All they seem to do is pass the time, watching dancers, strippers and other trivial entertainment. Therefore, far from achieving what Genet's work was attempting to do, we see Edward and Gaveston, as I have argued earlier, continuously circumscribed back into society's narrative.

Yet the film ends victoriously. As I have argued earlier, the actual hero is the film is not King Edward but little Prince Edward and he is the character with whom the spectator is often asked to empathize. He is Jarman's 'eye in the castle' (Quinn-Meyler, 1996: 125) and it is often Prince Edward's gaze of surprise and disbelief which leads the spectator into the scene.

Arguably it is the film's ending – depicting Prince Edward in full drag, dancing on the cage of the dusty Isabella and Mortimer – which attains what Bersani has termed the 'meta-transgressive *dépassement* of the field of transgressive possibility itself' (1995: 163). Indeed this final image *is* Genet's prison cell, which has been referenced throughout the film in both the castle itself and Edward's dungeon, transcended by the young Prince. It is therefore important that the parameters of resistance have actually been shifted. Far from being an issue of sexual orientation, the focus now becomes one of gender performativity. Prince Edward is not simply rebelling against the imposition of dominant heterosexual norms, as that would still leave him socially positioned and restrained, but instead is presenting a revised subjectivity outside the theatre of normalcy.

Therefore, as I have argued, *Edward II* is not necessarily exalting a radical, separatist politics and, in many ways, the film can be read as showing the futility of such activity. While Edward and Gaveston exalt their love, their transgressive behaviour can only define itself against the dominant societal script and therefore does not succeed in transcending anything. The 'happy' ending of the film is, in this respect, not representing Prince Edward's resistance but his rejection or *dépassement* of social scripts altogether. As Genet achieves with Querelle, so Jarman achieves with Prince Edward.

8

AIDS AND ITS METAPHORS: (RE)IMAGING THE SYNDROME

AIDS was first diagnosed as 'Gay Related Immune Deficiency' (GRID) in the USA in 1982. One year later scientists renamed the condition 'Acquired Immune Deficiency Syndrome' (AIDS) when they identified the HIV virus which leads to AIDS. More than twenty years later medical science is still no closer to a cure – although treatment has improved greatly through the development of anit-viral combination therapies and protease inhibitors.

However, while medical science struggles to find a cure or a vaccine, the media continues to wrestle with the difficulties in representing AIDS in film, television and print. From its very inception AIDS has been a crisis in representation. As Susan Sontag points out, AIDS is difficult to represent because, strictly speaking, AIDS is not an illness with recognisable symptoms but is really a 'medical condition, whose consequences area spectrum of illnesses' (1991: 102). What the media commonly identifies as AIDS is not the condition itself but examples from the myriad of secondary infections which *may* infect a Person With AIDS (PWA). One of the most popular symbols of AIDS in the media has been the Karposi Sarcoma (KS) Lesion – a rare form of skin cancer which attacks *some* PWAs.

Douglas Crimp, therefore, makes the remarkable claim that 'AIDS does not exist apart from the practices which conceptualize it, represent it, and respond to it' (1987: 3). In other words, the media has constantly strained to represent a condition – whose consequences may be an array of illnesses – in a tangible form. In doing so the media has often portrayed AIDS inaccurately and has created many AIDS myths. More than twenty years after the discovery of the condition, many of these myths are still credited by the general public.

This chapter will review the cultural myths surrounding AIDS (AIDS as a 'gay' disease; AIDS as a direct result of promiscuity; AIDS as a plague/punishment; AIDS and gay shame; AIDS and abjection) and look at how these have coloured representations in the media. Drawing upon 'mainstream' examples from popular film, the chapter will consider the difficulty in representing the syndrome without either re-enforcing the cultural misconceptions about the condition or dehumanising the PWA. Finally the chapter will consider these debates in relation to Jarman's cinema which not only attempts to challenge many of the inaccuracies surrounding the representation of AIDS but also avoids the difficulty of representing the body infected by the virus.

AIDS as a 'Gay' Disease

From its earliest inception, AIDS has been identified as a gay disease – an inaccuracy which, unfortunately, many people still harbour (see Watney, 1997: 32). From its earliest acronym GRID, AIDS has been linked to homosexuality. The connotation has always been that AIDS has somehow grown out of, or developed, from the 'disease' of homosexuality itself (Sharrock, 1997: 356). Soap operas, pulp novels and pot-boiler theatre of the 1980s and early 1990s often employed the gay character's revelation of his HIV status as a standard plot twist, implying that, as a gay man, developing AIDS was not only inevitable but somehow intrinsically linked to homosexuality itself. In the 1980s GAY came to stand for 'Got Aids Yet?'.

One of the earliest slang phrases for AIDS was 'Gay Plague'. This not only suggested that AIDS developed out of homosexuality but also implied that homosexuality itself was a form of disease from which the heterosexual majority must be protected (Sharrock, 356-7). Indeed, as Simon Watney points out, AIDS-phobia has re-emphasised the original idea of the homosexual as someone/something which 'emerged in the last century at the interstices of a host of overlapping discourses concerning sickness, contamination and genetic throwbacks, and was regarded as the most concrete evidence of the results of indecency, depravity and uncleanliness' (1997: 49). The conflation of AIDS with gay men has not simply emphasised that AIDS 'is' a gay disease but has suggested that homosexuality itself is a pathological condition.

AIDS and Promiscuity

Despite the fact that AIDS should not really even be classified as an STD at all (it's a blood disease rather than a venereal disease), the syndrome has always been read as the corollary of promiscuity. Although originally this was predominantly linked to gay promiscuity, the perception has changed to include heterosexual promiscuity as well. People 'get' AIDS because they have too many sexual partners or fail to maintain 'long'-term relationships. As Watney suggests, AIDS is related to sex 'in a quantitative rather than qualitative way' (1997: 12).

Leo Bersani quotes a terrifying piece of 'AIDS paranoia' which, although written by a man of 'supposed' medical science, only serves to demonstrate the public misperception of AIDS as a result of promiscuity:

These people (the 'gays') have sex twenty to thirty times a night [...] A man comes along and goes from anus to anus and in a single night will act as a mosquito transferring infected cells on his penis. When this is practised for a year, with a man having three thousand sexual intercourses, one can readily understand this massive epidemic that is currently upon us.
(Professor Opendra Narayan, The John Hopkins Medical School, quoted in Bersani, 1987: 1)

Despite crediting gay men with stallion-like sexual process who, in a decade preceding Viagra, can apparently manage to have penetrative sex twenty to thirty times a night, Professor Narayan is also confusing two different fears in his AIDS paranoia. Narayan is not simply citing a fear of sexual contagion but asserting a horror of sexual promiscuity.

Sexual promiscuity discomforts many people for two reasons. The first is the psychic distress of promiscuous sex which signifies non-climactic sex or unsatisfying sex. Promiscuity is often described as 'whorelike' behaviour because female prostitutes will have non-climactic (an-orgasmic) sex within their occupation. Because the sex drive is so closely linked to both the death drive and also the life essence or life force, to violate its supremacy through non-climactic activity is to signify a form of psychic death or dehumanization. The second reason is a cultural one. The promiscuous subject is in direct violation of sexual monogamy which is exalted as the ideal state by the contemporary Western institutions of religion, education and politics. Queer promiscuity challenges the chocolate box image of the house and family.

However, one of the most inaccurate issues raised by Narayan in his lament of the 'gay misquito' is the issue of 'public sex' which he is confusing with the issue of 'safe' sex. This fantastic 'gay mosquito' can (presumably) only have sex with twenty to thirty people if he is in a gay bathhouse or sauna. Time and time again people point the finger at the bathhouses and saunas as the cause of the AIDS contagion. Even Alan Sinfield makes the overly simplistic suggestion that the AIDS epidemic was not as immense in Britain as in the USA because 'Britons had not developed, or been allowed to have, bath-houses and backrooms' (1998: 91). However, it can only be speculated how much unsafe sex either takes or took place in the bathhouses. Sinfield is correct in citing them as a supreme risk in the days before safer-sex education but what is worrying is the implication that public sex is synonymous with unsafe sex. A cursory inspection of lifestyle magazines and other media will discover a wealth of horror stories about young men and women who contracted the HIV virus after their first sexual encounter or when they were in a 'committed' relationship. Indeed, one of the reasons people usually offer as to why they took sexual risks was that they thought they were in love. They thought the person they were with was special.

Therefore, it could be argued that a large number of cases of infection occur within the intimate security of the 'home' as opposed to the breathless promiscuity of the bathhouse. Setting up a dichotomy between house/home (which signifies monogamy and security) and places of public sex and cruising (which signify sickness and debauchery) is too simplistic and only supports the cultural myth of AIDS resulting from promiscuity.

However, in the eyes of many people, AIDS is still considered to be the result of promiscuity. Simon Watney cites an opinion poll which appeared in the widely read *News of the World* newspaper which found '56.8 per cent of readers in favour of the idea that 'AIDS carriers' should be 'sterilised and given treatment to curb their sexual appetite' (Watney, 1997:

138). In some people's eyes (albeit *News of the World* readers' eyes) AIDS is intrinsically related to promiscuous sex and, according to Scottish Health Minister John MacKay, the only solution to the epidemic is just to not have sex:

> We are going to be asked to spend a lot of money on a disease which could easily be prevented by people changing their lifestyles [...] I think this is a straightforward moral issue.
>
> (quoted in Watney, 1997: 49)

The issue of HIV transmission is therefore confused with moral issues about the unacceptability of promiscuity. This, however, only diverts attention from the actual problem of HIV infection into moralistic rantings about the importance of house/home and monogamy versus depraved/sick, queer public sex. In this respect AIDS, more than any other medical condition, has revived a Dark Ages moralism in which sickness is viewed as the apt punishment for depravity. As Watney suggests, AIDS has returned many of us to 'the pre-modern world, with disease restored to its ancient theological status as punishment' (Watney, 1997: 204).

AIDS as a Punishment or Plague

Susan Sontag points out that AIDS is particularly susceptible to wilful impositions of plague metaphors because, unlike influenza for example, AIDS is thought to target only specific groups of morally reprehensible people (1991: 142). William Buckley offers a charming suggestion which, given the *News of the World* poll cited by Watney, may well be the view shared by many people:

> Everyone detected with AIDS should be tattooed in the upper fore-arm, to protect common needle users, and on the buttocks to prevent the victimization of other homosexuals.
>
> (William F. Buckley, quoted in Crimp, 1987: 8)

Not only does Buckley's terrifying suggestion incite images of Nazism but it demonstrates how he believes that *only* intravenous drug users or homosexuals will have contracted the virus.

This raises another key issue in that AIDS is often thought to affect only people who – from a moralistic point of view – have supposedly 'brought the trouble on themselves'. These people contract HIV and develop AIDS because they engaged in disreputable behaviour. Indeed, one of the most frightening developments in AIDS debates is the concept of the 'innocent victim'. These PWAs are, for example, people who have had blood transfusions with infected blood or babies who have been born with the virus. While in no way wishing to detract from the horror of these situations, it should be pointed out that the concept of the 'innocent victim' raises a tendentious binary between those PWAs who are 'innocent' and the others who, by implication, are 'not innocent' or even 'guilty' (see Crimp and Rolston, 1990: 53). PWAs who contracted the disease through sexual contact are, supposedly, 'not innocent' and deserve everything they get. Therefore, one of the main social issues which AIDS has created is a form of 'erotophobia': a fear of, or shame for, a particular expression of sexuality.

AIDS and Shame: The Cult of Barebacking

One of the most frightening, recent trends in gay culture has been the cult of 'bare-backing' or unprotected fucking. Like anything reasonably shocking it has been exploded by the media and if there even is much of a cult – which many people involved in metropolitan gay life actually doubt – it is probably between seropositive men for whom the hypothetical risk of re-infection is something they are prepared to tolerate.

However, journalists have consistently stressed that barebackers eroticise the danger or risk of unprotected anal sex. There is, apparently, a thrill for many gay men in believing that they are being infected (or might be infected) by the HIV virus (Signorile, 1997). The problem with such a portrayal though is that, like all the other misrepresentations considered so far, it gives the general public a chance to throw their hands in the air and lament the abject horror of queer lifestyles. Not only does the unfortunate name of 'barebacking' connote ideas of horse-riding and, by implication, the horrors of bestiality, but it also re-emphasises the misnomer of AIDS as a gay disease. The barebackers eroticise the risk of being infected because the virus is intrinsically linked to homosexuality. By virtue of engaging in unprotected homosexual sex these men are supposedly more at risk than a heterosexual couple who engage in condomless intercourse. Even the fact that the name 'barebacking' was coined to describe the activity testifies to a belief in the correlation between homosexuality and AIDS. There is, of course, no equivalent title for reckless heterosexuals who engage in unprotected sex.

However, the issue should not be that some gay men are choosing to have un-safe sex but *why* these men are engaging in such risky behaviour. Walt Odets suggests that taking sexual risks is linked to low self image:

> The conflict, shame, humiliation, guilt (and often, the unmitigated self-hatred) that so many gay men feel about being homosexual and about this fundamental human need for anal sex are all feelings that have become seamlessly woven into too many gay men's feelings about the epidemic.
>
> (1997: 129)

Michael Warner corroborates Odets's theory and suggests that un-safe sex (especially the high risk activity of getting fucked without a condom) is inextricably linked not just to low self-esteem but to gay shame. 'Getting fucked is both clouded and intensified by shame' (Warner, 1999: 212). Like the initial belief of Genet's Querelle, many gay men still consider getting fucked as the ultimate – yet tantalising – form of degradation. Many consider that it is shameful to be fucked yet this shame only intensifies the experience. American slang has even coined the phrase 'bottom shame' to describe gay men who won't admit that they enjoy being on the receiving end (see Richardson, 2003c).

Homophobes consider anal sex (or buggery) to be the ultimate subjugation of a man. Many gay men have absorbed this prejudice and have developed a form or 'erotophobia' in which they attempt to deny some of the variants of gay sexuality. Therefore, one possible result of 'bottom shame' is that some gay men have eroticised the supposed degradation of the activity. And the ultimate degradation is, of course, being infected by the virus while submitting to the 'suicidal ecstasy' of being penetrated. However, these men will probably then deny that the 'shameful' event has even taken place thus leading to further risk taking in a cycle of shame and denial.

Representing Possible Secondary Infections rather than AIDS

The most problematic of all the AIDS myths is the way in which the media has constantly sought to 'collapse the issue of HIV virus infection – a blood disease affecting the body's immune defence system – into the symptoms of individual opportunistic infections which result from severe damage to the body's immunological defences' (Watney, 1997: 34). The virus itself is never addressed in issues of media representation. Instead AIDS is viewed as coterminous, if not even synonymous, with the disfiguring opportunistic infections which *may* attack the PWA.

However, the media's conflation of AIDS with physical deterioration is often inaccurate. As Mark Nash points out (1994: 100), the terrifying unpredictability of AIDS is that it may disfigure and wrack one body while leaving another's physical beauty untarnished. This was evidenced in Cyril Collard's drama *Les Nuits Fauves* (Savage Nights) – a film which deliberately contradicted the clichéd representations – by portraying the HIV+ protagonist as healthy and vibrant (see next section: 'Representing AIDS').

Understandably, therefore, many people are terrified of such an insidious medical condition. What exactly is AIDS? How can it be identified? How can we delineate infected bodies from un-infected bodies? In light of this, media representations of AIDS have strained to produce tangible images which allow the spectator to delineate the infected from the un-infected. In many ways, media representations of Persons With AIDS have followed a similar pattern to the early media representations of gays and lesbians. Like media portrayals of sexual orientation, representations of AIDS have strained to make visible something which is actually in-visible. In doing so, the media has already established a visual rhetoric – an AIDS shorthand – which allows the spectator to identify the virus which has infected the character's body. Spectators of Hollywood films have learned to read K.S. lesions as symbolic of AIDS. In a similar fashion to the way popular media conflated sexuality with gender transitivity in order to represent homosexuality, the representations of AIDS have emphasised the possible opportunistic infections in order to identify a PWA.

AIDS and Abjection

The final AIDS myth is the connection between AIDS and the horror of abjection. Persons With AIDS are constantly represented as the spectre of the 'living dead' who dare to transgress proper boundaries and infiltrate the domain of the living (Hanson, 1991: 324). Society must abject these bodies in order to maintain its own purity.

AIDS, therefore, has recently been conflated with everything unclean and unsound which society must shove to the margins. Politicians constantly list the problems of a major city as being: homelessness, drugs, prostitution, muggings, vandalism and, of course, AIDS. Such statements conflate AIDS – a medical condition which may infect anyone – with issues of physical threat located in an inner city slum. In this respect, AIDS is represented as a crime or violence – something which upsets the safe and proper boundaries, messing up law and order, and, as such, must be abjected. As Tim Dean summarises, 'America pushes AIDS – and the social groups seen as representing AIDS – to the outside of its psychic and social economies, treating them exactly like shit' (1993: 87).

It is here that Foucault's work on the body is illuminating. In order for AIDS to offer a physical threat – like muggings or vandalism – it must be considered a corporeal issue. Media representations have constantly attempted to show AIDS as something which not only infects but affects and disfigures bodies (see section: 'Representing AIDS').

In a much-cited passage, Foucault elaborates on how the body is subjugated and controlled by the various mechanisms of culture and industry:

The body is directly involved in a political field; power relations have an immediate hold upon it: they invest it, train it, torture it, force it to carry out tasks, to perform ceremonies and to emit signs.

(1991: 25)

In short, there cannot be a body without the cultural systems of meaning which reify it.

However, for the body to belong to these mechanisms of power – to be a working body, a reproductive body or a culturally readable body – it must conform to the 'net-like organisation' (Foucault, 1980: 98) of the norm. Disciplinary power 'hierarchizes in terms of value the abilities, the level, the 'nature' of individuals. It introduces, through this 'value-giving' measure, the constraint of a conformity that must be achieved' (Foucault, 1991: 183).

The acceptable, normal bodies are therefore productive bodies but are also subjugated by the normalising regime. When bodies are sick or unhealthy they do not gel with the regimes of subjugation and therefore are not bodies which are either successfully productive or designated as normal. A body must conform to cultural expectations or else it simultaneously enjoys the liberation from subjugation but also the loss of social citizenship.

The problem with the PWA is that this body destabilises the binary of sick/healthy or natural/unnatural. It is the polymorphous nature of the disease, that a HIV+ body may be both productive and attractive or, on the other hand, may be wretched and disfigured by the disease which evokes the horror of abjection by confusing the boundaries of sick/healthy, productive/unproductive. Therefore, in seeking to represent AIDS, the media has sought to make this 'abjection' visible and AIDS has consistently been represented as a monstrous body. This representation ensures that PWAs do not offer the insidious threat of living-dead vampires who secretly infiltrate society but instead are recognisable monsters who can be abjected to the margins.

Representing AIDS

In reaction to the cultural prejudices surrounding AIDS, Hollywood and mainstream television unleashed a deluge of 'AIDS awareness films' in the late 1980s and early 1990s. Films such as *An Early Frost* (1985), *Buddies* (1985), *Parting Glances* (1986), *Our Sons* (1991), *Longtime Companion* (1991), *Philadelphia* (1993) and *It's My Party* (1993) attempted to break down the AIDS myths and stereotypes of Persons With AIDS.

The genre of these films was the melodrama or 'weepy': sentimental tear-jerkers which asked the audience to empathise with the victims, who were usually unthreatening and loveable, and weep tears of pity at the end of the film. The films all aimed to promote an understanding of a PWA as a 'person' rather than seeing him/her as an abject monster. However, while the films attempted to break down many of the cultural prejudices about AIDS (especially gay men suffering from AIDS) they, unfortunately, also strengthened many of the AIDS myths.

One of the most financially successful of the AIDS melodramas was *Philadelphia* which tells the story of Andy Beckett (Tom Hanks) – a lawyer who is fired from his law firm when the firm's partners discover that he has AIDS. The partners, however, do no admit that they have fired Beckett because of his medical condition and attempt to disguise the dismissal with accusations of work incompetence. The rest of the film portrays Beckett's legal battle with the firm to gain compensation for unfair dismissal.

Although *Philadelphia* demonstrates many admirable qualities in its attempt to portray a delicate issue, it also inadvertently helps to support many of the cultural prejudices or AIDS myths. Firstly, the film does little to challenge the misnomer of AIDS as a gay disease. Andy Beckett is gay identified and the film implies that the main reason Beckett was fired was homophobia and not AIDS-phobia. As Dennis Allen suggests, *Philadelphia* emphasises 'the lesion as the symbol of homosexuality' (1995: 624) throughout its narrative. The film, therefore, confuses two prejudices and, in doing so, implicitly conflates homosexuality with AIDS.

Secondly, films such as *Philadelphia*, *Longtime Companion* and *It's My Party* link AIDS to promiscuity or public sex. During one of the courtroom scenes in *Philadelphia*, counsel implies that Beckett contracted the HIV virus during a casual fuck in a gay porno cinema. This casual encounter occurred around 1984/85 and Beckett admits that, at that time, he was unaware of how HIV was transmitted or that it led to a fatal condition. *Longtime Companion* makes the issue even more explicit by representing only the monogamous couple as uninfected and healthy by the end of the film.

In this respect, the films imply that AIDS is a form of punishment of plague for disreputable (gay) behaviour. *Philadelphia* inadvertently emphasises this in the scene where Beckett is asked to unbutton his shirt in the courtroom to reveal the K.S. lesions on his torso (discussed in greater detail below). One of the partners of the law firm remarks that Beckett 'brought this on himself' and the implication is that the partner is not simply referring to the courtroom degradation that Beckett, through seeking compensation, has arguably brought upon himself but to Beckett's medical condition itself which is supposedly the result of his promiscuity. Although 'brought this on himself' is uttered by a villain of the film, the narrative does little to dispute the logic of the statement.

Therefore, it could be argued that a film like *Philadelphia* is inherently homophobic or, at least, can fuel a homophobic interpretation. Rather than inspiring sympathy and understanding for the PWA, *Philadelphia* simply represents a gay monster who, through his own fault, has brought a terrible disease upon himself and, like all monsters, is conveniently dead by the end of the film.

This issue of 'monstrousness' is a key aspect in the AIDS awareness melodramas as it could be argued that they support one of the biggest misconceptions about AIDS: collapsing the virus with the most horrific of the possible secondary infections. All these films focus upon the opportunistic infections that disfigure the body rather than attempting to represent the ubiquitous presence of the virus itself. Indeed one of the most disturbing aspects of these films is that they usually emphasise the disfigured body of the PWA and, in doing so, often degrade the person. The spectator doesn't see a person, merely a monstrous, disfigured body. *Our Sons*, *It's My Party* and *Philadelphia* all document the disfigurement brought about by AIDS, focusing in particular on the horrific K.S. lesions.

Susan Sontag argues that the most terrifying illnesses are those which jeopardise physical beauty. While cholera may have killed fewer people in Western Europe in the nineteenth century than smallpox, it was more feared because of the suddenness with which it struck and the indignity of its symptoms:

Fulminant diarrhoea and vomiting, whose result anticipated the horror of post-mortem decomposition. Within several hours radical dehydration shrank the patient into a wizened caricature of his or her former self, the skin turned bluish-black (overwhelming, transfixing fear is still, in French, *une peur bleue*), the body became cold; death followed the same day or soon after.

(1991: 125)

Sontag points out that the most feared illnesses are those which strike the face as, in contrast to the body, the face represents not only the expression of the mind, heart and soul but is also inextricably connected to Western culture's theories of beauty and sexual appreciation (ibid.). As Sontag explains, devotional art with its representations of saints crucified may represent the body as wracked or tortured but the face is usually serene as it gazes up to heaven 'not registering pain or fear; already elsewhere' (ibid.: 126).

This ruination of the face and physical attractiveness is emblazoned on the screen in a particularly chilling scene in *It's My Party* where Brandon (one of the lead characters) recalls, through a series of flashbacks, how a friend committed suicide during the final stages of AIDS. The first flashback represents the friend while in the blossom of gay, Aryan youth with tan and gym-buffed muscles. This image is then immediately juxtaposed with the image of the boy as a cadaverous, grey AIDS victim. The camera, identifying with Brandon's viewpoint, explores in close up, the horrific lesions now savaging the boy's original beauty.

Arguably the most savage and dehumanising representation of a Person With AIDS is the courtroom scene in *Philadelphia* where Beckett is asked to unbutton his shirt to reveal his skeletal torso cluttered with K.S. lesions. The scene employs the editing conventions of horror films as the moment of revelation if momentarily delayed so the spectator can see the courtroom's horrified reaction, inciting the imagination to depths of horror, before finally revealing the actual representation. Throughout the scene the camera takes Beckett's point of view and the spectator sees the courtroom gasping in horror at Beckett's appearance and, when the spectator eventually sees the monstrous spectacle of the K.S. lesions, it is in a mirror reflection. Beckett is forced to confront his own monstrosity in the mirror image.

Films such as *Philadelphia* and *It's My Party* demonstrate the tightrope line which must be walked when representing AIDS. Although it is important to represent the horror of the syndrome, the filmmaker often renders a medical condition visible by focusing on opportunistic infections and, in doing so, can dehumanise the subject and rob him of dignity. Understandably, AIDS activists have attacked photographic portraits of AIDS victims, 'noting how they strip their subjects of dignity and take pleasure in bringing to light visible evidence of the invisible virus in, say, the lesions of Karposi's Sarcoma' (Paul Julian Smith, 1993: 18).

However, while the majority of AIDS awareness melodramas represent the condition *as* the secondary infections, another alternative is to challenge all the prejudices and misconceptions through humour. This was the approach employed in *Jeffrey* (1994) – a successful film developed from Paul Rudnick's hugely popular off-Broadway play. It tells the story of Jeffrey, a gay man living in contemporary New York, who decides that he will give up sex because he can't face either the worry of contracting HIV or becoming emotionally involved with someone HIV+ who might become sick. However, Jeffrey's plan of celibacy is disrupted when he falls for Steve. Unfortunately Jeffrey also learns that Steve is HIV+. The rest of the play/film is an often hilarious trip through self-help evangelist groups, Gay Pride marches and fantasy dream sequences as Jeffrey, in fear of becoming involved with someone who might become sick, tries to suppress his feelings for Steve.

Edmund White warns against representing AIDS with humour, stating that 'humour suggests that AIDS is just another calamity to befall Mother Camp' (quoted in Baker, 1994: 205). Although the use of humour to represent disease is not a new invention (Renaissance dramas from Fletcher and Beaumont to Shakespeare abound with puns upon different venereal diseases) this method of representation always seems to evade the issue by evading the seriousness. *Jeffrey* offers the spectator a surreal vision of AIDS wracked, 1990s New York life and employs distancing effects such as the inclusion of Mother Theresa and freeze frame action. Yet Alan Sinfield correctly suggests that one of the main problems with *Jeffrey* is the way Jeffrey, reluctant to become involved with someone who is HIV+, is virtually bullied into dating Steve through peer pressure (Sinfield, 1998: 100 and 1999: 320). This is not a satisfactory way of addressing the delicate relations between positive and negative men.

Even more dissatisfying is the way *Jeffrey* retreats into a fantasy ending. When Jeffrey finally articulates that he wants to be Steve's boyfriend they enjoy a surreal dinner date (Mother Theresa is the cocktail bar pianist and the presence of AIDS is represented metaphorically through candles and red balloons). By the conclusion of the film, both Jeffrey and Steve toss a red balloon around the room before eventually flicking it away altogether. AIDS, however, cannot simply be flicked away like the red balloon. Steve may become sick in the near or distant future and although Jeffrey offers a very comforting fantasy it cheats the spectator and side-steps the issue.

The third problem with representing AIDS is that, rather than degrade the subject or trivialise the issue with humour, the filmmaker can eroticise or glamorise the condition. AIDS can be as fashionable as consumption; the new bohemian disease as evidenced in the musical *Rent*, based on the libretto of Puccini's opera *La Bohème*. Indeed Thomas Waugh suggests that in a lot of AIDS dramas 'the person with AIDS is shown not only as sexual but also in several instances as downright sexy [...] The buddy protagonist of *Buddies* is seen more often in his underwear in the single film than Clara Bow was in her entire career' (Waugh, 2000: 223).

This was a criticism levelled at Collard's *Les Nuits Fauves* which represented the bisexual (anti)hero Jean (played by Collard himself) as extremely sexy and attractive. Not only does Jean fuck Laura without a condom (without telling her that he's seropositive) but, after he does tell her, she *still* wants to have unprotected sex. Arguably, such imagery only serves to emphasise the eroticism of risk and implies that AIDS is not only glamorous but very sexy. Unsurprisingly, critics such as Simon Watney (1993b) and Paul Julian Smith (1993) were critical of *Les Nuits Fauves*, with Smith drawing attention to Collard's 'narcissistic disavowal' (1993: 18).

Jarman's cinema, however, offers an alternative to these representations by avoiding the issue of the body of the PWA but without either resorting to breezy humour or glamorising the condition.

AIDS in Jarman's Cinema

As all of the AIDS awareness films analysed so far demonstrate, there is a problem with representing AIDS. Not only do these films inadvertently support many of the AIDS myths (such as AIDS is a 'gay' disease, AIDS as a punishment for promiscuity) but they represent the virus only in terms of the grotesque secondary infections which may attack the body. In doing so they either risk dehumanising the subject and rendering him/her monstrous or else they sidestep the issue with humour or by glamorising the condition.

Jarman's representation is extremely different in that his cinema manages to evoke a sense of the virus's ubiquitous threat without focusing on the secondary infections which attack the body. Jarman's cinema therefore avoids re-emphasising the cultural misconceptions of AIDS but, remarkably, also evokes a sense of the body without featuring the body itself.

Sinfield has pointed out that most artistic representations of AIDS have, with few exceptions, been American (1998: 90-91; 1999: 328). Britain has not (yet?) experienced the tidal wave of the AIDS pandemic and so the British artistic response has been rather more muted. This, however, is not relevant to Jarman as he is one of the few artists addressing the issue of AIDS while himself being a PWA. Writing about Hollywood representations Jarman said:

> No 90 minutes could deal with the 8 years HIV takes to get its host. Hollywood can only sentimentalise it, it would all take place in some well-heeled west-coast beach hut – the reality would drive the audience out of the cinema [...] Even documentaries cannot tell you of the constant, all consuming nagging, of the aches and pains. How many times I've stopped to touch my inflamed face even while writing this page, there's nothing grand about it, no opera here, just the daily grind in a minor key.
>
> (2000: 290)

Therefore, as can only be expected, Jarman's films approach the issue of representing AIDS in a subtle fashion. Instead of representing the syndrome as a concoction of possible symptoms wracking a body, Jarman's films are invested with a sense of the insidious and ubiquitous threat of the virus.

Firstly, red images can be traced throughout Jarman's films but most notably in *Edward II*. The colour features in nearly every scene and is picked up in Isabella's dresses, in Gaveston's shirt, in the lighting during the card scene and, even in the Annie Lennox scene where everything has a blanched, heavenly colour, there is still the burning red lip stain on Lennox's lips. The effect of this is to suggest the ubiquitous threat of the virus rather than condensing the condition into one quantifiable group of specific infected bodies. AIDS is always a lurking threat in the film, something colouring every scene with its lurking presence.

Edward II, however, makes this imagery even more explicit by representing blood as a dominant image within the film. Gaveston and Spencer are beaten to bloody pulps while Edward and Spencer coat themselves in blood before dealing with Gaveston's murderer. Therefore the emphasis is, correctly, upon AIDS as blood disease rather than an STD. This threat of AIDS as a blood contagion is emphasised most violently in the scene where Isabella shreds Kent's jugular with her vampire fangs thus affirming the idea of a lethal contagion transferred through blood. The scene also challenges the vampire slurs that have been levelled at gay men. In *Edward II*, it is the campily feminine Isabella who is the sexually voracious vampire (Isabella's insatiable heterosexuality has already been emphasised cruelly in the scene where she cannot resist Gaveston's flirtations). Isabella's vamprisim, emphasises that the pandemic is not a gay plague but a lethal, blood contagion.

In Chapter 5 I attempted to defend the understandable criticisms of misogyny which Isabella's vampirism has inspired, by suggesting that the scene denotes gender transgression. Kent becomes the penetrable, leaky, abject body who is fucked by Isabella's fangs. In this respect the scene offers a queer image which not only challenges the gender dichotomies but disturbs the idea of a sexual identity as well. In the midst of the AIDS pandemic the idea of a gay or straight sexual identity politics becomes curiously redundant. Many people do not think of their identity in terms of *how* they have sex rather than *with whom*. Indeed Jonathan Dollimore even speculates that eventually, if an AIDS vaccine cannot be developed, 'it may even be that a 'straight' and 'gay' pair doing penetrative sex might be classified as more alike than (for example) two gay pairs in which one is doing penetrative sex and the other is not' (2001: 18). Jarman's vampire scene emphasises that there is little benefit gained from a 'sexual identity' when there is a constant risk of a pandemic transferred through blood or sexual fluids. Ironically it has taken a lethal syndrome like AIDS to mobilise queer theory's insistence upon the futility of sexual taxonomies.

This image of the 'death fuck' is then echoed later in Edward's nightmare where he dreams of his execution – having a red-hot poker shoved up his ass as his face blazes scarlet (another red image) and he howls in agony. The scene is one of the most brutal in the film and draws very obvious connections between penetrative sex and AIDS related death. Yet Jarman softens the blow of this image by representing it only as a dream. In the narrative, Edward does not actually die as the gaoler Lightborn throws the poker into the water and kisses Edward softly on the lips. This is one of the most sentimental images in Jarman's canon and, arguably, one of the weakest. It can be read as replacing sexual desire with saccharine love – as Larry Kramer advocated in dramas such as *The Normal Heart*. Yet this image is the companion scene to Isabella's vampirism. The connecting thread is Lightborn, whom Isabella had previously tried to seduce with a kiss but who rejected her advances. Now Lightborn tenderly kisses Edward instead.

The effect of such imagery is Jarman's queer resignification of gay clichés. Isabella is a metaphor for heterosexuality which is represented as being all the things normally associated with homosexuality – depravity, insatiability and violence. Lightborn, on the other hand, is a metaphor for homosexuality but is represented as the very opposite. Yet such imagery is not simply a petulant challenge to gay slurs but, given the AIDS metaphors contained in every scene, is an emphasis of the danger of *sexual acts* rather than the importance of *sexual identifications*. Jarman's imagery insists that AIDS cannot be considered a gay disease but correctly affirms that it is a blood disease transferred through specific acts which exchange bodily fluids.

Interestingly, this 'blood metaphor' also appears in Jarman's earlier work *Caravaggio*. *Caravaggio* predates Jarman's positive HIV test, yet the fear of the disease was presumably haunting Jarman, as it was a sexually active gay man in the mid eighties. *Caravaggio* offers two similar scenes in which the characters penetrate each other's bodies and exchange blood. In the early fight scene Ranuccio stabs Michele who then smears his blood across Ranuccio's face and declares them both to be 'blood brothers'. Then, in the film's climax, Michele slashes Ranuccio's throat who, in return, wipes his blood across Michele's face before falling limp into Michele's arms. Both scenes testify to the threat of death in the midst of a contagion transferred through fluids or can also be read as emblematic of Jarman's interest in sadomasochistic eroticism, especially given than both scenes are preceded by Ranuccio's wicked grin, as if in anticipation of the pleasure of sexualised violence.

However, both scenes feature a salient symbol of the film's imagery: Michele's knife. The knife is both a symbol of death – Michele eventually uses it to slash Ranuccio's throat – but, paradoxically, it is also a symbol of life. Michele, in two scenes, uses his knife to aid his painting by both scratching an arc on his canvas and also using his blade to apply thick, impasto paint. Michele, at one point, remarks that his painting has captured 'pure spirit in matter'. In other words, he has captured a life force/essence in his inanimate painting. Therefore Leo Bersani and Ulysse Dutoit argue that the film demonstrates how, 'sexuality is the self-lacerating passage from life to death, from images of phenomena to 'pure spirit' hidden in art' (1999: 75).

Yet the curious aspect about *Caravaggio* is that the film does not so much evoke a sense of life in death but the concept of corporeal transcendence – sexuality as liberation rather than annihilation. The male body dominates the film in the same way it does in Caravaggio's art. Michele paints while shirtless and his flesh – moist with sweat – glistens in his sultry studio. The muscles and sinews of the actual Caravaggio paintings are sculpted with the most intense chiaroscuro so that his art is almost a surgical analysis of the body or a sense of penetrating deep within the body's very fibres. This sense of penetration is emphasised by Michele actually stabbing his art with his knife. Yet it is only through this sense of death – of penetration of the body – that a sense of transcending the confines of the body is achieved. Caravaggio's art is both the 'pure spirit' and also 'matter' – as if through ravaging the physical the artist can achieve a sense of oblivion within the physical. Whether we term this a sense of 'death or in life' or a spiritual transcendence it is emblematic of a release from the confines of the body. The images testify that sexuality (especially in the midst of the AIDS contagion) is not linked to death but a sense of life-in-death. We can, however, only speculate that this philosophy was providing a reassuring fantasy for Jarman at a time in his life when he suspected his seropositive status. Yet these themes, which are implied in *Caravaggio*, become major concerns in Jarman's later works *The Garden* and *Blue*.

The Garden is more hermetic than *Edward II* or *Caravaggio*. It offers clandestine references to AIDS throughout but is also famous for containing some of the most violent scenes which Jarman ever created. At the end of the film it is obvious that there is another threat upon the garden other than the harassment by the church and the military. The queer lovers, who in the previous scene lay dead from crucifixion, carry burning torches to join the figures seated at yet another parody of The Last Supper (a motif which has occurred throughout the film). All the figures hold small candles upon their heads and the scene echoes the torchlight parades which are often held in major cities on AIDS Awareness Day. This scene is immediately followed by an image of still, blood-red liquid thus linking crucifixion – the most horrible of deaths – with that of AIDS.[1] The Biblical analogy then continues as Michael Gough reads Jarman's poem, 'I walk in this garden':

> I walk in this garden holding the hands of dead friends
> Old age came quickly for my frosted generation.
> Cold, Cold, they died so silently.
> Did the forgotten generation scream
> Or go full of resignation, quietly protesting their innocence
> Cold, Cold, they died.
> We linked hands at four a.m deep under the city.
> You slept on; never heard the sweet flesh song.
> I have no words.
> My shaking hands can not express this fury.
> Sadness is all I have.
> No words.
> Matthew fucked Mark, fucked Luke, fucked John
> Who lay in the bed that I lie on.
> Touch fingers again as you sing this song.
> Cold, cold, they died.
> Sweet garden of vanished pleasures
> Come back next year.

The poem has a Poe-like quality in its haunting refrain but, undoubtedly, its most striking image is the Apostles of Christ 'gang-banging' each other on the bed which the speaker now occupies. Understandably, various critics interpreted this as tastelessly blasphemous. Although throughout *The Garden* a parallel has been drawn between the queer lovers and the life of Christ, exposing the 'queer' (used in its broadest sense) or non-normative life which Jesus and his disciples led as they rejected traditional, heterocentrist society, the final stanza links the idea of sex and death within the matrix of Christian belief.

The core of Christian faith is exemplified in the Eucharist when Christians receive bread/wafers and wine, symbolising the body and blood of Christ which have been broken and shed for mortals' salvation. By receiving these gifts Christians believe they will attain eternal *spiritual* life. The road to salvation is therefore found within the flesh. The vampire myth is, of course, the Christian doctrine reversed as eating *actual* flesh and drinking actual blood promotes an eternal life of the flesh but an annihilation of the spirit or soul. In Jarman's representations, however, it is the absorption of the flesh, through sexual union, which leads to spiritual transcendence. Sexual union – partaking of someone else's flesh – leads not to a corporeal immortality but a liberation of the soul or spirit for the Biblical apostles who have now attained the Christian supremacy of being in the garden. These themes of transcendence and the relationship between body and spirit are developed more fully in Jarman's last feature: *Blue*.

Blue

I have tried to point out that there is a difficulty in representing AIDS. The syndrome has been portrayed as synonymous with the range of possible opportunistic infections and representations have focused on the body, not only rendering the body abject from hegemonic society but consolidating the already existing links between gay sex and death. AIDS has been viewed in terms of quantitative, public fucking and those who test positive have supposedly brought it upon themselves. Artistic representations have attempted to challenge these prejudices directly but have often resulted, inadvertently, in re-enforcing many of the AIDS myths or else have breached artistic integrity by retreating into fantasy endings or unduly eroticising the positive bodies in order to overthrow the stereotyped spectre of monstrosity.

Jarman's films, by contrast, raise the subject more subtly by featuring AIDS metaphors throughout the narrative. *Blue*, however, is devoted entirely to AIDS and its effects. Jarman was nearly blind when he made the film and so only one visual metaphor is used throughout the film: the blue screen. Although Jarman's cinema is only ever slightly indebted to traditional filmmaking techniques, *Blue* goes even further and breaks every traditional cinematic code. Even more than the other Jarman films, *Blue* draws upon the legacy of modern art and, for the entire duration of the film, the cinema screen is a virtual colour field painting reminiscent of the huge canvases of Abstract Expressionism.

Like all artists studying at the Slade, Jarman would have been required to research the techniques and philosophies of the abstract expressionists – notably Barnett Newman, Jackson Pollock, Robert Motherwell, Franz Kline and Mark Rothko. Abstract Expressionism, perhaps more than any other movement, epitomised the Clement Greenberg concept of modern art which sought to 'purify' the properties of the art form (see Chapter 2 'Queer Cinema'). For Greenberg, modern art should surrender to the exclusivity of its own physical medium. The spectator was supposed to lose himself in the vast colour field painting and experience a sense of transcendence.

At its best, Abstract Expressionism suggested transcendence and spirituality. The paintings confronted the existentialist dilemma of being and death – the terrifying sense of oblivion or nothingness in life – but yet the spectator should lose himself in the enormous, monochromatic colour field and achieve a sense of universal transcendence. More than any other movement, Abstract Expressionism represented modernist detachment – a detachment which is free from the threat of being shivered by aesthetic manipulation.

Originally 'aesthetics' referred to sensual, bodily reactions although its public perception has been cluttered by notions of effeteness or 'artistic sensibility' by such cultural icons as Oscar Wilde. The sensual bodily reaction, which the spectator experiences from a work of art, is an aesthetic response. When we see a 'beautiful' object we try to ascribe beauty to it as something inherent. Yet when our judgement is questioned we always retreat into the defence of 'it is beautiful – to me'. As Terry Eagleton has famously summarised, 'aesthetics is born as a discourse of the body' (1990: 13) and so something looks beautiful, sounds beautiful or tastes/smells beautiful. From this stems the medical 'an-aesthetic' which dulls the corporeal senses.

The colour field painting of Abstract Expressionism supposedly frees the spectator from aesthetic reaction as it contains no element of representation. The eye is simply flooded with colour and the senses drown. This is, of course, a stolidly masculine discourse as the body is epistemologically construed as feminine. The truly masculine subject is therefore one which transcends the constraining senses of the body. A colour field painting supposedly facilitates this transcendence so that the spirit can become lost within the huge, colour field painting. This is the phallic fantasy of the Kantian sublime which, as Susan Buck Morss summarises:

> Kant's transcendental subject purges himself of the senses which endanger autonomy not only because they unavoidably entangle him in the world, but, specifically, because they make him passive [...] instead of active.
>
> (1992: 9)

Indeed, Abstract Expressionism has even been linked to ideas of autogenesis as the male subject loses his present body within the colour field and attains a psychic rebirth. It is therefore not at all ironic that colour field paintings, despite their modernist detachment and valiant refusal of commoditization, often became the property of Wall Street offices – that most masculine of environments – as their size suited a boardroom wall. In this respect they became fetishized aspects of commodity rather than commodity in its original guise. Therefore, as Eva Cockcroft famously pointed out, Abstract Expressionism, precisely because it claimed to be purely abstract art, became the ideal weapon of the American Cold War (Cockcroft, 1992: 89). By giving their painting an individualist emphasis and eliminating recognisable subject-matter, the Abstract Expressionists succeeded in creating an important new art movement. They also contributed, whether they knew it or not, to a political phenomenon as the supposed divorce between art and politics served America's needs in the cold war.

However, the artist who satirised Abstract Expressionism was Yves Klein who, together with Pierro Manzoni and Andy Warhol, can be seen as representative in the shift toward postmodernity. In the field of fine art, postmodernism can be distinguished from the Greenbergian definitions of modernism in its belief that there is actually nothing for art to reflect (we live in a world of hyper-reality) so the modernist canon of 'art which calls attention to art itself' is irrelevant. There is no actual reality which is not, in some way, a form of representation anyway. While 'Abstract Expressionists wanted to erase the past and invent an original culture' (Shapiro and Shapiro, 1990: 9), postmodernism maintained an ironic stance against the very idea of changing the world as the world itself can be read as nothing more than a fiction or reassuring fantasy or myth. Therefore postmodern art, exemplified by Warhol, did not seek to free the spectator from the confines of the body but sought to an-aesthetise the body through the frantic proliferation of modern day images. For example, one of Warhol's most famous silk screen canvases shows a repetition of the electric chair washed with a pretty colour. As the spectator gazes on Warhol's repetitive images of the electric chair, she/he is de-sensitised to one of the most horrific inventions of the twentieth century. At the heart of such imagery is a dystopian pessimism as the spectator is not asked to enter sublimity but to simply suffer an aesthetic suffocation.

Yves Klein, however, does not offer Warhol's dystopia or Manzoni's intense cynicism (Manzoni is famous for selling cans of 'artist's shit' for huge sums of money) but reconfigures the idea of the body and representation within the swirl of postmodernism. Although Klein's blue colour field canvases have the look of Abstract Expressionism (notably Barnett Newman) they are subtly different. On an immediate level, Klein's canvases are curiously sensual and glisten with a voluptuous paint which Klein manufactured using a resin called 'rhodopas' which bound pigments without dulling their luminosity. This paint - 'International Klein Blue' or 'IKB' — eventually developed sexual connotations from Klein's performance art pieces where he had his nubile and pliant female nudes coat themselves in blue paint and writhe around on the canvas. Historically, the colour blue has held connotations of purity as the Madonna's robes were conventionally always blue as seen in paintings from Perugino to Raphael. Klein, however, was subverting this, so although he creates a painting which seems to offer a transcendence of the body, it is simultaneously affirming the sexualised body. Writing about Klein's now infamous anthropometries (his performance art pieces with the female nudes), Sidra Stich suggests that:

> Klein thus focuses attention on the core of the body, the locus of bodily functions that lies outside the control of the conscious mind. Once again, there is a displacement from mind to body, from intellect to sensibility. The body is made manifest as the vital and vitalizing center of human existence.
>
> (1995: 175)

As can be seen in all of Jarman's features, this making the body 'manifest as the vital and vitalizing centre of human existence' appealed to his sensibilities. Michael O'Pray points out that the very title of *Blue* is intended to be a sexual pun as well:

> There was little doubt that he was playing with the double meaning of the word 'blue' as he was also enthusiastic at the time to make *Edward II* a 'blue' film with explicit sex in an almost pantomime rendering of the tragedy.
>
> (1996: 201)

Therefore, like Klein's work, *Blue* was not offering the 'dispassionate sensibility' (Porton, 1996: 150) or modernism but, as Peter Wollen suggests, is 'intensely sensual' (2000: 124), despite avoiding the representation of the physical body. While the IKB colour and the title carry sexual connotations, the film conveys all the resonances of the body without actually having to represent the body on screen. As Paul Julian Smith suggests, 'Jarman brilliantly eludes the double bind of representing AIDS – bearing witness to illness but avoiding...the invasive intrusions of the documentary gaze. We learn to stop looking and start listening instead' (1993: 19).

The opening lines of the film emphasise the physical as the narrator reports a near collision with a cyclist:

I step off the kerb and a cyclist nearly knocks me down.
Flying in from the dark he nearly parted my hair.

Yet later the film asserts that 'Blue transcends the solemn geography of human limits' as the IKB monochrome facilitates a transcendence of the corporeal and an absorption into a world of pure spirit. Rather than show gruelling images of bodies ravaged by the disease and avoid the inevitable sentimentality, Jarman addresses the question of representation itself. The film echoes the ambivalent title of the queer cinema anthology 'How Do I Look?' as the question refers not only to *how* the spectator should look at the image of the continuous blue screen but also suggests the invisibility which queers, especially queer men with AIDS, experience. One of *Blue*'s narrators asks 'How are we perceived, if we are perceived at all? For the most part we are invisible'. Asking 'How Do I Look?' is only necessary because the queer subject – especially one suffering from AIDS – is invisible and is therefore denied subjectivity and relegated to the abject status of PWA.

However, by not representing the body, *Blue* uses the colour field as a metaphor (O'Pray, 1996: 206). In this respect, although the film may attempt to transcend corporeality, the spectator is not drawn into an existential void of modernism, wherein the masculine intellect is separated from the uncontrolled body, but is instead focused on the issue of postmodern identifications in relation to AIDS. The omnipresent blue screen can be read as a metaphor for the ubiquitous threat of AIDS which therefore makes other sexual identification politics redundant. The film suggests this by featuring a weird chant or queer voices all expressing cultural, political, sexual and gender paradoxes:

I am a mannish
Muff-diving
Size queen
I am a cock-sucking
Straight acting

Lesbian man
With ball crushing bad manners

The chant suggests that identity, in light of the AIDS pandemic, is now fragmented into a myriad of revolving performative identifications. The last threat of unity is only provided, sadly, by the crisis of AIDS. As Lee Edelman argues, 'queer and AIDS are interconnected, because each is articulated through a postmodernist understanding of the death of the subject and both understand identity as a curiously ambivalent site' (1994: 96). *Blue* emphasises this even further by the way the term 'blue' itself shifts in meaning throughout the film. Sometimes 'blue' is a character, sometimes a metaphor, sometimes an emotional state. The film signifies the death of an established (sexual) identity in the midst of the pandemic and insists that alternative forms of identification make more strategic sense.

In many ways *Blue* seems to mobilise the paradoxical politics of synthesising individuality with group collectivity. The film does not insist upon the auto-destructive identity category of 'PWA' but instead stresses the ubiquitous threat of the virus. As Smith suggests, 'released from the image which is, *Blue* tells us, 'the prison of the soul', new and disturbing identities proliferate and are projected onto the blank, blue screen' (1993: 19).

Blue is undeniably one of Jarman's most accomplished films. It seems to address insurmountable difficulties but foregrounding the spiritual while maintaining a sense of the corporeal. In many ways it signifies how Jarman's canon has evolved full circle. While the early works, such as *Sebastiane*, were often baroque, *Blue* is minimalist and controlled. Most importantly, the issue of the body, foregrounded to such an extreme in *Sebastiane*, now becomes something implied through means other than visual representation.

Surprisingly, given the degree of physical trauma which Jarman was suffering when he made the film, *Blue* is also one of his most tranquil films. It is ironic that the turmoil of AIDS led to a film of such unique beauty. *Blue* does not emphasise the death of the subject through sexual activity but instead stresses the exaltation of the spirit through love. In many ways the film is the summation of what Jarman has been trying to achieve throughout all his films: desire and love configured beyond the confines of the essentialist, physical subject, the separation of desire from gender and the dissolution of fixed identity. Perhaps the final comment should be Bersani and Dutoit's who assert that *Blue* does not simply offer a sense of bogus sublimity, not a mediation on death. Instead the film asserts the very opposite and offers 'a kind of liberating spirituality in life' (1999: 74).

Note

1. In the 'AIDS awareness melodrama' *It's My Party*, Nick (the protagonist dying of AIDS) dedicates a wall of his house to photographs of all his friends who have died of AIDS. The wall consists of photographs of the dead friends arranged around a sculpture of Christ crucified. Sontag (1991: 126) points out that only in images of Christ do we see complete and utter suffering which expressed not only through the body but through the face.

CONCLUSION

In 1998, Matthew Shepard, a 21 year-old gay student from Laramie Wyoming, was pistol whipped by two homophobic men and left tied to a fence. He was discovered, eighteen hours later, by a passing cyclist and was rushed to hospital. Shepard later died. Such horrendous displays of homophobic violence hardly suggest that homophobia is subsiding or that the need for queer militancy has gone. If anything, such open and violent manifestations of hatred only serve to emphasise that homophobia still blazes throughout the Western World and that militant action is required. More importantly, for academic scholars of sexualities, such terrifying examples of homophobia do little to support the political relevance of the abstract debates known as 'queer theory'. What is the political use of theorising sexuality as a performative effect when queer identified students are being pistol whipped to death?

Therefore, for many 'queer' identified people, the immediate response which the Shepard murder inspires, is a desire for more aggressive identity politics. Gays appalled by Shepard's murder would understandably want to proclaim that 'gay is good' and scream other slogans of gay pride in the face of their oppressors. Indeed, most people would feel inspired to initiate extreme forms of queer political action – the 'bash-back' approach of those that have been hurt and so will hurt others in return. Yet the efficacy of such political action is debatable. Queer may understandably wish to 'bash-back' but is 'bashing' really a suitable approach towards a fellow human being and, more importantly, does it actually achieve anything?

These issues undoubtedly influence any queer identified artist attempting to make queer-themed images. On the one hand the artist may be driven by his political rage and heterophobia. After all, identifying as queer – with all its connotations of shame and indignity – is nothing if not a political action. The queer artist may feel that making aggressive images of queer militancy will stir the spectators to 'OutRage' and inspire political action. Queers don't want to be merely tolerated and, in order to achieve their goals, they will bludgeon everyone with slogans of queer pride.

Yet on the other hand, the artist is driven by his/her own personal vision. In the case of queer-themed work the artist may be intrigued by the psycho-social dimensions of sexuality, especially the all consuming power of desire and the way in which it may be a 'dangerous' solvent of seemingly stable identities.

This book has argued that the most intriguing aspects of Jarman's work arise from the tension between his personal artistic vision and his burning, political activism. Throughout the chapters, I have argued that Jarman's films should not simply be read as retaliatory political slogans which are supposed to stir the spectator to 'OutRage'. Instead Jarman's cinema has wrestled with the tension between rage-fuelled activism and 'queer' as a philosophical theory.

The rage and stalwart political activism is evident throughout Jarman's work. Yet rage can only achieve so much and 'challenges' can only challenge for a certain period of time. Although activism fuels the narrative of many of Jarman's most famous films, this often only succeeds in trapping the queer heroes within the crippling position of victimhood. The homophobes may inspire disgust but the heroes often inspire little more than pity.

Therefore, this book has not focused on Jarman's representation of political activism but on his broader examination of the philosophical and cultural debates of queer. In doing so it has attempted to widen the debates on Jarman's cinema and augment the existing body of writing which has often simply praised Jarman's cinema because of its political resistance. Throughout all the chapters the readings have been influenced by the tension which exists (and, for the foreseeable future, probably always will exist) between queer theory and activism. While theory attempts to deconstruct the monolith of heterosexuality by exposing incoherencies in the sex, gender, sexuality matrix, activism is fuelled by a sense of petulant retaliation. Jarman's films evidence the same tension. There is a blazing desire to 'bash back' but yet the sub-textual themes of Jarman's work (such as his examination of alternative paradigms of gender, re-examination of subjectivity and the prescription of sexuality/desire to the gendered body) offer a more intriguing 'queer' dimension.

Chapters 3 and 4 have analysed the dominant 'types' of male heroes represented throughout Jarman's cinema, arguing that Jarman never represents bodies simply to appeal to gay tastes or excite the reveries of a gay identified spectator. Instead his cinema constantly questions how culture attempts to prescribe sexual desire to the gendered body. As is evidenced in *Caravaggio*, *Sebastiane*, *The Garden*, and *The Angelic Conversation*, Jarman's images are as much interested in interrogating the basis of sexual attraction as re-inforcing conventional ideas of gender based sexuality.

However, while Jarman's cinema constantly questions the idea of sexuality circumscribed by gender, his images also interrogate the concept of traditional masculinity. Jarman's constant foregrounding of submissive, masochistic male bodies (from Sebastian to Caravaggio to King Edward) forces the spectator to question how culture maintains paradigms of masculinity. In many ways, therefore, Jarman's cinema is an exploration of the images of masculinity which have dominated gay culture. Throughout his films the images re-evaluate the body as it has been prescribed by cultural traditions. His male masochists challenge normative masculinity while his rough trade boys question the identifications of 'gay' and 'straight' and their relation to class and social mobility. Therefore, what we find in Jarman's cinema is not simply the eroticisation of bodies but the idea of sexual desire as something more than the body; sexuality not prescribed by the traditionally gendered body.

Chapter 4 was an analysis of Jarman's representation of the female body and an attempt to defend accusations of 'gay male misogyny' levelled at his work. Examining Jarman's representation of Tilda Swinton's body, the chapter argued that Jarman was not simply conforming to stereotypical gay male misogyny and representing a monstrous woman against which the gay male heroes could define their masculinity. Instead Jarman was using Swinton's famous androgyny and her command of Brechtian acting style in order to expose a distance between femininity, as stylization, masquerade and artifice, and the body of Swinton the actor beneath the performance. In this respect the chapter developed themes raised in the previous chapters: the gendering the of the body and how this supports the traditional heterosexual matrix.

Developing this theme, Chapter 5 considered how *The Angelic Conversation* did not represent the female body at all, thus avoiding both the misogyny and gynephobia implicit in the original sonnets but also eliding homosexual and homosocial relations. The chapter argued that the final 'bliss' of the film is a return to the Kristevan inspired concept of the semiotic chora: a time of pre-oedipal, ungendered love. In this respect, *The Angelic Conversation* can be seen to illuminate the theme implicit in all of Jarman's cinema: the tension between desire circumscribed by the body versus desire beyond the gendered body.

Chapter 5 'The Legacy of Jean Genet on Film' was inspired by some passing comments from film critics who described Jarman as 'Saint Genet' (MacCabe, 1991:4) or suggested that 'Jarman's work is illuminated by the world Genet revealed' (Gardner, 1996: 39). The chapter tried to link common themes between the world of Jean Genet, as represented in the films *Un Chant D'Amour* and *Querelle*, and Jarman's cinema, arguing that Jarman is a successor to Genet's 'proto-queer' sensibility. Both Jarman and Genet can be seen to question the political efficacy of conventional identity groups, especially the gay/straight divide. While identity groups offer a recognised gay identity this is still a marginalised identity. Therefore neither Jarman nor Genet are attempting to simply invert traditional equations and render everything which society deems to be abject into something beautiful. Instead their representations emphasize a liberation from the very system of taxonomic equations itself.

Chapter 6 'AIDS and its Metaphors: (Re)Imaging the Syndrome' outlined the cultural prejudices surrounding the AIDS virus (what I termed 'AIDS Myths') and examined the approaches which artists and filmmakers employed in representing the virus. While most mainstream film representations strengthened AIDS prejudices, trivialised the condition or dehumanised the PWA, Jarman approached the issue metaphorically. *Blue* is arguably one of Jarman's most accomplished films and definitely one of the best meditations on the AIDS pandemic. The film manages to surmount the difficulties in representing the virus by maintaining a sense of the 'every day' and the physical through the voice-over narration while avoiding the prickly issue of representing the infected body.

It is sadly ironic that *Blue* – a film devoted entirely to the ravages of AIDS – should actually illuminate so many of the themes implied in

Jarman's earlier work. *Blue* not only questions the relevance of sexual identity politics but it also challenges the very notion of identity itself with 'Blue' being at one point a character and at another time a state of emotion.

Surprisingly, given the fact that Jarman was suffering such extreme ill health at the time of filming, *Blue* does not actually suggest the death of the subject – the clichéd connection between sex and death – but celebrates the joy of the human spirit in love. In many ways, *Blue* can be read as the summation of what Jarman was implying throughout much of his cinema: desire and love configured beyond the confines of the physical subject; the separation of desire from the parameters of gender and the dissolution of fixed identity. In short, Jarman's cinema continually represents alternative paradigms of gender performativity, an examination of the power dynamics implicit in sexual relations and a representation of sexuality which moves in excess of recognised taxonomies and its conventional prescription by the sexed body.

I have asserted in Chapter 1 that I believe 'queer' was unfortunate in happening too early. Academics were introduced to queer theory in the early 1990s and this has fostered some interesting (and on-going) debate. Yet realising these theories in every day life or within artistic representation has been a much more difficult task. Many people were (and still are) struggling with the idea of gay and lesbian identities. What these people did not need in the early 1990s was 'queer' questioning the very concept of identity itself. When disadvantaged groups are in oppressed situations they need stability of identity not mobility. Therefore, without sufficient understanding of what 'queer' was trying to achieve, its politics were often read as those of vanguard militancy and, of course, such aggressive politics can only be sustained for so long. The same is evident in much queer-themed art.

Therefore, shortly after Jarman's death, there was another death, more silent, and less publicly acknowledged, also occurring: the Queer New Wave was floundering. As Ruby Rich describes:

> The New Queer Cinema was a more successful term for a moment than a movement. It was meant to catch the beat of a new kind of film and video-making that was fresh, edgy, low-budget, inventive,

unapologetic, sexy and stylistically daring. The godfather of the movement was the late great Derek Jarman who pronounced himself finally able to connect with an audience thanks to the critical mass of the new films and videos that burned a clearing in the brush.

(2000: 22)

Reviewing recent queer(ish)-themed films such as *Boys Don't Cry* and *The Talented Mr. Ripley*, Rich asks, 'Is either one a New Queer Cinema Product? I think not. If only because no such thing can exist any more' (ibid.: 25).

The promising beginning of the new queer wave faltered almost immediately after the first rush of films. *Swoon* was Kalin's only queer masterpiece, Todd Haynes's *Velvet Goldmine* dealt with gay themes of 'camp' and gender-bending while his recent homage to Douglas Sirk, *Far From Heaven*, is 'queer' only in the sense that its images seek to 'make strange' bourgeois American life or evoke a Brechtian/Sirkian sense of distanciation in the spectator (see Richardson, 2006). Similarly, Gus Van Sant returned to camp sensibility in *To Die For* and most recently effaced his directorial style altogether by remaking, scene by scene, Hitchcock's *Psycho*.

Queer Cinema was unconcerned with positive images. Queerness was not necessarily 'good' or 'bad' it just was. Likewise, the imagery always asserted that sexuality was multiple and not fixed. It took as its premise a politics of anti-identity and attempted to overthrow the established boundaries. However, queer cinema was nothing it not didactic and all its images were inspired by a passionate hatred of the brutal acts of homophobia occurring throughout the Western World. A sense of rage burned throughout all the films.

However, were Jarman still alive today, it is almost certain that he would not have abandoned his unique queer sensibility. What gives Jarman's art its power is the way in which it erodes the boundaries between his personal and artistic life. The personal, political and the artistic are indistinguishable in Jarman's work and his sexuality inflected everything he created. For Jarman, queer was not simply something to shock the public or something to appeal to gay audiences; it was his personal, political and artistic life.

When Brian Sewell dismissed the 1996 retrospective of Jarman's work mounted at the Barbican, stating that 'without the alchemist, there is no alchemy" (*Evening Standard*, 16:5, 1996), he was not only being unfair but inaccurate. Although Jarman saw film as an alchemical conjunction, his art was not simply the meretricious fool's gold of the alchemist. Despite stressing anti-realism, aestheticism and spectacle, below the surface of the 'fool's gold' was art forged from an all consuming political passion and his own personal, artistic vision. Jarman, more than any other director working in the field of Queer Cinema, made films which were personal and true. A cinema inspired by both queer politics and queer poetics.

FILMOGRAPHY

À Bout de Souffle (dir: Jean-Luc Godard, France, 1959)

Alien (dir: Ridley Scott, USA, 1979)

Aliens (dir: James Cameron, USA, 1986)

Angelic Conversation, The (dir: Derek Jarman, UK, 1985)

Bar Girls (dir: Lauren Hoffman, 1994, USA)

Belle de Jour (dir: Luis Bunuel, Italy-France, 1967)

Billy's Hollywood Screen Kiss (dir: Tommy O'Haver, USA, 1998)

Birds, The (dir: Alfred Hitchcock, USA, 1963)

Bitter Tears of Petra Von Kant (dir: Rainer Werner Fassbinder, Germany, 1972)

Blade Runner (dir: Ridley Scott, USA, 1982)

Blue (dir: Derek Jarman, UK, 1993)

Bonnie and Clyde (dir: Arthur Penn, USA, 1967)

Broadway Damage (dir: Victor Mignatti, USA, 2000)

Broken Hearts Club, The (dir: Greg Berlanti, USA, 2000)

Bronenosets Potemkin (Battleship Potemkin) (dir: Sergei Eisenstein, Russia, 1925)

Buddies (dir: Arthur J. Bresson, USA, 1985)

Butch Cassidy and the Sundance Kid (dir: George Roy Hill, USA, 1969)

Camille (dir: George Cukor, USA, 1936)

Caravaggio (dir: Derek Jarman, UK, 1986)

Carrie (dir: Brian de Palma, USA, 1976)

Casablanca (dir: Michael Curtiz, USA, 1943)

Chant d'Amour, Un (dir: Jean Genet, France, 1950)

Chariots of Fire (dir: Hugh Hudson, USA, 1981)

Chien Andalou, Un (dir: Luis Bunuel and Salvador Dali, France, 1928)

Claire of the Moon (dir: Nicole Conn, USA, 1992)

Compulsion (dir: Richard Fleischer, USA, 1959)

Edward II (dir: Derek Jarman, UK, 1991)

Early Frost, An (dir: John Erman, USA, 1985)

Far From Heaven (dir: Todd Haynes, USA, 2003)

Frankie and Johnny (dir: Gary Marshall, USA, 1991)

Garden, The (dir: Derek Jarman, UK, 1990)

Gods and Monsters (dir: Bill Condon, USA, 1998)

Hellraiser (dir: Clive Barker, USA, 1987)

Hours and the Times, The (dir: Christopher Munch, USA, 1992)

Imitation of Life (dir: Douglas Sirk, USA, 1959)

Incredibly True Adventures of Two Girls in Love, The (dir: Maria Maggenti, USA, 1995)

It's My Party (dir: Randall Kleiser, USA, 1993)

Jeffrey (dir: Christopher Ashley, USA, 1994)

Jubilee (dir: Derek Jarman, UK, 1978)

Killing of Sister George, The (dir: Robert Aldrich, UK, 1968)

Last of England, The (dir: Derek Jarman, UK, 1987)

Lethal Weapon (dir: Richard Donner, USA, 1987)

Life and Death of Colonel Blimp, The (dir: Michael Powell and Emeric Pressburger, 1945, UK)

Living End, The (dir: Greg Araki, USA, 1992)

Longtime Companion (dir: Norman René, USA, 1990)

Long Goodbye, The (dir: Robert Altman, USA, 1973)

Love and Death on Long Island (dir: Richard Kwietniowski, UK, 1996)

Making Love (dir: Arthur Hiller, USA, 1982)

Matrix, The (dir: Wachowski Bros., USA, 1999)

My Hustler (dir: Andy Warhol, USA, 1965)

My Own Private Idaho (dir: Gus Van Sant, USA, 1991)

Nuits Fauves, Les (Savage Nights) (dir: Cyril Collard, France, 1993)

Our Sons (dir: John Erman, USA, 1991)

Orlando (dir: Sally Potter, UK, 1993)

Orphée (dir: Jean Cocteau, France, 1950)

Paris is Burning (dir: Jennie Livingston, USA, 1991)

Parting Glances (dir: Bill Sherwood, USA, 1986)

Philadelphia (dir: Johnathon Demme, USA, 1993)

Pierrot Le Jeu (dir: Jean-Luc Goddard, France, 1965)

Poison (dir: Todd Haynes, USA, 1991)

Psycho (dir: Gus Van Sant, USA, 1998)

Querelle (dir: Rainer Werner Fassbinder, Germany, 1982)

Riddle of the Sphinx (dir: Laura Mulvey and Peter Wollen, UK, 1975)

Rope (dir: Alfred Hitchcock, USA, 1948)

Scorpio Rising (dir: Kenneth Anger, USA, 1963)

Sebastiane (dir: Derek Jarman, UK, 1976)

Sleep (dir: Andy Warhol, USA, 1964)

Star Wars (dir: George Lucas, USA, 1977)

Strictly Ballroom (dir: Baz Luhrman, Australia, 1992)

Sunset Boulevard (dir: Billy Wilder, USA, 1950)

Swoon (dir: Tom Kalin, USA, 1992)

Tea and Sympathy (dir: Vincente Minnelli, USA, 1956)

Tempest, The (dir: Derek Jarman, UK, 1979)

Terminator, The (dir: James Cameron, USA, 1984)

Thelma and Louise (dir: Ridley Scott, USA, 1991)

To Die For (dir: Gus Van Sant, USA, 1995)

Tongues Untied (dir: Marlon Riggs, 1991)

Trick (dir: Jim Fall, USA, 1999)

Untouchables, The (dir: Brian de Palma, USA, 1987)

Velvet Goldmine (dir: Todd Haynes, USA, 1998)

War Requiem (dir: Derek Jarman, UK, 1988)

Weekend, Le (dir: Jean-Luc Godard, France, 1967)

Wittgenstein (dir: Derek Jarman, UK, 1993)

Wizard of Oz, The (dir: Victor Fleming and King Vidor, USA, 1939)

BIBLIOGRAPHY

Aaron, Michele (ed.) (2004) *New Queer Cinema: A Critical Reader*
(Edinburgh: Edinburgh University Press).

Abelove, Henry (1993) 'From Thoreau to Queer Politics', *The Yale
Journal of Criticism*, 6:2.

Alderson, David (2000) 'Desire as Nostalgia: the novels of Alan
Hollinghurst' in David Alderson and Linda Anderson (eds.) *Territories
of desire in queer culture: Refiguring contemporary boundaries* (Manchester:
Manchester University Press).

Almaguer, Tomás (1993) 'Chicano Men: A Cartography of Homosexual
Identity and Behaviour' in Abelove *et al.* (eds.) *The Lesbian and Gay
Studies Reader* (New York: Routledge).

Altman, Dennis (1972) *Homosexual Oppression and Liberation* (Sydney:
Angus and Robertson).

Anfam, David (1990) *Abstract Expressionism* (London: Thames & Hudson).

Arroyo, José (1993) 'Death, Desire and Identity: The Political
Unconscious of New Queer Cinema' in Joseph Bristow and Angelia
R. Wilson (eds.) *Activating Theory: lesbian, gay and bisexual politics*
(London: Lawrence & Wishart).

_____ (1997) 'Film Studies' in Andy Medhurst and Sally R. Munt (eds.)
Lesbian and Gay Studies: A Critical Introduction (London: Cassell).

Aumont, Jacques; Bergala, Alain; Marie, Michel; Vernet, Marc (1992)
Aesthetics of Film, translated and revised by Richard Neupert, (Austin:
University of Texas Press).

Babuscio, Jack (1984) 'Camp and Gay Sensibility' in Richard Dyer (ed.)
Gays and Film (New York: Zoetrope).

Bad Object-Choices (eds.) (1991) *How do I Look? Queer Film and Video* (Seattle: Bay Press).

Bader, Eleanor (1993) 'Coping and Caring: Films on the AIDS Crisis', *Cineaste*, 19: 4.

Baker, Rob (1994) *The Art of AIDS: From Stigma to Conscience* (New York: Continuum).

Baudrillard, Jean (1983) *Simulations*, translated by Paul Foss, Paul Patton and Philip Beitchman, (New York: Semiotext(e)).

Bawer, Bruce (1993) *A Place at the Table: the gay individual in American Society* (New York: Touchstone Books).

Beck, Ulrich and Beck-Gernsheim, Elisabeth (1995) *The Normal Chaos of Love* (Cambridge: Polity Press).

Bell, David and Binnie, Jon (2000) *The Sexual Citizen: Queer Politics and Beyond* (Cambridge: Polity Press).

Belsey, Catherine (1980) *Critical Practice* (London: Methuen).

Benjamin, Walter (1936) 'The Work of Art in the Age of Mechanical Reproduction' reprinted in (1992) Francis Fraschina and Jonathan Harris (eds.) *art in modern culture: an anthology of critical texts* (London: Phaidon Press Ltd.).

Berger, John (1972) *Ways of Seeing* (Middlesex: Penguin Books Ltd.).

Bergman, David (1993) 'Introduction' in David Bergman (ed.) *Camp Grounds: Style and Homosexuality* (Amherst: University of Massachusetts Press).

Berlant, Lauren and Freeman, Elizabeth (1997) 'Queer Nationality' in Michael Warner (ed.) *Fear of a Queer Planet: Queer Politics and Social Theory* (Minneapolis: University of Minnesota Press).

_____ and Warner, Michael (1998) 'Sex in Public' in Michael Warner *Publics and Counterpublics* (New York: Zone Books).

Bersani, Leo (1987) 'Is the Rectum a Grave?', *October*, 43, Winter.

_____ (1995) *Homos* (Cambridge, Massachusetts: Harvard University Press).

_____ (1995b) 'Loving Men' in Maurice Berger, Brian Wallis and Simon Watson (eds.) *Constructing Masculinity* (New York and London: Routledge).

_____ and Dutoit, Ulysse (1999) *Caravaggio* (London: BFI Publishing).

Biga, Tracy (1996) 'The Principle of non-narration in the films of Derek Jarman' in Chris Lippard (ed.) *By Angels Driven: The Films of Derek Jarman* (Trowbridge: Flicks Books).

Blachford, Greg (1981) 'Male Dominance and the Gay World' in Kenneth Plummer (ed.) *The Making of the Modern Homosexual* (London: Hutchinson).

Blake, Nayland (1995) 'In a Different Light' in Nayland Blake, Laurence Rinder and Amy Scholder (eds.) *Visual Culture, Sexual Identity, Queer Practice* (San Francisco: City Light Books).

Bordo, Susan (1999) *The Male Body: A New Look at Men in Public and in Private* (New York: Farrar, Strauss and Giroux).

Brassell, R. Bruce (1992) 'Gay Hustler: Gay Spectatorship as Cruising' in *Wide Angle*, 14:2.

Bray, Alan (1988) *Homosexuality in Renaissance England* (London: Gay Men's Press).

Brett, Philip *et al.* (eds.) (1994) *Queering the Pitch: The New Gay and Lesbian Musicology* (London and New York: Routledge).

Bristow, Joseph (1997) *Sexuality* (London and New York: Routledge).

Bronski, Michael (1997) 'Why gay men still have unsafe sex: beauty, self-esteem and the myth of HIV negativity' in Joshua Oppenheimer and Helena Rickitt (eds.) *Acting on AIDS: sex, drugs & politics* (London: Serpent's Tail).

Brownworth, Victoria (1996) 'Tying the knot of the hangman's noose: the case against marriage', *Journal of Gay, Lesbian and Bisexual Identity*, 1: 91-8.

Bruzzi, Stella (2000) 'Two Sisters, the Fogey, the Priest and his Lover: Sexual Plurality in 1990s British Cinema', in Murphey, Robert (ed.) *British Cinema of the 90s* (London: BFI).

Buck-Morss, Susan (1992) 'Aesthetics and Anaesthetics: Walter Benjamin's Artwork Essay Reconsidered', *October*, 62, Fall.

Bürger, Peter (1984) *Theory of the Avant-Garde* (Manchester: Manchester University Press).

Burston, Paul (1995) *What are you looking at? Queer Sex, Style and Cinema* (London: Cassell).

_____ and Richardson, Colin (eds.) (1995) *A Queer Romance: lesbians, gay men and popular culture* (London and New York: Routledge).

Butler, Judith (1999) *Gender Trouble: Feminism and the Subversion of Identity* 2nd edition (London and New York: Routledge).

_____ (1991) 'Imitation and Gender Insubordination' in Diana Fuss (ed.) *Inside/Out: Lesbian Theories, Gay Theories* (London and New York: Routledge).

_____ (1993) *Bodies that Matter: On the Discursive Limits of 'Sex'* (London and New York: Routledge).

Callaghan, Dympna (1996) 'The terms of gender: 'gay' and 'feminist' *Edward II*' in Valerie Traub, M. Lindsay Kaplan and Dympna Callaghan (eds.) *Feminist readings of early modern culture: emerging subjects* (Cambridge: Cambridge University Press).

Campbell, Jan (2000) *Arguing with the Phallus: Feminist, Queer and Postcolonial Theory* (London and New York: Zed Books).

Camus, Renaud (1981) *Tricks: 25 Encounters*, translated by Richard Howard (New York: Saint Martin's Press).

Cassetti, Francesco (1999) *Theories of Cinema: 1945 – 1995*, translated by Francesca Chiostri and Elizabeth Gard Bartolini-Salimbeni, with Thomas Kelso (Austin: University of Texas Press).

(charles), Helen (1993) 'Queer Nigger': Theorizing 'White' Activism' in Joseph Bristow and Angelia R. Wilson (eds.) *Activating Theory: lesbian, gay and bisexual politics* (London: Lawrence & Wishart).

Chedgzoy, Kate (1995) 'The past is our mirror: Marlowe, Shakespeare, Jarman' in Kate Chedgzoy *Shakespeare's Queer Children* (Manchester: Manchester University Press).

Chee, Alexander (1991) 'A Queer Nationalism', *Out/Look: National Lesbian and Gay Quarterly*, 11.

Clark, T. J. (1994) 'In Defense of Abstract Expressionism', *October*, 69, Summer.

Clum, John M. (1993) 'And Once I Had It All': AIDS Narratives and Memories of an American Dream' in Timothy F. Murphy and Suzanne Poirier (eds.) *Writing AIDS: Gay Literature, Language, and Analysis* (New York: Columbia University Press).

_____ (1999) *Something for the Boys: Musical Theatre and Gay Culture* (New York: Palgrave).

_____ (2000) *Still Acting Gay: Male Homosexuality in Modern Drama* (New York: St. Martin's Griffin).

Cockcroft, Eva (1992) 'Abstract Expressionism: Weapon of the Cold War' in Francis Fraschina and Jonathan Harris (eds.) *art in modern culture: an anthology of critical texts* (London: Phaidon Press Ltd.).

Connor, Steve (2001) 'The Shame of being a man', *Textual Practice*, 15:2.

Cook, Matt (1996) 'Derek Jarman's Written Work', *Derek Jarman: A Portrait* (London: Thames & Hudson).

Copjec, Joan (1989) 'The Orthopsychic Subject: Film Theory and the Reception of Lacan' in *October*, 49, Summer.

Craft, Christopher (1984) ''Kiss Me With Those Ruby Lips': Gender and Inversion in Bram Stoker's *Dracula*, *Representations*, 8, Fall.

Creed, Barbara (1987) 'From Here to Modernity: Feminism and Postmodernism', *Screen*, 28:2, Spring.

_____ (1993) *The Monstrous Feminine: Film, Feminism, Psychoanalysis* (London and New York: Routledge).

_____ (1993b) 'Dark Desires: Male masochism in the horror film' in Steven Cohan and Ina Rae Hark (eds.) *Screening the Male: Exploring masculinities in Hollywood Cinema* (London and New York: Routledge).

_____ (1999) 'Lesbian Bodies: Tribades, Tomboys and Tarts' in Janet Price and Margrit Shildrick (eds.) *Feminist Theory and the Body: A Reader* (Edinburgh: Edinburgh University Press).

Creekmur, Corey and Doty, Alexander (eds.) (1995) *Out in Culture: Gay, Lesbian and Queer Essays on Popular Culture* (Durham: Duke University Press)

Crimp, Douglas (1987) 'AIDS: Cultural Analysis/Cultural Activism', *October*, 43, Winter.

_____ and Rolston, Adam (eds.) (1990) *AIDS demographics* (Seattle, WA: Bay Press).

_____ (1993) 'Right On, Girlfriend!' in Michael Warner (ed.) *Fear of a Queer Planet: Queer Politics and Social Theory* (Minneapolis: University of Minnesota Press).

Crisp, Quinten (1986) *The Naked Civil Servant* (London: Michael Joseph).

Cossen, Steve (1991) 'Queer', *Out/Look: National Lesbian and Gay Quarterly*, 11.

Darke, Chris (1993) *'Blue'* (Film Review), *Sight and Sound*, 3:10, October.

David, Hugh (1997) *On Queer Street: A Social History of British Homosexuality 1895-1995* (London: Harper Collins).

Davis, Glyn (2002) 'Greg Araki' in Yvonne Tasker (ed.) *Fifty Contemporary Filmmakers* (London and New York: Routledge).

_____ (2004) 'Camp and Queer and the New Queer Director: Case Study – Gregg Araki' in Michele Aaron (ed.) *New Queer Cinema: A Critical Reader* (Edinburgh: Edinburgh University Press).

Davis, Mike (1990) *City of Quartz: Excavating the Future in Los Angeles* (London: Verso).

De Duve, Thierry (1989) 'Yves Klein, or The Dead Dealer', translated by Rosalind Krauss, *October*, 49, Summer.

De Lauretis, Teresa (1991) 'Queer Theory: Lesbian and Gay Sexualities', *differences: A Journal of Feminist Cultural Studies*, 3:2.

_____ (1994) *The Practice of Love: Lesbian Sexuality and Perverse Desire* (Bloomington and Indianapolis: Indiana University Press).

Dean, Tim (1993) 'The Psychoanalysis of AIDS', *October*, 63, Winter.

_____ (2000) 'Lacan Meets Queer Theory' in Tim Dean *Beyond Sexuality* (Chicago and London: University of Chicago Press).

DiLallo, Kevin and Krumholz, Jack (1994) *The Unofficial Gay Manual: Living the Lifestyle (Or at Least Appearing To) (New York: Doubleday)*.

Dillon, Steven (2004) *Derek Jarman and Lyric Film: The Mirror and the Sea* (Austin: University of Texas Press).

Doane, Mary Ann *(1987) The Desire to Desire: The Woman's Film of the 1940s* (Bloomington: Indiana University Press).

_____ (1991) 'Film and Masquerade: Theorizing the Female Spectator' in Mary Ann Doane *Femmes Fatales: Feminism, Film Theory, Psychoanalysis* (London and New York: Routledge).

Dollimore, Jonathan (1991) *Sexual Dissidence: Augustine to Wilde, Freud to Foucault* (Oxford: Clarendon Press).

_____ (1995) 'Sex and Death', *Textual Practice*, 9:1.

_____ (1996) 'Bisexuality, heterosexuality and wishful theory', *Textual Practice*, 10:3.

_____ (1997) 'Bisexuality' in Andy Medhurst and Sally R. Munt (eds.) *Lesbian and Gay Studies: A Critical Introduction* (London: Cassell).

_____ (2001) *Sex, Literature and Censorship* (Cambridge: Polity Press).

Doty, Alexander (1993) *Making Things Perfectly Queer: Interpreting Mass Culture* (Minneapolis: University of Minnesota Press).

_____ (1998) 'Queer Theory' in John Hill and Pamela Church Gibson (eds.) *The Oxford Guide to Film Studies* (Oxford: Oxford University Press).

_____ (2000) *Flaming Classics: Queering the Film Canon* (New York and London: Routledge).

Dover, Kenneth J. (1980) *Greek Homosexuality* (New York: Random House-Vintage).

Dutton, Kenneth (1995) *The Perfectible Body: The Western Ideal of Physical Development* (London: Cassell).

Dyer, Richard (1982) 'Don't Look Now', *Screen*, 23: 3-4, September-October.

_____ (1984) 'Stereotyping' in Richard Dyer (ed.) *Gays and Film* (London: Zoetrope).

_____ (1987) 'Judy Garland and Gay Men' in Richard Dyer *Heavenly Bodies: Film Stars and Society* (London: MacMillan).

_____ (1988) 'Children of the Night: Vampirism as Homosexuality, Homosexuality as Vampirism' in Susannah Radstone (ed.) *Sweet Dreams: Sexuality, Gender and Popular Fiction* (London: Lawrence & Wishart).

_____ (1990) *Now You See It: Studies on Lesbian and Gay Film* (London and New York: Routledge).

_____ (1991) 'Believing in Fairies: The Author and The Homosexual' in Diana Fuss (ed.) *Inside/Out: Lesbian Theories, Gay Theories* (London and New York: Routledge).

_____ (1992) *Only Entertainment* (London and New York: Routledge).

_____ (1993) 'Seen to be believed: some problems in the representation of gay people as typical' in Richard Dyer *The Matter of Images* (London and New York: Routledge).

_____ (1993b) 'Homosexuality and Film Noir' in *The matter of Images*.

_____ (1997) 'Heterosexuality' in Andy Medhurst and Sally R. Munt (eds.) *Lesbian and Gay Studies: A Critical Introduction* (London: Cassell).

_____ (2002) *the culture of queers* (London and New York: Routledge).

Eagleton, Terry (1990) *The Ideology of the Aesthetic* (London: Blackwell).

Edeleman, Lee (1994) *Homographesis: Essays in Gay Literary and Cultural Theory* (London and New York: Routledge).

Edge, Sarah (2000) 'Images of the self: semiotic 'chora' in recent post-feminist theory' in Dan Felming (ed.) *Formations: A 21st Century Media Studies Textbook* (Manchester and New York: Manchester University Press).

Ellenzweig, Allan (1992) *The Homoerotic Photograph* (New York: Columbia University Press).

Ellis, Jim (1999) 'Queer Period: Derek Jarman's Renaissance' in Ellis

Hanson (ed.) *Outtakes: Essays on Queer Theory and Film* (Durham and London: Duke University Press).

_____ (2001) 'The Erotics of Citizenship: Derek Jarman's *Jubilee* and Isaac Julien's *Young Soul Rebels*', *Southern Quarerly*, 39:4.

_____ (2001) 'Conjuring *The Tempest*: Derek Jarman and the Spectacle of Redemption', *GLQ: A Journal of Lesbian and Gay Studies, 7:2.*

Epstein, Steven (1989) 'Gay Politics, Ethnic Identity: The Limits of Social Constructionism', *Socialist Review*, 17, May-August.

_____ (1996) 'A Queer Encounter: Sociology and the Study of Sexuality' in Steven Seidman (ed.) *Queer Theory/Sociology* (Oxford: Blackwell).

Ewing, William A. (1994) *The Body: Photoworks of the Human Form* (London: Thames and Hudson Ltd.).

Farmer, Brett (2000) *Spectacular Passions: Cinema, Fantasy, Gay Male Spectatorships* (Durham and London: Duke University Press).

Florence, Penny (1994) 'We are here but are we queer?: Lesbian Filmmaking versus Queer Cinema Conference, London, 12 March 1994', *Screen*, 35:3, Autumn.

Forest, Benjamin (1995) 'West Hollywood as symbol: the significance of place in the construction of a gay identity', *Environment and Planning D: Society Space*, 13.

Forster, E. M. (1972) *Maurice* (Harmondsworth: Penguin).

Foster, Hal (1991) 'Armor Fou', *October*, 56.

_____ (1993) 'Postmodernism in Parallax', *October*, 63, Winter.

_____ (1996) *The Return of the Real* (Cambridge, Mass: MIT Press).

Foucault, Michel (1978) *The History of Sexuality: Volume 1*, translated by Robert Hurley (Harmondsworth: Penguin).

_____ (1980) 'Two Letters' in C. Gordon (ed.) *Power/Knowledge: Selected Interviews and Other Writings, 1972-1977* (New York: Routledge).

_____ (1985) *The History of Sexuality: Volume 2, The Use of Pleasure,* Translated by Robert Hurley (New York: Random Press).

_____ (1991) *Discipline and Punish: The Birth of the Prison* (London: Penguin Books).

Freud, Sigmund (1957) 'Leonardo Da Vinci and a Memory of His Childhood' in *Standard Edition of the Complete Psychological Works of Sigmund Freud: Volume 11*, translated by James Strachey (London: Hogarth Press).

_____ (1961) 'The Economic Problem of Masochism' (1924) in *Standard Edition of the Complete Psychological Works of Sigmund Freud: Volume 19* (London: Hogarth Press).

_____ (1961) 'A Child is Being Beaten' (1919) in *Standard Edition of the Complete Psychological Works of Sigmund Freu: Volume 17* (London: Hogarth Press).

_____ (1984) 'On Narcissism: An Introduction' in *On Metapsychology: The Theory of Psychoanalysis* (Harmondsworth: Penguin).

Frye, Marilyn (1983) *The Politics of Reality: Essays in Feminist Theory* (Trumansberg, NY: Crossing Press).

Fuss, Diana (1991) (ed.) *Inside/Out: Lesbian Theories, Gay Theories* (New York: Routledge).

Fuery, Patrick (2000) *new developments in film theory* (London: MacMillan Press Ltd.).

Gammon, Lorraine and Marshment, M (eds.) (1988) *The Female Gaze* (London: The Women's Press).

Gamson, Joshua (1996) 'Must Identity Movements Self-Destruct? A Queer Dilemma' in Steven Seidman (ed.) *Queer Theory/Sociology* (Oxford: Blackwell).

Gardner, David (1996) 'Perverse Law: Jarman as gay criminal hero' in Chris Lippard (ed.) *By Angels Driven: The Films of Derek Jarman* (Trowbridge: Flicks Books).

Garland, Rodney (1953) *The Heart in Exile* (London: W. H. Allen).

Genet, Jean (1990) *Querelle of Brest*, translated by Gregory Steatham (London and Boston: Faber & Faber).

_____ (1988) *Our Lady of the Flower,* translated by Gregory Steatham (London: Grove Press).

Gever, Martha; Greyson, John and Parmar, Pratibha (1991) *Queer Looks: Perspectives on Lesbian and Gay Film and Video* (London and New York: Routledge).

Giles, Jane (1991) *The Cinema of Jean Genet: Un Chant D'Amour* (London: BFI).

Glass, Honey (1997) 'Queer', *Sight and Sound*, 10, October.

Goodman, Lizbeth (1990) 'Subverting Images of the Female: Feminist Theatre Interview No. 3 – Tilda Swinton', *New Theatre Quarterly*, 6, August.

_____ (1993) 'Death and dancing in the Live Arts: performance, politics and sexuality in the age of AIDS', *Critical Quarterly*, 35:27, Summer.

Gray, Francine du Plessix (1981) 'The Escape from Fashion', *The Dial 2*, 9, September.

Griffiths, Robin (2006) 'Introduction: Queer Britannia – a century of sinema' in Robin Griffiths (ed.) *British Queer Cinema* (London and New York: Routledge).

Grosz, Elizabeth (1995) *Space, Time and Perversion: The Politics of Bodies* (Sydney: Allen and Unwin).

Greenberg, Clement (1967/86) 'Where is the Avant-Garde' in *Collected Essays Vol. 4: Modernism with a Vengeance* (Chicago: University of Chicago Press).

_____ (1990) 'Towards a Newer Laocoon' in Shapiro and Shapiro (eds.) *Abstract Expressionism: A Critical Record* (New York: Cambridge University Press).

_____ (1992) 'Modernist Painting' in Francis Fraschina and Jonathan Harris (eds.) *art in modern culture: an anthology of critical texts* (London: Phadion Press Ltd.).

Grundman, Roy (1990) 'Longtime Companion' (Film Review), *Cineaste*, XVII:1.

_____ (1993) 'The Fantasies We Live By: Bad Boys in *Swoon* and *The Living End*', *Cineaste*, March.

Guibert, Serge (1983) *How New York Stole the Idea of Modern Art: Abstract Expressionism, Freedome, and the Cold War*, translated by Arthur Goldhammer (Chicago and London: University of Chicago Press).

Gunning, Tom (1990) 'The Cinema of Attractions: Early Film, its Spectator and the Avant-Garde' in Thomas Elsaesser (ed.) *Early Cinema: Space, Frame, Narrative* (London: BFI).

_____ (1998) 'Early American Film' in John Hill and Pamela Church Gibson (eds.) *The Oxford Guide to Film Studies* (Oxford: Oxford University Press).

Hall, Stuart (1992) 'The Question of Cultural Identity' in Stuart Hall and Tony McGrew (eds.) *Modernity and its Futures* (Cambridge: Polity Press).

Halperin, David M. (1990) *One Hundred Years of Homosexuality and Other Essays on Greek Love* (London and New York: Routledge).

_____ (1993) 'Is There a History of Sexuality?' in Abelove *et al.* (eds.) *The Lesbian and Gay Studies Reader* (London and New York: Routledge).

_____ (1995) *Saint Foucault: Towards a Gay Hagiography* (Oxford: Oxford University Press).

Hamilton, Marybeth (1995) *The Queen of Camp: Mae West, sex and popular culture* (London: HarperCollins).

Hansen, Miriam (1986) 'Pleasure, Ambivalence and Identification: Valentino and Female Spectatorship', *Cinema Journal*, 24: 4.

Hanson, Ellis (1991) 'Undead' in Diana Fuss (ed.) *Inside/Out: Lesbian Theories, Gay Theories* (London and New York: Routledge).

_____ (1999) 'Introduction: Out Takes' in Ellis Hanson (ed.) *Outtakes: Essays on Queer Theory and Film* (Durham and London: Duke University Press).

Harris, Diana and Jackson, MacDonald (1997) 'Stormy Weather: Derek Jarman's *The Tempest*', *Film Literature Quarterly*, 25:2.

Hart, Linda and Dale, Joshua (1997) 'Sadomasochism' in Andy Medhurst and Sally R. Munt (eds.) *Lesbian and Gay Studies: A Critical Introduction* (London: Cassell).

Hawkes, David (1996) ''The Shadow of this time': The Renaissance Cinema of Derek Jarman' in Chris Lippard (ed.) *By Angels Driven: The Films of Derek Jarman* (Trowbridge: Flicks Books).

Hayes, Susan (1996) 'Coming Over All Queer', *New Statesman and Society*, 16, September.

Haynes, Todd (1985) 'Homoaesthetics and *Querelle*', *Subjects/Objects*, 3.

Hayward, Susan (2001) *Cinema Studies: The Key Concepts* 2nd Edition (London and New York: Routledge.

Healy, Murray (1996) *Gay Skins* (London: Cassell).

Heath, Stephen (1981) *Questions of Cinema* (London: MacMillan Press Ltd.).

_____ (1982) *The Sexual Fix* (London: MacMillan Press Ltd.).

Heller, Agnes (1985) *The Power of Shame: A Rational Persepctive* (London and New York: Routledge).

_____ (1995) *Family Plots* (Philadelphia: Pennsylvania University Press).

Hennessy, Rosemary (1993) 'Queer Theory: A Review of the *differences'* special issue and Wittig's *The Straight Mind'*, *Signs: Journal of Women in Culture and Society*, 18.

Hill, John (1998) 'Film and Postmodernism' in John Hill and Pamela Church Gibson (eds.) *The Oxford Guide to Film Studies* (Oxford: Oxford University Press).

_____ (1999) 'The Avant-Garde: *The Last of England*' in John Hill *British Cinema in the 1980s* (Oxford: Clarendon Press).

Hollinghurst, Alan (1998) *The Swimming Pool Library* (London: Vintage).

_____ (1999) *The Spell* (London: Vintage).

_____ (2005) *The Line of Beauty* (London: Picador).

Ingram, Gordon Brent *et al.* (eds.) (1997) *Queers in Space: Communities/Public Places/ Sites of Resistance* (Seattle: Bay Press).

Irigaray, Luce (1985) *This Sex Which Is Not One*, translated by Gillian C. Gill (Ithaca, NY: Cornell University Press).

_____ (1991) *Marine Lover of Friedrich Nietzsche*, translated by Gillian C. Gill (Ithaca, NY: Cornell University Press).

Jagose, Annamarie (1996) *Queer Theory* (Melbourne: Melbourne University Press).

Jameson, Frederic (1984) 'Postmodernism or The Cultural Logic of Late Capitalism', *New Left Review*, 146.

Jarman, Derek (1984) *Dancing Ledge*, Shaun Allen (ed.) (London and New York: Quintet Books).

_____ (1991) *Modern Nature: The Journals of Derek Jarman* (London: Century).

_____ (1992) *At Your Own Risk: A Saint's Testament* (London: Century).

_____ (2000) *Smiling in Slow Motion*, Keith Collins (ed.) (London: Century).

Jay, Karla and Young, Allen (eds.) (1992) *Out of the Closets: Voices of Gay Liberation* (London: Gay Men's Press Ltd.).

Jones Mars, Adam (1983) 'Introduction: Gay Fiction and the Reading Public' in Adam Mars-Jones (ed.) *Mae West is Dead: Recent Lesbian and Gay Fiction* (London and Boston: Faber & Faber).

Kaplan, E. Ann (1983) 'Is the Gaze Male?' in E. Ann Kaplan *Women and Film: Both Sides of the Camera* (London and New York: Routledge).

Kaye, Richard A. (1996) 'Losing his religion: Saint Sebastian as contemporary gay martry' in Peter Horne and Reina Lewis (ed.) *Outlooks: Lesbian and Gay Sexualities and Visual Culture (London and New York: Routledge).*

Kimball, Roger (1990) *Tenured Radicals: How Politics Has Corrupted Our Higher Education* (New York: Harper & Row).

Kipnis, Laura (1998) 'Adultery', *Critical Inquiry*, 24.

Klinger, Barbara (1994) 'Mass Camp and the Old Hollywood Melodrama Today' in Barbara Klinger *Melodrama and Meaning: History, Culture and the Films of Douglas Sirk* (Bloomington: Indiana University Press).

Kramer, Larry (1986) *The Normal Heart* (London: Methuen).

_____ (1997) 'Sex and Sensibility', *The Advocate*, 27 May.

Krauss, Rosalind (1985) *The Originality of the Avant-Garde and other Modernist Myths* (Cambridge, Mass: MIT Press).

_____ (1993) *The Optical Unconscious* (Cambridge, Mass: MIT Press).

Kristeva, Julia (1982) *Powers of Horror: An Essay an Abjection*, translated by Leon S. Roudiez (New York: Columbia University Press).

_____ (1986) *The Kristeva Reader*, Toril Moi (ed.) (Oxford: Blackwell Publishers Ltd.).

_____ (1987) *Tales of Love*, translated by Leon S. Roudiez (New York: Columbia University Press).

Lacan, Jacques (1977) *Écrits: A Selection*, translated by Alan Sheridan (London: Tavistock Publications).

_____ (1985) 'The Meaning of the Phallus' in Juliet Mitchell and Jacqueline Rose (eds.) *Feminine Sexuality: Jacques Lacan and the École Freudienne* (New York: Norton).

_____ (1986) *The Four Fundamental Concepts of Psychoanalysis*, translated by Alan Sheridan (Middlesex: Penguin).

_____ (1988) *The Seminar: Book I. Freud's Papers on Technique 1953-54*, translated with notes by John Forrester (Cambridge: Cambridge University Press).

_____ (1988) *The Seminar: Book II. The Ego in Freud's Theory and the Technique of Psychoanalysis, 1954-55*, translated by Sylvana Tomaselli with notes by John Forrester (Cambridge: Cambridge University Press).

_____ (1993) *The Psychoses: The Seminar of Jacques Lacan Book III, 1955-56*, Jacques Miller (ed.), translated with notes by Russell Grigg (London and New York: Routledge).

Lang, Robert (1997) '*My Own Private Idaho* and The New Queer Road Movie' in Steven Cohan and Ina Rae Hark (eds.) *The Road Movie Book* (London and New York: Routledge).

Lapsley, Robert and Westlake, Michael (1988) *Film Theory: An Introduction* (Manchester: Manchester University Press).

Laskawy, Michael (1991) '*Poison* at the Box-Office: An Interview with Todd Haynes', *Cineaste*, 18.

Lauritsen, John and Thorstad, David (1974) *The Early Homosexual Rights Movement* (New York: Time Change Press).

Lehring, Gary (1997) 'Essentialism and the Political Articulation of Identity' in Shane Phelan (ed.) *Playing with Fire: Queer Politics, Queer Theories* (London and New York: Routledge).

Lilly, Mark (1993) 'Jean Genet: The Autobiographical Works' in Mark Lilly *Gay Men's Literature in the Twentieth Century* (London: MacMillan Press Ltd.).

_____ (1993b) 'David Leavitt: *The Lost Language of Cranes*' in Mark Lilly *Gay Men's Literature in the Twentieth Century* (London: MacMillan Press Ltd.).

Lippard, Chris (1996) 'Introduction' in Chris Lippard (ed.) *By Angels Driven: The Films of Derek Jarman* (Trowbridge: Flicks Books).

Lucas, Ian (1998) *OutRage: An Oral History* (London: Cassell).

Lombardo, Patrizia (1994) 'Cruellement Bleu', *Critical Quarterly*, 36:1.

Lucie-Smith, Edward (1995) *Movements in art since 1945: Issues and Concepts* (London: Thames and Hudson).

Lyotard, Jean-François (1984) *The Postmodern Condition: A Report on Knowledge*, translated by Geoff Bennington and Brian Massumi (Minneapolis: University of Minnesota Press).

MacCabe, Colin (1991) '*Edward II*: Throne of Blood', *Sight and Sound*, 1:6.

_____ (1992) 'A Post-National European Cinema: A Consideration of Derek Jarman's *The Tempest* and *Edward II*' in Duncan Petrie (ed.) *Screening Europe: Image and Identity in Contemporary European Cinema* (London: BFI Working Papers).

_____ (1994) 'Derek Jarman – Obituary', *Critical Quarterly*, 13:1.

Malinowitz, Harriet (1993) 'Queer Theory: Whose Theory?', *Frontiers*, 13.

Manning, Toby (1999) 'Gay Culture: Who Needs It?' in Mark Simpson (ed.) *Anti-Gay* (London: Cassell).

Mason, Angela (1999) 'Sparks fly over *Queer As Folk*', *Pink Paper*, 5 March.

McIntosh, Mary (1997) 'Seeing the World from a Lesbian and Gay Standpoint' in Lynne Segal (ed.) *New Sexual Agendas* (London: MacMillan Press Ltd.).

McMahon, Joseph H. (1980) *The Imagination of Jean Genet* (Connecticut: Greenwood Press Publishers).

Medhurst, Andy (1984) 'Notes on Recent Gay Film Criticism' in Richard Dyer (ed.) *Gays and Film* (New York: Zoetrope).

_____ (1991) 'That Special Thrill: Brief Encounter, Homosexuality and Authorship', *Screen*, 32:2, Summer.

_____ (1997) 'Camp' in Andy Medhurst and Sally R. Munt (eds.) *Lesbian and Gay Studies: A Critical Introduction* (London: Cassell).

Mercer, John (2003) 'Homosexual Prototypes: Repetition and the Construction of the Generic in the Iconography of Gay Pornography', *Paragraph*, 26: 1&2.

Merck, Mandy (1993) 'More of a Man' in Mandy Merck *Perversions: Deviant Readings* (London: Virago Press).

_____ (1996) 'Figuring out Andy Warhol' in Jennifer Doyle *et al.* (eds.) *Pop Out: Queer Warhol* (London and Durham: Duke University Press).

Metz, Christian (1985) 'From The Imaginary Signifier' in Gerald Mas and Marshall Cohen (eds.) *Film Theory and Criticism: Introductory Reading* (Oxford: Oxford University Press).

Meyer, Moe (1994) 'Introduction' in Moe Meyer (ed.) *The Politics and Poetics of Camp* (London and New York: Routledge).

Miller, D. A. (1993) 'Sontag's Urbanity' in Abelove *et al.* (eds.) *The Lesbian and Gay Studies Reader* (London and New York: Routledge).

Miller, Jacques-Alain (1980) 'Teachings of the Case Presentation' in *Returning to Freud: Clinical Psychoanalysis in the School of Lacan,* translated and edited by Stuart Schneiderman (New Haven: Yale University Press).

Mills, Katie (1997) 'Revitalizing The Road Genre: *The Living End* as an AIDS Road Film' in Steven Cohan and Ina Rae Hark (eds.) *The Road Movie Book* (London and New York: Routledge).

Moran, James M. (1996) 'Gregg Araki: Guerilla Film-Maker for a Queer Generation', *Film Quarterly*, 50:1.

Morton, Donald (1995) 'Birth of the Cyberqueer', *PMLA*, 110:3.

Moor, Andrew (2000) 'Spirit and Matter: Romantic Mythologies in the Films of Derek Jarman' in David Alderson and Linda Anderson (eds.) *Territories of desire in queer culture: Refiguring contemporary boundaries* (Manchester and New York: Manchester University Press).

Mulvey, Laura (1975) 'Visual Pleasure and Narrative Cinema', *Screen*, 16:3.

_____ (1981) 'Afterthoughts on 'Visual Pleasure and Narrative Cinema' inspired by *Duel in the Sun*', *Framework*, 6.

_____ (1986) 'Contribution to 'The Spectatrix'', *Camera Obscura*, 20-1.

Munt, Sally R. (2000) 'Shame/Pride Dichotomies in *Queer As Folk*', *Textual Practice*, 14:3.

Murray, Timothy (1993) 'Dirtier Still? Wistful gazing and homographic hieroglyphs in Jarman's *Caravaggio*' in Timothy Murray *Like a film: ideological fantasy on screen, camera and canvas* (London and New York: Routledge).

Nash, Mark (1985) 'Innocence and Experience', *Afterimage*, 12.

_____ (1994) 'Chronicle(s) of a death foretold, notes apropos of *Les Nuits Fauves*', *Critical Quarterly*, 36:1, Spring.

Neale, Steve (1993) 'Masculinity as Spectacle: Reflections on men and mainstream cinema' in Steve Cohan and Ina Rae Hark (eds.) *Screening the Male: Exploring Masculinities in Hollywood Cinema* (London and New York: Routledge).

Nunokawa, Jeff (1991) '"All the Sad Young Men": AIDS and the Work of Mourning' in Diana Fuss (ed.) *Inside/Out: Lesbian Theories, Gay Theories* (London and New York: Routledge).

Odets, Walt (1997) 'Why we do not do primary prevention for gay men' in Joshua Oppenheimer and Helena Rickett (eds.) *Acting on AIDS: sex, drugs and politics* (London: Serpent's Tail).

Okewole, Seun (1992) 'Tom Kalin', *Sight and Sound*, 2:5, September.

Oldfield, Simon (2001) 'Wrestling with Francis Bacon', *Oxford Art Journal*, 24:1.

O'Pray, Michael (1991) 'Damning Desire', *Sight and Sound*, 1:6, October.

_____ (1996) *Derek Jarman: Dreams of England* (London: BFI Publishing).

_____ (1996b) 'The British Avant-Garde and Art Cinema from the 1970s to the 1990s' in Andrew Higson (ed.) *Dissolving Views: Key Writings on British Cinema* (London: Cassell).

O'Quinn, Daniel (1999) 'Gardening, History and the Escape from Time: Derek Jarman's *Modern Nature*', *October*, 89.

Oswald, Laura (1983) 'The Perversion of the I/Eye in *Un Chant D'Amour*', *Enclitic*, 7:2.

Paechter, Carrie (1998) *Educating the Other: Gender, Power and Schooling* (London: The Falmer Press).

Paglia, Camille (1995) *Vamps and Tramps* (London: Viking).

_____ (1998) *The Birds* (London: BFI).

Parker, Andrew (1996) 'The Construction of masculinity within boys' physical education', *Gender and Education*, 8:2.

Parkes, James Cary (1996) 'Sexuality and the Gay Sensibility', *Derek Jarman: A Portrait* (London: Thames and Hudson).

Patton, Cindy (1993) 'Tremble, Hetero Swine!' in Michael Warner (ed.) *Fear of a Queer Planet: Queer Politics and Social Theory* (Minneapolis: University of Minnesota Press).

_____ (1997) 'Queer peregrinations' in Joshua Oppenheimer and Helena Rickitt (eds.) *Acting on AIDS: Sex, drugs & politics* (London: Serpent's Tail).

Peake, Tony (1999) *Derek Jarman* (London: Little, Brown and Company).

Penn, Donna (1995) 'Queer: Theorizing Politics and History', *Radical History Review*, 62.

Phillips, Anita (1998) *A Defense of Masochism* (London: Faber & Faber).

Pinfold, Michael John (1998) 'The Performance of Queer Masculinity in Derek Jarman's *Sebastiane*', *Film Criticism*, 23:1.

Porton, Richard (1996) 'Language games and aesthetic attitudes: style and ideology in Jarman's late films', in Chris Lippard (ed.) *By Angels Driven: The Films of Derek Jarman* (Trowbridge: Flicks Books).

Probyn, Elspeth (1997) 'Michel Foucault and the Uses of Sexuality' in Andy Medhurst and Sally R. Munt (eds.) *Lesbian and Gay Studies: A Critical Introduction* (London: Cassell).

Pronger, Brian (1990) *The Arena of Masculinity: Sports, Homosexuality and the Meaning of Sex* (London: Gay Men's Press).

Queen, Carol A. (1992) 'Strangers at Home: Bisexuals in the Queer Movement', *OutLook*, 16.

Quinn-Meyler, Martin (1996) 'Opposing "Heterosoc": Jarman's counter-hegemonic activism' in Chris Lippard (ed.) *By Angels Driven: The Films of Derek Jarman* (Trowbridge: Flicks Books).

Rayns, Tony (1973) 'Un Chant D'Amour', *Monthly Film Bulletin*, 40.

_____ (1985) 'Submitting to Sodomy: Propositions and Rhetorical Questions about an English Film-Maker', *Afterimage*, 12, Autumn.

Rechy, John (1963) *City of Night* (New York: Grove).

Restany, Pierre (1982) *Yves Klein*, translated by John Shepley (New York: Harry N. Abrams).

Rich, B. Ruby (1992) 'Queer Cinema', *Sight and Sound*, 2:5, September.

_____ (1993) 'Reflections On A Queer Screen', *GLQ: A Journal of Lesbian and Gay Studies*, 1.

_____ (2000) 'Queer and Present Danger', *Sight and Sound*, 10:3, March.

Richardson, Niall (2003) 'Queer Masculinity: The Representation of John Paul Pitoc's Body in *Trick*', *Paragraph*, 26:1&2, March/July.

_____ (2003b) 'Effeminophobia', *AXM*, February.

_____ (2003c) 'Bottom Shame', *AXM*, March.

_____ (2006) '*Poison* in the Sirkian System: The Political Agenda of Todd Haynes's *Far From Heaven*', *Scope: International Journal of Film Studies*, Issue 6, October.

Riviere, Joan (1986) 'Womanliness and the Masquerade' in Victor Burgin *et al.* (eds.) *Formations of Fantasy* (London and New York: Routledge).

Robertson, Pamela (1997) 'Home and Away: Friends of Dorothy on the road in Oz' in Steven Cohan and Ina Rae Hark (eds.) *The Road Movie Book* (London and New York: Routledge).

Rodowick, David N. (1982) 'The Difficulty of Difference', *Wide Angle*, 5:1.

_____ (1988) *The Crisis of Political Modernism: Criticism and Ideology in Contemporary Film Theory* (Urbana: University of Illinois Press).

Rosenberg, Harold (1990) 'The American Action Painters' in Shapiro and Shapiro (eds.) *Abstract Expressionism: A Critical Record* (Cambridge: Cambridge University Press).

Ross, Andrew (1989) 'Uses of Camp' in *No Respect: Intellectuals and Popular Culture* (London and New York: Routledge).

Rubin, Gayle (1975) 'The Traffic in Women: Notes on the "Political Economy" of sex' in Rayna R. Reiter (ed.) *Toward an Anthropology of Women* (New York: Monthly Review Press).

_____ (1993) 'Thinking Sex' in Abelove *et al.* (eds.) *The Lesbian and Gay Studies Reader* (London and New York: Routledge).

Rumaker, Michael (1979) *A Day and a Night at the Baths* (Bolinas, California: Grey Fox).

Rushdie, Salman (1992) *The Wizard of Oz* (London: BFI).

Rushton, Richard (2002) 'Cinema's double: some reflections on Metz', *Screen*, 43:2, Summer.

Russo, Vito (1981) *The Celluloid Closet: homosexuality in the movies* (New York: Harper & Row).

Saalfield, Catherine and Navarro, Ray (1991) 'Shocking Pink Praxis: Race and Gender on the ACTUP Frontiers' in Diana Fuss (ed.) *Inside/Out: Lesbian Theories, Gay Theories* (London and New York: Routledge).

Sacher-Masoch, Leopold (2000) *Venus in Furs* (Harmondsworth: Penguin).

Samuels, Jacinth (1999) 'Dangerous Liaisons: Queer Subjectivity, Liberalism and Race', *Cultural Studies*, 13:1, January.

Sartre, Jean Paul (1952) *Saint Genet: comédien and martyr* (Paris: Gallimard).

_____ (1966) *Being and Nothingness*, translated by Hazel Barnes (New York: Washington Square Press).

_____ (1979) 'On the Fine Arts Considered as Murder' in Peter Brooks and Joseph Halperin (eds.) *Genet: A Collection of Critical Essays* (New Jersey: Prentice Hall).

Savage, Jon (1991) 'Tasteful Tales', *Sight and Sound*, 1:6, October.

_____ and Julien, Isaac (1994) 'Queering the Pitch: a conversation', *Critical Quarterly*, 36:1, Spring.

Savoy, Eric (1994) 'You Can't Go Homo Again: Queer Theory and the Foreclosure of Gay Studies', *English Studies in Canada*, 20.

Sedgwick, Eve Kosofsky (1985) *Between Men: English Literature and Male Homosocial Desire* (New York: Columbia University Press).

_____ (1991) *Epistemology of the Closet* (Berkeley: University of California Press).

_____ (1993) *Tendencies* (Durham: Duke University Press).

_____ (1993b) 'Gosh, Boy George, you must be awfully secure in your masculinity', in Maurice Berger, Brian Wallis and Simon Watson (eds.) *Constructing Masculinity* (New York and London: Routledge).

_____ (1998) 'A Dialogue on Love', *Critical Inquiry*, 24, Winter.

Seidman, Steven (1996) 'Introduction' in Steven Seidman (ed.) *Queer Theory/Sociology* (Oxford: Blackwell).

_____ (1997) 'Identity and Politics in a 'Postmodern' Gay Culture: Some Historical and Conceptual Notes' in Michael Warner (ed.) *Fear of a*

Queer Planet: Queer Politics and Social Theory (Minneapolis: University of Minnesota Press).

Shakespeare, William (1963) *Sonnets* (Martin Seymour-Smith ed.) (Oxford: Heinemann Educational Books).

Shapiro, David and Shapiro, Cecile (1990) 'Introduction: A Brief History' in Shaprio and Shapiro (eds.) *Abstract Expressionism: A Critical Record* (New York: Cambridge University Press).

Sharrock, Cath (1997) 'Pathologizing Sexual Bodies' in Andy Medhurst and Sally R. Munt (eds.) *Lesbian and Gay Studies: A Critical Introduction* (London: Cassell).

Shaviro, Stephen (1993) 'Masculinity, Spectacle and the Body of Querelle' in Stephen Shaviro *The Cinematic Body* (Minneapolis: University of Minnesota Press).

Shingler, Martin (1995) 'Masquerade or Drag? Bette Davis and the ambiguities of gender', *Screen*, 36:3, Autumn.

Showalter, Elaine (1987) *The Female Malady: Women, Madness and English Culture, 1830-1980* (London: Virago).

Siegel, Lee (1998) 'The gay science: queer theory, literature, and the sexualisation of everything', *The New Republic*, 9, November.

Signorile, Michelangelo (1997) 'Bareback and Reckless', *Out*, July.

Silverman, Kaja (1992) *Male Subjectivity at the Margins* (London: New York).

Simpson, Mark (1994) *Male Impersonators* (London: Cassell).

_____ (1999) 'Gay Dream Believer: Inside the Gay Underwear Cult' in Mark Simpson (ed.) *Anti-Gay* (London: Cassell).

Sinfield, Alan (1989) *Literature, Politics and Culture in Post-War Britain* (Oxford; Blackwell).

_____ (1992) *Faultlines* (Berkeley: University of California Press).

_____ (1992b) 'What's in a Name?', *Gay Times*, May.

_____ (1994) *The Wilde Century: Effeminacy, Oscar Wilde and the Queer Movement* (New York: Columbia University Press).

_____ (1994b) *Cultural Politics: Queer Readings* (London: Routledge).

_____ (1998) *Gay and After* (London: Serpent's Tail).

_____ (1999) Out on Stage: Lesbian and Gay Theatre in the Twentieth Century (New Haven and London: Yale University Press).

_____ (2000) 'The Production of gay and the return of power' in Richard Philips, Diane Watt and David Shuttleton (eds.) *de-centring sexualities: politics and representations beyond the metropolis* (London and New York: Routledge).

Sitney, P. Adams (ed.) (1978) *The Avant-Garde Film: A Reader of Theory and Criticism* (New York: New York University Press).

Smith, Anna Marie (1997) 'The Centring of Right-Wing Extremism Through the Construction of an "Inclusionary" Homophobia and Racism' in Shane Phelan (ed.) *playing with fire: queer politics, queer theories* (London and New York: Routledge).

Smith, Murray (1998) 'Modernism and the avant-gardes' in John Hill and Pamela Church Gibson (eds.) *The Oxford Guide to Film Studies* (Oxford: Oxford University Press).

Smith, Paul Julian (1993) 'Blue and the Outer Limits', *Sight and Sound*, 3:10, October.

Smyth, Cherry (1992a) 'Queer Questions', *Sight and Sound*, 2:5, September.

_____ (1992b) 'Trash Femme Cocktail', *Sight and Sound*, 2:5, September.

_____ (1992c) *Lesbians Talk Queer Notions* (London: Scarlet Press).

Snaith, Guy (2003) 'Tom's Men: The Masculinization of Homosexuality and the Homosexualization of Masculinity at the end of the Twentieth Century', *Paragraph*, 1:1&2, March/July.

Sontag, Susan (1983) 'Notes on Camp' in *A Susan Sontag Reader* (New York: Vintage Books).

_____ (1991) *Illness as Metaphor/AIDS And Its Metaphors* (London: Penguin Books).

Spago, Tamsin (1999) *Foucault and Queer Theory* (Cambridge: Icon Books Ltd.).

Spelman, Elizabeth (1982) 'Woman as Body: Ancient and Contemporary Views', *Feminist Studies*, 8:1, Spring.

Stacey, Jackie (1987) 'Desperately Seeking Difference', *Screen*, 28:1, Winter.

_____ (1991) 'Promoting Nationality: Section 28 and the Regulation of Sexuality' in Sarah Franklin, Celia Lury and Jackie Stacey (eds.) *Off Centre: Feminism and Cultural Studies* (London: Harper Collins).

Stich, Sidra (1994) *Yves Klein* (Ostfildern: Cantz).

Storper, Michael and Susan Christopherson (1987) 'Flexible Specialization and Regional Industrial Agglomerations: The Case of the US Picture Industry', *Annals of the Association of American Geographers*, 77:1.

Studlar, Gayle (1988) *In the Realm of Pleasure: Von Sternberg, Dietrich and the Masochistic Aesthetic* (New York: Columbia University Press).

Suárez, Juan A. (1996) *Bike Boys, Drag Queens and Superstars: Avant-Garde, Mass Culture, and Gay Identities in the 1960s Underground Cinema* (Bloomington and Indianapolis: Indiana University Press).

Sullivan, Andrew (1996) *Virtually Normal: an argument about homosexuality* (London: Picador).

Talvacchia, Bette (1993) 'Historical Phallicy: Derek Jarman's *Edward II*', *The Oxford Art Journal*, 16:1.

Taubin, Amy (1993) 'Queer male cinema and feminism' in Pam Cook and Philip Dodd (ed.) *Women and Film: A Sight and Sound Reader* (London: Scarlet Press).

Taylor, Affrica (19970 'A Queer Geography' in Andy Medhurst and Sally R. Munt (eds.) *Lesbian and Gay Studies: A Critical Introduction* (London: Cassell).

Thody, Philip (1969) 'Jean Genet and the Indefensibility of Sexual Deviation', *Twentieth Century Studies*, 2.

Thomas, Calvin (1996) *Male Matters* (Urbana and Chicago: University of Illinois Press).

_____ (2000) 'Straight with a Twist' in Calvin Thomas (ed.) *Straight with a Twist: Queer Theory and the Subject of Heterosexuality* (Urbana and Chicago: University of Illinois Press).

Thompson, Mark (ed.) (1992) *Leatherfolk: Radical Sex, People, Politics and Practice* (Boston: Alyson).

Tillman, Lynne (1987) 'Love Story', *Art in America*, January.

Tweedie, James (2003) 'The suspended spectacle of history: the tableau vivant in Derek Jarman's *Caravaggio*', *Screen*, 44:4, Winter.

Tyler, Carol-Ann (1991) 'Boys Will Be Girls: The Politics of Gay Drag' in Diana Fuss (ed.) *Inside/Out: Lesbian Theories, Gay Theories* (London and New York: Routledge).

Ulrich, Karl Heinrich (1994) *The Riddle of 'Man-Manly' Love: The Pioneering Work on Male Homosexuality, 2 volumes,* translated by Michael A. Lombardi-Nash (Buffalo, NY: Prometheus Books).

Walker, Alexander (1985) *National Heroes: British Cinema in the Seventies and Eighties* (London: Harap).

Warner, Michael (1992) 'From Queer to Eternity: An Army of Theorists Cannot Fail', *Village Voice Literary Supplement*, June.

_____ (1993) 'Introduction' in Michael Warner (ed.) *Fear of a Queer Planet: Queer Politics and Social Theory* (Minneapolis: University of Minnesota Press).

_____ (1999) *The Trouble with Normal: Sex, Politics and the Ethics of Queer Life* (Cambridge, Massachusetts: Harvard University Press).

_____ (2002) 'Something Queer About the Nation State' in Michael Warner *Public and Counterpublics* (New York: Zone Books).

Watney, Simon (1982) 'Hollywood's Homosexual World', *Screen*, 23: 3-4, September-October.

_____ (1992) 'School's Out' in Diana Fuss (ed.) *Inside/Out: Lesbian Theories, Gay Theories* (New York and London: Routledge).

_____ (1993) 'Emergent Sexual Identities and HIV/AIDS' in Peter Aggleton, Peter Davies and Graham Hart (eds.) *AIDS: Facing the Second Decade* (London: The Falmer Press).

____ (1993b) 'The French Connection', *Sight and Sound*, 3:6, June.

____ (1994) 'Queer Epistemology: activism, 'outing' and the politics of sexual identities', *Critical Quarterly*, 36:1, Spring.

____ (1997) *Policing Desire: Pornography, AIDS and the Media* (London: Cassell).

____ (1997b) 'Lesbian and Gay Studies in the Age of AIDS' in Andy Medhurst and Sally R. Munt (eds.) *Lesbian and Gay Studies: A Critical Introduction* (London: Cassell).

Waugh, Thomas (2000) 'Erotic Self-Images in the Gay Male AIDS Melodrama' in Thomas Waugh *The Fruit Machine: Twenty Years of Writings on Queer Cinema* (Durham and London: Duke University Press).

Weir, John (1999) 'Going In' in Mark Simpson (ed.) *Anti-Gay* (London: Cassell).

Weiss, Andrea (1992) *Vampires and Violets: Lesbians in the Cinema* (London: Jonathan Cape).

Weeks, Jeffrey (1985) *Sexuality and Its Discontents: Meanings, Myths and Modern Sexualities* (London: Routledge).

White, Edmund (1993) *Genet* (London: Chatto and Windus).

Wilde, Oscar (1994) *The Picture of Dorian Gray* in *The Complete Works of Oscar Wilde* (Glasgow: HarperCollins).

Willemen, Paul (1981) 'Anthony Mann: Looking at the Male', *Framework*, 15-17.

____ (1994) 'The Fourth Look' in Paul Willemen *Looks and Frictions* (London: BFI Publishing).

Williams, Linda (1993) 'Second Thoughts on *Hard Core*: American Obscenity Law and the Scapegoating of Deviance' in Pamela Church Gibson and Roma Gibson (eds.) *Dirty Looks: Women, Photography, Power* (London and New York: Routledge).

Wilson, Angelia R. (1997) 'Somewhere Over the Rainbow: Queer Translating' in Shane Phelan (ed.) *Playing with Fire: Queer Politics, Queer Theories* (London and New York: Routledge).

Wilson, Elizabeth (1993) 'Is Transgression Transgressive?' in Joseph Bristow and Angelia R. Wilson (eds.) *Activating Theory: lesbian, gay, bisexual politics* (London: Lawrence & Wishart).

Wilson, John Dover (1966) 'Introduction' in John Dover Wilson (ed.) *The Sonnets* by William Shakespeare (Cambridge: Cambridge University Press).

Wollen, Peter (1975) 'The Two Avant-Gardes' in Peter Wollen *Readings and Writings: Semiotic Counter Strategies* (London: Verso).

_____ (2000) 'Blue', *New Left Review*, 6, November/December.

Wood, Aylish (1998) 'Deviant Imaging: Lesbian/Gay/Queer – Film Conference, University of Warwick, 23 May 1998', *Screen*, 39:4, Winter.

Woods, Chris (1995) *State of the Queer Nation: A Critique of Gay and Lesbian Politics in 1990s Britain* (London: Cassell).

Woods, Gregory (1993) 'The injured sex: Hemingway's voice of masculine anxiety' in Judith Still and Michael Worton (eds.) *Textuality and Sexuality: Reading Theories and Practices* (Manchester and New York: Manchester University Press).

_____ (1999) *A History of Gay Literature: The Male Tradition* (New Haven and London: Yale University Press).

Worth, Fabienne (1993) 'Of Gayzes and Bodies: A Bibliographical Essay on Queer Theory, Psychoanalysis and Archeology', *Quarterly Review of Film and Video*, 15:1.

Wyatt, Justin (1993) 'Cinematic/Sexual Transgression: An Interview with Todd Haynes', *Film Quarterly*, 46:3.

_____ (1998) *Poison* (Trowbridge: Flicks Books).

_____ (2002) 'Todd Haynes' in Yvonne Tasker (ed.) *Fifty Contemporary Filmmakers* (London and New York: Routledge).

Wymer, Rowland (2005) *Derek Jarman* (Manchester: Manchester University Press).

Yingling, Thomas (1991) 'AIDS in America: Postmodern Governance,

Identity and Experience' in Diana Fuss (ed.) *Inside/Out: Lesbian Theories, Gay Theories* (London and New York; Routledge).

_____ (1994) 'Wittgenstein's Tumour: AIDS and the national body', *Textual Practice*, 8:1.

INDEX